Harvard Historical Studies

Published under the direction
of the Department of History
from the income
of the Henry Warren Torrey Fund

Volume XCII

A Donor and Saints. Saint Nicholas's Church, Troyes.

The Religions of the People
in
Sixteenth-Century Champagne

A.N. Galpern

Harvard University Press
Cambridge, Massachusetts
and London, England
1976

Copyright © 1976 by the President and Fellows of Harvard College
All rights reserved
Printed in the United States of America
Library of Congress Cataloging in Publication Data
Galpern, A   N   1939–
    The religions of the people in sixteenth-century
Champagne.

    (Harvard historical studies; 92)
    Bibliography: p.
    Includes index.
    1. Champagne—Social conditions. I. Title.
II. Series.
HN438.C5G34   309.1'44'3028   75-35993
ISBN 0-674-75836-6

To my mother and to the memory of my father

Acknowledgments

I am grateful for the patient wisdom of William Bouwsma, the incisive but tempered criticism of Hans Rosenberg, and the sustained encouragement of Richard Herr and Gene Brucker. Joyce Galpern and Seymour Drescher read and reread successive drafts of the manuscript and mitigated its flaws. Robert Cook, Natalie Davis, François Furet, Léon-E. Halkin, Charles Ledit, and Emmanuel Le Roy Ladurie also offered valuable aid. Nancy Lyman Roelker provided a penetrating critique and Madeleine Rowse Gleason unstintingly gave of her superb editorial talents. None of them is responsible for the interpretations that are offered, or the errors that may remain. Among French archivists I am indebted to the friendship of Gildas Bernard and the helpfulness of Françoise Bibolet. The Social Science Research Council and the University of California, Berkeley, generously sent me to Champagne, and the University of Pittsburgh's faculty research fund and Center for International Studies made a second trip possible. Howard Ziegler's fine maps were underwritten by the university provost's fund, and Michel Vuillemin and Jean-Paul Colomb were kind enough to give me copies of their photographs for publication. An earlier version of parts of chapter 2 and 3 appeared in *The Pursuit of Holiness*, edited by Charles Trinkaus with Heiko Oberman, and published by E. J. Brill (Leiden, 1974), who have granted their permission for the use of this material here.

Contents

Illustrations

Frontispiece (*facing title page*)
  A Donor and Saints. Saint Nicholas's Church, Troyes. By permission of the Caisse nationale des monuments historiques
Following page 93:

1. *The Entombment of Christ,* at Chaource. Photograph by Jean-Paul Colomb, with permission

2. *The Pietà* of Bayel. By permission of the Caisse nationale des monuments historiques

3. *The Madonna of the Grapes.* Saint Urban's Church, Troyes. Photograph by Michel Vuillemin, with permission

4. *The Visitation.* Saint John's Church, Troyes. By permission of the Caisse nationale des monuments historiques

5. *The Beautiful Cross of Neuvy-Sautour.* By permission of the Caisse nationale des monuments historiques

6. *Saint Agnes.* Saint Nicholas's Church. Troyes. By permission of the Caisse nationale des monuments historiques

7. *Christ at the Column.* Saint Nicholas's Church, Troyes. Photograph by Michel Vuillemin, with permission

Maps

1. Physical map of Champagne

2. Towns and villages, diocesan boundaries, French frontier

3. Troyes

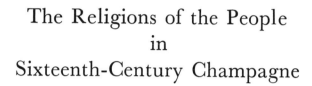

The Religions of the People
in
Sixteenth-Century Champagne

1 / The Problem and the Province

Lucien Febvre, both as a scholar and as an evangelist, fired the imagination of more than one generation of young people to pursue an integrated approach to social history. He urged the examination of the widest possible range of archival sources, in order to explore the reciprocal relationships between the material and cultural dimensions of the life of the many.[1] But Febvre did not perhaps give due weight to the influence of political on religious change, and in any event his work on sixteenth-century French religion has been more praised than emulated. Johan Huizinga used chronicles and works of art to evoke the dreams and fears of an age, in his arresting if avowedly incomplete image of the autumn of the Middle Ages.[2] We honor the memory of these men by seeking inspiration from their work.

Religion in sixteenth-century France has been relatively neglected because this was not a part of Europe where the partisans of a new faith overcame the defenders of the old one, or where the sovereign withdrew his allegiance from Rome for reasons of state, or where the Catholic church initiated and sustained its own program of reform. French Calvinists, after briefly challenging Catholic supremacy, had to endure a long and bitter struggle for survival. The country's rulers, whatever their religious needs or lack of them, never forgot the political benefits of the papal connection. And its bishops were too jealous of their relative autonomy to accept direction from Rome, too varied in their interests to join in a strictly Gallican reform.

As an organized movement directed by the church on a national level, the Catholic Reformation came to France only in the seventeenth century. In a way it came too late. By then much of the earlier, sixteenth-century fervor was ebbing, meaning that the reformers became as occupied in reviving a flagging interest in religion as in trying to contain strong religious feelings within the channels of or-

1. See especially his *Le problème de l'incroyance au XVIe siècle; la religion de Rabelais* (Paris, 1942), *Au coeur religieux du XVIe siècle* (Paris, 1957), and *Combats pour l'histoire* (Paris, 1953).
2. *The Waning of the Middle Ages*, trans. F. Hopman (London, 1924).

thodoxy. Their effort, despite its limitations, has been studied much more thoroughly than the earlier period.[3] Historians prefer institutions in movement to those in inertia, and they are partial as well to the greatness of seventeenth-century France. But the earlier period warrants consideration precisely because of the lack of clerical leadership, which makes it easier to study the laity. Scholars continue to tax the sixteenth-century European people with "a profound misunderstanding of the essential character of Christianity." Jean Delumeau, the author of this phrase, argues that "on the eve of the Reformation the average Occidental," by whom he means primarily but not exclusively the peasant, "had only been superficially Christianized."[4] This is to judge religiosity by a yardstick that had not yet been applied to the people, rather than to search for the norms that actually existed and that presumably reflected social needs and cultural traditions. It is also to postulate a gulf between the religious behavior of a small, thoughtful elite and the mass of the illiterates without asking whether, on the eve of the Reformation, the spiritual needs and aspirations of most of the privileged, and most of the people, may not have been divisible by common religious denominators. A.L. Rowse wrote of "the penumbra of superstition and custom which was the religion of the people" in Tudor Cornwall.[5] Perhaps instead of shadows we can find a set of practices and beliefs that was no less (and no more) coherent than in other periods of history.

I propose to begin by characterizing the traditional strain in religious behavior, which was dominant at the beginning of the century, for one part of France, and by interpreting that behavior as a continuing and lingering response to the crisis of the late Middle Ages. An attempt, however tentative, to intertwine the dual lines of economic and political inquiry on the one hand, and religious inquiry on the other, seems timely, given the significant but somewhat cloistered work in these two fields for the pre-Reformation period.[6] Then

3. Jean Delumeau, *Le Catholicisme entre Luther et Voltaire* (Paris, 1971), provides a comprehensive bibliography. Pierre Deyon, *Amiens, capitale provinciale; étude sur la société urbaine au 17e siècle* (Paris, 1967), includes an excellent treatment of the social history of religion.

4. *Catholicisme*, pp. 257 and 237: an otherwise skillful discussion of the ways in which the Catholic Reformation may be studied.

5. *Tudor Cornwall*, rev. ed. (New York, 1969), p. 257.

6. For cogent syntheses and comprehensive bibliographies see Jacques Heers, *L'Occident aux XIVe et XVe siècles; aspects économiques et sociaux* (Paris, 1966), which is especially strong on urban life; Francis Rapp, *L'église et la vie religieuse en Occident à la fin du Moyen Age* (Paris, 1971), a highly successful survey of a subject now coming

we shall observe Catholics who modify their religious practices but remain orthodox, and infer their shifts in belief. This section, together with an examination of the genesis of the Protestant movement, will bring those changes that occur within the majority confession into sharper focus, as we ask the following two well-worn but still eminently worthwhile questions: Why did traditional religion seem less plausible, as a means of expression and a system of belief, to some people at mid-century than it had to their fathers or grandfathers? In what ways, conversely, did the social changes of the period undermine the foundations of the established faith? The matter of heresy has a special place in a study devoted primarily to orthodoxy. By clarifying those links in the chain of Catholicism that contemporaries regarded as weak, it helps us to understand the developments that were underway within the established religious order, independently of the challenge from outside. On the other hand, many committed Catholics responded to the Protestants in ways that recall aspects of late-medieval religiosity. Their reactions demonstrate that there is no single equation for the relationship between social change and religious choice, and permit an evaluation of the degree of change that took place in popular religion over the course of the century.

But what portion of a country whose population was approaching sixteen million souls does one choose for the exploration of these problems? Given the diversity of France, no city and its hinterland, no diocese or province could be considered either representative of the kingdom as a whole, or a mean between extremes. Still, some places were more distinctive, more alive with their own individuality, than others. The wheatlands of the Ile-de-France, which were abundant enough to insure the greatness of Paris, stand out even in a country known for its rural wealth. The mercantile centers of Rouen and Lyons — one for the Atlantic, the other for overland trade — were rich and vibrant cities, parts of the wider, European world. The cloistered interior of Brittany lived on its meager agricultural resources and its rich, particularistic traditions. The list could be extended, but not indefinitely. It is unlikely ever to include Champagne.

---

under intensive scholarly inquiry; and Bernard Guenée, *L'Occident aux XIVe et XVe siècles: les états* (Paris, 1971), a masterful essay that rests on a long tradition of research.

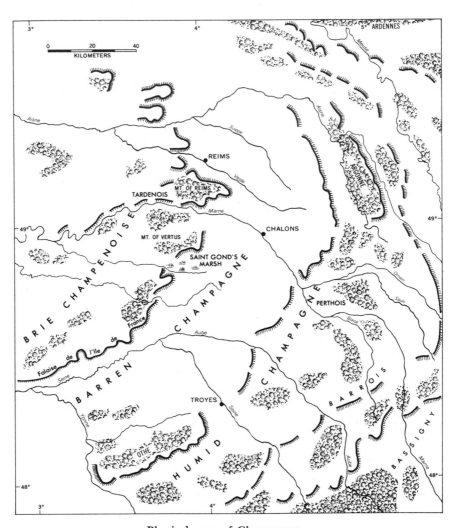

Physical map of Champagne

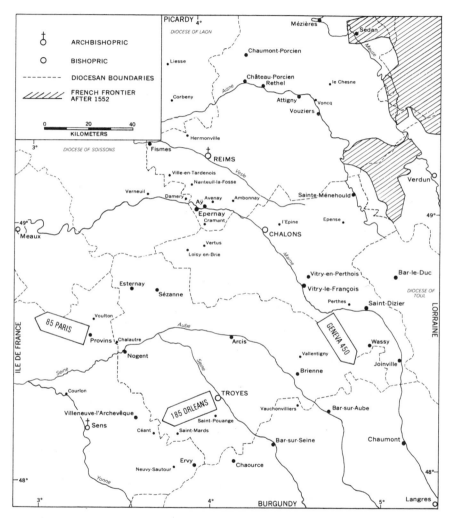

The distance from Provins to Paris, and from Troyes to Orléans, is direct; from Vitry to Geneva, via "the route of the ministers," it is indirect and approximate.

Towns and villages, diocesan boundaries, French frontier

For the great moments and special qualities of this province, by
and large, lay buried in the past. True, Reims was still in some ways
the clerical capital of France. The kings came to its cathedral for coronation, to be anointed by the archbishops with the sacred chrism
and acclaimed by peers and people as their God-given sovereigns. But
the city's claims to intellectual eminence and political influence during the time of the last Carolingians had been progressively overshadowed by the lights of Paris from the founding of the Capetian
dynasty onwards. In the southern part of the province the counts of
Champagne, vassals stronger than the twelfth-century Capetian kings,
brought both power and civilization to Troyes, and enlivened Provins and Bar-sur-Aube as well. But the counts' lineage petered out in
the course of the thirteenth century, and finally expired with an only
daughter who married into the royal family in 1284. The crown,
which had been progressively asserting its tutelage over the county,
now set itself to make Champagne royal domain, and succeeded def-
initively in 1361.[7] Finally, the fairs of Champagne — Bar, Troyes,
Provins, and Lagny-sur-Marne — were once the hub of European
commerce. They had grown from farmers' markets at the beginning
of the eleventh century into significant commercial centers by at-
tracting Flemish and Northern French merchants, who had expensive
woolens to sell. The Flemings in turn drew Italians, who offered
silks, spices, and dyes in return for the cloth that they took back to
Mediterranean Europe. Merchants came from the rest of France,
from Spain, and after 1250 from Germany as well. By this time, however, the Italians were beginning to enter the clothing industry themselves, and had less and less use for the fairs. Their chief merchant
houses, meanwhile, were establishing branches in Bruges, making it
unnecessary for the Flemings to travel part way to Italy. Fortunately,
the Champagne fairs acquired a new purpose as financial market-
places, where currency was exchanged and loans negotiated. But after
1320 the increasing supply of gold relative to silver disorganized the
European money markets and ruined the Italian bankers operating
in Champagne. The next generation of bankers set themselves up in
Paris, abandoning the fairs of Champagne, which abruptly and ir-
revocably shrank to the size of the local markets.[8]

By the sixteenth century Champagne was at once too far from Paris

7. Robert Fawtier, *Les Capétiens et la France* (Paris, 1942), pp. 122–127.
8. R.H. Bautier, "Les foires de Champagne, recherches sur une évolution historique,"
in *La Foire,* Recueils de la Société Jean Bodin, 5 (Brussels, 1953), 97–148.

and not far enough — too far to be galvanized by the capital and share in its animation, too close to enjoy life on its own. Reims and Troyes, the poles of the province, were three days' ride from Paris for a purposeful but not hard-pressed traveler, Châlons-sur-Marne another half-day by the river route.[9] Champagne had no university until the cardinal of Lorraine founded one at Reims in 1547 to help defend the faith, no provincial estates, and no parlement. Both as a high court of appeals and as the administrative agent of the royal will, the parlement was a crucial institution, which gave strength and character to a province. Generally speaking, then, for matters judicial, political, and intellectual, Champagne depended on guidance from outside.[10]

The province that I have chosen was one of the more prosaic parts of France, and is worth studying for the very reason that it was unlikely to have bred a religious climate all its own. Although long removed, by the sixteenth century, from the main currents of trade, it was not at all isolated from new fashions and new ideas. For its plains offer an easy passage from the English Channel and the Low Countries toward Mediterranean Europe. They also open the roads from the Rhine, which have first probed the gaps between the ancient massifs that watch over the northeastern flank of France, into broad highways to Paris. Champagne's vocation, ever since men have settled the area, has been to link more important places to one another. The Romans took full advantage of its accessibility and, improving on the work of the Gauls, built a dense network of roads through the region. With their eyes on Britain and the middle Rhine, they developed Reims into a more important center of transit than Paris. It was the position of the fairs on the north-south route that made their international role possible. Then, as Paris affirmed its hegemony, the

9. Charles Estienne, *La guide des chemins de France* (2 vols., Paris, 1935–1936), II, 51–69. Jean Bonnerot, Estienne's modern editor, states on p. 8 that Estienne's daily distances, 10 to 15 *lieues* (roughly 50 to 75 kilometers), were calculated for the well-limbered pedestrian and could be doubled by a rider — but the rider would have to be a messenger who rode for his living. M.N. Boyer, "A Day's Journey in Medieval France," *Speculum*, 26 (1951), 602–604, puts a day's journey for purposeful riders, who could be accompanied by pedestrians, since they did not hamper the trip, at about 50 kilometers. R.H. Bautier, "Recherches sur les routes de l'Europe médiévale: 1. De Paris et des foires de Champagne à la Méditerranée par le Massif Central," *Bulletin philologique et historique . . . du Comité des travaux historiques et scientifiques,* 1960, vol. I, p. 102, allows 30 to 35, or even 40, kilometers a day to the medieval merchant convoy, which would have meant five days to the Champagne towns.

10. Bernard Guenée, "Espace et état dans la France du bas Moyen Age." *Annales: E. S. C.,* 23 (1968), 754–755, demonstrates the hegemony of Parisian administration over north-central France.

east-west direction across the province became predominant, a trampling ground for armies as well as a carrier of goods.

In addition, Champagne was hardly wealthy, nor yet truly poor. It is easier to build a good road than to grow a bumper crop on the chalk plains that stretch in a broad north-south belt from the Suippe, a tributary of the Aisne, to slightly below the Seine, between its confluence with the Aube and Troyes. The chalk lies bare at the surface, giving no soil and draining the rainwater down through its fissures so well that the ground is bone dry. Life is necessarily concentrated along the several rivers that flow west, toward the bottom of the Parisian Basin, and along the line of springs that feed the rivers, at the base of the chalk slopes. Villages succeed one another at short intervals on both sides of each river. This was one of the most clear-cut champion, or open-field, regions of Europe, in which the peasants lived in big village clusters and were linked together by a tight communal organization that governed the working of the land. For champion and Champagne are both derived from *campus* and mean open country. The peasants pastured their stock on the valley bottoms, and then drove the animals up behind the villages to manure the higher ground and make it suitable for cereals other than wheat, the luxury grain, which their soil was still too poor to support. The farther back from the valley, the drier the ground, which in many places was good for sheep walks at best, and sometimes for nothing at all. Yet we must not be overdramatic. Early settlers found it easier to work this light soil than the hard, impermeable clays in other parts of the Basin which drain very poorly, even though they promise better yields. Great cemeteries provide evidence of the Celts who came here more than five hundred years before Caesar. The sheep's fleece, in Christian times, would be sold in the river towns, and provide the raw materials for a clothing industry. Champagne's ill-repute, in good measure, postdates our period. The seventeenth-century demographic crisis dealt a severe blow to the countryside, drying up villages on the poorest soils and increasing the emphasis on sheep relative to crops. North of the Marne, moreover, the movement of armies in this time of frequent warfare drove peasants to seek permanent security in Reims and other towns.[11] The chalk country never recovered. Barren

11. Jean-Marie Pesez and Emmanuel Le Roy Ladurie, "Le cas français vue d'ensemble," *Villages désertés et histoire économique, XIe–XVIIIe siècle* (Paris, 1965), pp. 214–227.

Champagne (*Champagne pouilleuse*) is what geographers have called it, ever since the eighteenth-century *Encyclopedia* popularized the mordant phrase.[12] Today commercial fertilizer has made possible the development of large, productive farms. They are owned and worked by a few, so that the countryside remains solitary.

Barren Champagne is far from the whole of the province. Its plains dip very gradually toward the west, and then disappear abruptly below the *Falaise de l'Ile-de-France,* a cuesta that faces the chalk surface. Rock fragments and soil have been weathered down the scarp to create a mixed soil at the base which rewards intensive cultivation. Reims and Epernay command the gaps which the Vesle and Marne rivers, respectively, have chiseled through the cuesta. The "Mountain of Reims," north of Epernay, the "Mountain of Vertus" to the south, and the "River," the Marne's right bank between the villages of Aÿ and Damery, have carried vineyards since Roman times. In our period clerical and bourgeois proprietors of Reims owned most of this land, including the Mountain of Vertus, as far as Cramant. Below this point the bourgeois of Châlons were dominant. Farther south, the vine disappears from the slopes, because the closest sizeable town, Troyes, was still too far away to have encouraged its development, and farther, too, than Châlons or Reims from potential buyers in the Low Countries.

Given the northern latitude, the cuesta's wine is more a tribute to the industry and ingenuity of growers and proprietors than a free gift from nature's bounty. The grapes are threatened, from year to year, by frosts in the spring or fall, and by the dearth or overabundance of a rainfall whose vigor depends on the uncertain struggle between maritime and continental influences. During the sixteenth century the still wines of this area enjoyed no special reputation. Drinkers did not distinguish them from the products of the other good, and extensive, vineyards of "France" — by which they meant the central portion of the Parisian Basin, near and north of the Marne-Seine. The educated palate, in fact, preferred the heady, deep-red wines of Beaune to the delicate, light-colored French ones, which tasted of vinegar in bad years, and in good ones still had to be drunk while young. More casks from Burgundy passed through Châlons

12. Roger Dion, "Le 'bon' et 'beau' pays nommé Champagne pouilleuse," *L'information géographique,* 25 (1961), 211. Dion makes an admirable and more than half-convincing attempt to rehabilitate the region.

and Reims en route to the Low Countries than originated locally. In the latter part of the century an intensive improvement of the cuesta's vineyards began. The process led, over a hundred years, to the careful mélange of must from both mountains and the River, which, bottled and made effervescent, conquered the world. Until then, "Champagne" meant the plain, not the wine.[13]

The southern portion of the cuesta loses altitude, and in places is almost effaced. The Aube River, nevertheless, chose the path of least resistance by curving southeast so as to turn the cuesta's flank. It intercepts the Seine, but gives up its own name along the way. Having joined forces, the waters attack the southern edge of the cuesta only when they are reinforced by the Yonne. This river flows downstream from Burgundy and across the Sennois, a *petit pays* around Sens, which is not a part of Champagne.

Behind the southern half of the cuesta lies the clay-covered Brie plateau, which in its turn slopes down as the Seine swings north to meet the Marne just above Paris. The chalk is now far below the ground. The counts of Champagne were also counts of Brie, and their domain on the Marne reached close to the gates of Paris. But we shall be somewhat less acquisitive than they were. The western part of the Brie, with its covering of loess, is excellent farmland, a pride of the Parisian region; the less favored eastern part belongs to us. Why else would it be called Barren Brie? "The solidarity that economic exchanges create," Marc Bloch pointed out, linked this area to Champagne.[14] Within it, just south of the Marne, the clay turns back rain with as much intensity as the chalk on the other side of the cuesta gulps it down, making for Humid Brie, an area of forest and marsh. The rest of the *Brie champenoise* was only somewhat less wet. Modern drainage has made it a prosperous agricultural region. In the past it mainly pastured sheep for the looms of Provins, a citadel town on a steep hill that rises just west of the cuesta. Behind the Mountain of Reims, on the western fringes of our area, is the richer region of the Tardenois.

If we turn now to the east of the chalk country we shall find a

13. Roger Dion, *Histoire de la vigne et du vin en France dès origines au XIXe siècle* (Paris, 1959), pp. 42–46, 229–237, 614–648.

14. "L'Ile-de-France," *Mélanges historiques* (2 vols., Paris, 1963), II, 710. Bloch argues that only "the hazards of feudal succession" fixed the boundaries of the counts' domains in Brie, and that there is no purpose in fixing a precise limit between western and eastern Brie, since neither nature nor history furnishes any.

second, broken cuesta. It faces a rather narrow, crescent-shaped region known as Humid Champagne, which is composed of heavy clays and greensand. The Argonne Forest, a raised "clay pie," occupies the northern half of the crescent, and separates Champagne from Lorraine.[15] The rest of Humid Champagne is depressed, lower than the chalk. Monastic houses began to clear its forests and drain its swampy lakes during the high Middle Ages. The choicest parts of the region are its river valleys, for the waters brought down rich periglacial debris from the plateau farther back, to create fertile terraces where they cross the crescent: the Perthois region between the Saulx-Ornain and the Marne, above Vitry; the Aube Valley above the town of Brienne; and the Barse Valley, between that stream and the Seine, above Troyes. The first and last, in the sixteenth century, sent grain downriver to Paris.[16]

The Othe Forest stands on the back slope of the southern edge of the cuesta, between Troyes and Sens. It provided wood to build the houses of Troyes, and bark for the tanner's trade. Above the city the waters of the Seine and its tributaries were clear enough to be used in making paper. This industry developed in the fourteenth century and reached its height soon after 1500, when it supplied the printing presses of Paris, Flanders, and England, as well as the local ones and those of Châlons and Reims.[17] Troyes, then, had more than the cloth string to its bow.

Just south of the Perthois, on the eastern edge of Humid Champagne along the Marne between Saint-Dizier and Joinville, ferruginous sands are found among the clay. Near these towns in the "Iron Country," and Wassy on the Blaise River, were many foundries.[18]

Rising to the southeast of Humid Champagne is hilly ground, called the Tonnerois between the Yonne and the Seine, and the Barrois from there to the Ornain. The Tonnerois, though part of the old county of Champagne, looked more to Sens and Auxerre than to

15. Paul Vidal de la Blache, *Tableau géographique de la France*, in E. Lavisse, ed., *Histoire de France*, vol. I, pt. 1 (Paris, 1903), p. 121.

16. Théophile Boutiot, "Notice sur la navigation de la Seine et la Barse," Société académique . . . du département de l'Aube: *Mémoires*, 20 (1856), 87. See also Micheline Baulant and Jean Meuvret, *Prix des céréales extraits de la mercuriale de Paris (1520–1698)* (2 vols., Paris, 1960–1962), I, 26 bis (plate 1).

17. Lucien Febvre and Henri-Jean Martin, *L'apparition du livre* (Paris, 1958), ch. 1. Louis Le Clert, *Le papier, . . . principalement à Troyes et aux environs depuis le quatorzième siècle* (2 vols., Paris, 1926).

18. For the extent of this industry, see the map of Cistercian metallurgical activity before 1300 in Rolf Sprandel, *Das Eisengewerbe im Mittelalter* (Stuttgart, 1968), p. 48.

Troyes; the Barrois is a rather complicated affair. Bar-le-Duc, on the Ornain, was a French possession of the archdukes of Lorraine, and Bar-sur-Seine had gravitated into the Burgundian orbit in the fifteenth century. Only Bar-sur-Aube, once the great fair town, was left for Champagne. Like its namesakes, this was an old citadel, commanding a river gate to the plains of Champagne and consuming and marketing the produce of the valley below, which includes wine where the slopes face the sun. The upper parts of the Barrois are heavily forested. They proved solitary enough for Saint Bernard, who became a monk at Clairvaux, south of Bar-sur-Aube, on the march of Champagne and Burgundy.

Upstream on the right bank of the Marne, finally, between Chaumont and Langres, lies the Bassigny, a wet clay region whose economy has always been dominated by livestock. Originally largely in the domain of the bishop of Langres, the Bassigny was considered part of Champagne in the sixteenth century and later, but sandwiched in between Burgundy and Lorraine it is eccentric to the rest of Champagne, and will be considered only rarely.

In short, Champagne was river towns on a dry central plain, bounded by ridges and woodland on either side. But despite its geographic core the province was neither an economic unit nor — in institutional terms — a religious one. For the chalk country between the Marne and Aube may have been suited for long-distance travel, but its lack of resources and chronic underpopulation discouraged regional contacts and split the province in two. This was the march between the Celtic peoples who gave their names to Sens and Reims, between Roman provinces, and finally the boundary between the archdioceses which had those same two cities for capitals. The ecclesiastical province of Reims stretched from the diocese of Châlons to the Low Countries. The archbishop-duke of Reims and the bishop-count of Châlons were powerful territorial lords, whom the counts in Troyes had never been able to subject. The province of Sens, for its part, included the diocese of Paris as well as Troyes. But our concern is not really the institutional structure of religion. In fact, to consider a single bishopric runs the danger of looking at the laity through the eyes of the clergy, instead of the other way around. Most important, since the sources are scattered, a comprehensive picture can emerge only by combining materials from several archival depots. And finally, the inclusion of a wider area enables us to glean a good deal of information on urban-rural religious relationships, though not enough, unfortunately, to study the countryside for its own sake.

Our evidence consists first of parish ledgers, which are most plentiful for the city of Troyes. They give the numbers and sometimes the names of participants in confraternities, the donations of parishioners to their church and the occasions on which they contributed, the relative éclat with which the various holidays were celebrated, and the effort and expense in building and embellishing the churches. Two hundred and fifty wills from the city and region of Reims not only name a specific place of burial and stipulate funeral arrangements, but make bequests to the poor and provisions for pilgrimages by relatives or palmers. Granted that a testator's motives, as he drew up his will in contemplation of death and more often than not in the face of it, were more narrowly religious than in the normal course of his life. I would nevertheless argue that he was drawing upon and emphasizing underlying feelings that were in him all the time. Granted, too, that the wills are not numerous enough to show the frequency of attitudes and gestures. Still, they do in their diversity demarcate the range of acceptable religious behavior. The information that they supply helps us to turn hints into hypotheses. The texts of mystery plays are a further body of evidence, to be read in conjunction with the iconography of stained-glass windows and statues that still grace scores of parish churches as well as the cathedrals of Champagne. The memoirs by contemporaries are crucial in interpreting as well as observing the religious scene. Official documents such as minutes of town council and cathedral chapter meetings enable us to establish the context and to master the detail of moments of effervescence, crisis, and decision. Almanacs, books of hours, and other works of devotion addressed to the faithful by local and Parisian printers complete this list. Taken together, this evidence should establish that in the matter of religious practice and belief the various parts of Champagne were complementary.

First, however, we need to survey more closely the condition of the province at the turn of the sixteenth century. Champagne was still slowly recovering from the depression of the late Middle Ages, which had developed from the end of the thirteenth century, when Europe's growing population outdistanced the supply of food. Famines early in the fourteenth century began the work of decimation, which the

Great Death of 1348 and its sequels continued. Of late some historians have preferred to talk of a process of economic transformation rather than of a crisis of depression; others have emphasized that many parts of Europe weathered this period well, and in some cases even prospered.[19] Champagne, like continental France in general, however, suffered greatly. Plague was not the only problem. The second half of the Hundred Years' War between England and France, and the war of supposedly disbanded but unpaid companies against the civilian population between campaigns, tortured the province, plundering merchants and driving peasants away from their farms. The crown, fighting for its life against the English, and undermined by the great lords, princes of the blood who hoped to commandeer what was left of France for their own purposes, could provide no protection to the lands in its own domain. Had the fairs of Champagne held their stature into the fifteenth century, they would still have come to grief.

The second half of the fifteenth century was a time of rebuilding for France, of peasants who left the mountain regions, which were again choked with people, for the fertile plains on which the wars had been fought.[20] Understandably they did not flock to Champagne. Robert Fossier's study of Humid Champagne proves that the rural population did not begin to recover its losses, by means of its own resources, until after 1470.[21] Reims, too, found it hard to make good the past. The linen and wool industries had significantly declined, though the vines were of course still there.[22] P. Desportes's demographic analysis evokes a sluggish town of small handicrafts and food trades, which served the clerical population of consumers. A headcount in 1482 by the municipal authorities, concerned about the grain supply in a difficult year, showed 10,678 residents, including the peasants of any means who had temporarily come in from the

19. Ernst Pitz, "Die Wirtschaftskrise des Spätmittelalters," *Vierteljahrschrift für Sozial- und Wirtschaftsgeschichte*, 52 (1965), 347–367; Heers, *L'Occident*, pp. 108–110, 151–155, 160–166, 171–174, and 180–181.

20. Ibid., pp. 112–113.

21. "Rémarques sur les mouvements de population en Champagne méridionale au XVe siècle," *Bibliothèque de l'Ecole des chartes*, 122 (1964), 196.

22. Louis Demaison, "Documents sur les draperies de Reims au Moyen Age," *Bibliothèque de l'Ecole des chartes*, 89 (1928), 17, cites a royal letter of 1490 calling for an inquiry in response to the inhabitants' request to establish a good drapery to help repopulate the city. P. Desportes, "La population de Reims au XVe siècle . . . ," *Moyen Age*, 72 (1966), 482, states that the textile industry was secondary in the city, which was not a "ville drapante."

countryside, but not the city's own "miserable and poor people who beg their life." They numbered more than 2,000. Four years later the crown introduced a garrison, because Maximilian, the German emperor, who liked to indulge himself in grand designs, was reported to be thinking of bringing an army before this "large but ill-populated city." Reims did not dwarf Châlons, which had a total of 9,228 inhabitants in 1517. Troyes was more prosperous and populous, with 15,309 residents and half again as many indigents as Reims in 1482, and 23,659 people all-told in 1500.[23] The city was embarked on a brief but bright moment in its history — thanks in part to the papermakers — which would last through the half-century.

If progress in most parts of Champagne was slow, then at least the general direction was clear — more people, increasing activity, and greater security too. For the French crown was strong once more, and its officers, while their kings played at war in Italy, exercised royal authority in a way that had not been seen for two hundred years. Until the religious wars of the late sixteenth century threatened France with disorganization once more, and a heady, expansive economy began to suffer from both monetary and demographic inflation, the people of Champagne would see better times than their forefathers had. But did their religion reflect the improvement of the present, or even expectations of the future, rather than the misfortunes that lay behind?

23. Ibid., p. 467, n. 23; BN, Collection Dupuy, 228, f. 115; BC, Châlons, BB 6 bis, f. 74; "Mémoires de Jean Foulquart, procureur de l'échevinage à Reims, 1479–1499," ed. Edouard de Barthélemy, *Revue de Champagne et de Brie*, 3 (1877), 290–291. These memoirs are the work of an outspoken defender of the royal prerogative in an archepiscopal town. Foulquart recounts the disorderly sermons of monks and gives details of the performance of mystery plays.

2 / The Late-Medieval Inheritance

The Quest for Prayer

In all of Champagne, there was no greater annual event than Corpus Christi at Reims. "The ancient custom" on this holiday, as the cathedral chapter proudly noted in a memorandum of 1601, was to stage "a most celebrated procession." The line of march began to form around Notre-Dame well before daybreak, when men from every guild and corporation in town assembled at the van. The torches they brought to identify and publicize their guilds were "taller and more decorated than in any other city of the kingdom." Farther back, eight or ten stout fellows readied themselves to lift a monumental symbol of the king. John II, at his coronation in 1350, had ordered that the largest torch in the procession be carried in his name. By 1601 this gaudy symbol of royal power stood — so the memorandum reads — eighty feet tall and weighed one hundred twenty pounds, according to the measurements of the time and place. Its surface was molded into fleurs-de-lis, and the royal coat of arms, on an escutcheon, hung from it. The purpose of the torch was "to excite the people to devotion and to pray for the king." His officers in the election of Reims followed directly behind it. At their side marched the clergy. Everyone "observed a very great order with all honor, reverence, and devotion, out of respect for the Holy Sacrament, which was being carried."

When the procession was over, the marchers attended Mass at the cathedral, which began once the royal torch was maneuvered into the choir, where the officers as well as the canons took seats. Next day the officers returned to attend a mass of the Holy Spirit, celebrated for the benefit of the king, and a requiem for his predecessors. They saw to it that each of the "canons, bourgeois, and [ordinary] inhabitants" who were present "in good number" received a card in the shape of the fleur-de-lis to make it crystal clear whom the service was for, and "to induce the people into devotion" for their ruler.[1]

1. BC, Reims, MS 1779, no. 35.

In the city of the coronation, the festival of God's Body had come to serve the needs of the king, which was hardly surprising, since royal propaganda was one of the fine arts of France. What the king seems to have needed most on these two days was the prayers of the Rémois, from the canons to the illiterate among the churchgoers, for whom the paper fleurs-de-lis were especially intended, since they could not have understood a written message. The king's needs were shared by his subjects, for the intense and persistent effort to solicit the prayers of others was a central theme of traditional religion in sixteenth-century Champagne.

The quest for prayer pursued the Catholic every day of his life. It called to him from the stained glass in church. "Guillemette, widow of the late Colas Vinot, has given this present window in the year 1522; pray God for those who live and for all the dead," reads the inscription at the bottom of a window portraying Saint Nicholas in the church of Saint-Parres-les-Tertres, near Troyes.[2] It colored the formal relations between the rich and the poor, who offered spiritual comfort in return for alms, as the following petitions to the municipal relief bureau of Châlons during the plague years from 1595 to 1597 make clear. The family of Hugues Chevalier, cooper, who is sick and unable to work, requests a weekly dole, and "will be held to pray God for you." Nicolas Perotin, farrier, and his family, in the same straits, "will be held to pray God for all." Stock phrases, these, put into the mouths of unfortunates by their betters, who insist upon such prayers because they think they need them, and expect them to work. One recurrent formula pledges those beset by hunger and disease to pray for "the prosperity and health" of their already comfortable benefactors. The exception comes from a shoemaker, a member of a trade whose practitioners, as we shall later see, were attracted by heterodox ideas. Jehan Vernison, confined to his house by the municipality because a neighbor had the plague, ended his plea with the observation: "and you will do good and justice."[3]

If prayers were sought by the living, they were exacted by the dead. The will of Jehan Richer, drawn at Reims in 1552, includes a three-livre bequest to his mother "so that she might have his soul to recommend in her prayers and orisons." In 1599 the widow of

2. Paul Biver, *L'école troyenne de peinture sur verre* (Paris, 1935), pp. 31–32, fig. 16.

3. AC, Châlons, GG 218 (1596).

Anthoine Manniere, merchant of Troyes, left five livres to each of her grandnephews and nieces, "in order to give them occasion to pray God for her soul." Gibrian Pirche, receiver in the *élection* (tax court) of Reims, and his wife, established an annual pension of 25 livres in 1538 for a daughter who was about to enter a nunnery "so that the said Jehanne be more inclined to pray and serve God our creator for the salvation of her soul and of her late relatives and friends, and for all others." This phrase, to be sure, is a formula that does not reveal the Pirches' inner thoughts, but tells us rather what they were expected to think. Only after Jehanne's religious obligations to her family have been stated does the contract note that the pension would also help provide for her material necessities. Prudent families often sent a girl to a convent to avoid the expense of dowering her; pious families, it would seem, regarded the daughter who became a nun as a spiritual asset. In 1544 the widow of the Rémois merchant Nicolas Aubert left 10 livres to each of her children in holy orders, explicitly requesting a quid pro quo of prayer only from the one who was a girl.[4]

The dead did not limit their appeal to family members. The linen cloth which during Lent covered the high altar of the parish church of Chaource, a small town south of Troyes, was embroidered with the figures of the four evangelists, and below them, with the admonition in red letters, "Pray for the soul of Jehan Arppel."[5] In 1532 Claude Berthier, bourgeois of Troyes, Nicole Dorigny, his curé at Saint John's, and Odard Hennequin, their bishop, together gave the parish 800 livres in order that the priest celebrating High Mass on Sundays and holidays turn to face the congregation, and ask them to say a Pater Noster and an Ave Maria for the three, Berthier's wife, their relatives, and all the parish dead.[6] Since the donors were of similar social origin, all members of prominent bourgeois families, their partnership in the endowment is not surprising. What merits our attention is the fact that a bishop felt the need for laymen's prayers. Cosme Clause, bishop of Châlons from 1574 to 1624, requested in the will he had drawn in the year of his death that "my body be buried in the middle of Saint Stephen's [Cathedral]

4. Richer: AD, Marne, 4E 16707; Manniere: AD, Aube, 2E 7/144; Pirche: AD, Marne, 4E 16694; Aubert: AD, Marne, 4E 16699.

5. AD, Aube, 108G 27: inventory (1502).

6. A. Assier, *Comptes de la fabrique de l'église Saint-Jean de Troyes* (Troyes, 1855), pp. 44–45.

Church, in the nave below the last vault near the steps of the great portal, so that my friends, seeing the tombstone on which my name will be written, remember to pray God for me, and give me holy water."[7] The captain (royal military officer) of Chaource, Henri de Foissy, and his wife gave a window of the Passion to the Church of Creney, near Troyes, in 1512, with an inscription that began with their names and ended with "pray God for them and for us all when we are gone."[8] Emile Mâle, the superlative historian of art, was struck, and more than a little offended, by the concern of donors of stained glass, at the end of the Middle Ages, to perpetuate their own memory. The only French inscription that he could consider "truly Christian" was in the village church of Montangon, near a tributary of the Aube, northeast of Troyes: "In 1553 good but unknown men have had this window mounted; they are not concerned to name their names here, but God knows them."[9] Surely most people in Champagne during the period would have considered such anonymity flippant rather than modest, arrogant rather than pious, because it meant that the donors felt no need for religious aid from their fellow Christians, and implied that they might not give any in return.

The town crier of Troyes, who walked the streets from midnight to two in the morning, announcing "Wake up, wake up, you who sleep, and pray God for the souls of the dead, whom he wants to forgive," typified an era.[10] His words convey the intense concern of Christians for the souls agonizing in purgatory, as well as the great opportunity they sensed, and the responsibility they felt, to abridge this suffering. "The day of the commemoration of the faithful, loyal departed," was the way a churchwarden of Troyes styled All Souls' Day in his receipt-book.[11] No wonder people bought indulgences so freely, both in the parish church and from monks traveling with a

7. AD, Marne, GG 215 and 216.

8. Biver, L'école troyenne, p. 99, fig. 77.

9. L'art religieux de la fin du Moyen Age en France, 5th rev. ed. (Paris, 1949), p. 162.

10. Théophile Boutiot, Histoire de la ville de Troyes et de la Champagne méridionale (5 vols., Paris, 1870–1880), III, 237; AC, Troyes, C 182 (1563–1564). In 1502 the bailiff of Chaumont and his wife donated a mill to found la clochette de nuit, a similar call for prayers for the dead (Emile Jolibois, Histoire de la ville de Chaumont [Paris, 1856], p. 94). For other such customs see François Lebrun, Les hommes et la mort en Anjou aux 17e et 18e siècles (Paris, 1971), p. 488, and Claude Fohlen, ed., Histoire de Besançon, I (Paris, Nouvelle Librairie de France, 1964), 667.

11. AD, Aube, 16G 65, f. 202v (Mary Magdalene's parish, 1557).

relic belonging to their abbey. Saint Nicholas's Church of Troyes had its indulgences printed in handbills and posted on every church door in the city and suburbs. Fourteen monasteries and other institutions paid the cathedral chapter of Troyes in 1501 for the privilege of offering indulgences in the diocese.[12] Hucksters could make extravagant claims for the efficacy of their relics only because laymen wanted very much to hear about and believe in the means by which one might be released from purgatory. Shady advertising always depends upon a tacit understanding between buyer and seller. The line between orthodox opinion and abuse was very fine, moreover, until the Council of Trent. An early sixteenth-century window in honor of the Eucharist at Saint Alpin's parish church of Châlons shows a priest celebrating Mass, while the small, naked figure of a soul ascends from the furnace of purgatory, to be wrapped by an angel in a white robe.[13] In 1564, immediately after Trent, the prelates of the ecclesiastical province of Reims, meeting in a council of their own, did decide to banish outside vendors of indulgences, though there is no evidence that they were successful. Four years later, in any event, the Rémois canon Gentien Hervet affirmed in his catechism that the sacrament of the Eucharist applied to the dead who merit it much more easily than to the living, because the faults of the former have been pardoned, and only their suffering remains.[14]

The Mobilization of the Community at Death

The importance that most men and women attached to their own funeral rites helps to show that Catholicism at the end of the Middle Ages was in large part a cult of the living in the service of the dead. A testator envisioned his "obsequies, services, and funerals" as he dictated his will. The prolixity of the formula suggests the elaborateness of these proceedings, which mobilized the spiritual resources of the community in the defense of the individual soul.

Damoiselle Guillemette Coquillart, wife of an attorney of Reims,

12. Saint Nicholas: AD, Aube, 17G 2, f. 69v (1525), 17G 15, f. 23 (1547); Cathedral: G 1573, f. 11.

13. Etienne Hurault, *Les vitraux anciens de l'église Saint-Alpin à Châlons-sur-Marne* (Paris, n.d.), p. 8.

14. Dom G. Marlot, *Histoire de la ville, cité et université de Reims* (4 vols., Reims, 1843), III, 370–373; G. Hervet, *Catéchisme et ample instruction de tout ce qui appartient au devoir d'un chrestien, . . .* (Paris, 1568), f. 64.

projected in 1542 what may have been the most elaborate funeral for a lay, private person in sixteenth-century Champagne. Her testament, by defining the limits which fervent piety and a full purse could reach, will serve as a foil for the rest. The notary found the lady, as his formula states, "dressed in her clothes, speaking with ease, going and coming"—in other words, well, and not in the immediate shadow of death. Like all testators, nevertheless, "thinking of sovereign matters, considering that nothing is more certain than death nor more uncertain than its hour, and not wanting to be deceased from this world intestate, but rather to provide for the salvation of her soul, she has made this testament and ordinance of last will and by it disposed of the goods that God has lent her, in the manner that follows."[15] She ordered, for the day of her death if possible, vigils at Saint Peter's, her parish, and then a high mass, the *grande recommandise* or full set of prayers for the commendation of her soul, and thirty low requiem masses. Her husband and her brother, meanwhile, whom she named as executors, were to distribute at their discretion eight setiers of rye and two puncheons of wine[16] to poor housewives, as soon after her death as they could.

On the day of burial, the clergy of Saint Peter's, not only the six canons but "all the other priests who regularly frequent the said church," together with those of Saint James's parish, would conduct the body from her home to church, and aid in chanting the appropriate psalms along the way.[17] The four mendicant orders then at Reims — the Franciscans, Dominicans, Augustinians, and Carmelites — were to join the convoy. Two two-pound torches, carried by young novice friars, would flank each of the processional crosses of the six churches. Adult friars, one from each order, would march at the sides of the bier, holding an edge of the cloth that covered it in one hand, and a candle in the other.

Damoiselle Coquillart "wanted and ordered" burial in the chapel of Saint Peter's confraternity, or pious lay association, in the parish church. The chapel served as a family burial place, since her mother's

15. AD, Marne, 4E 16670, ff. 49–53 (1542).

16. A *poinçon* (puncheon) of wine was equivalent to about 200 liters. The setier of grain, 156 liters at Paris, was generally a slightly smaller measure in the towns of Champagne. See Nicolas de Lamare, *Traité de la police*, . . . (2nd ed., 4 vols., Paris, 1722–1738), II, 744–745.

17. The words in quotation are from the will of Nicole Coquebert, whose will in other respects is similar to the one we are considering. AD, Marne, 4E 278* (1550).

remains already lay there, and her sister-in-law had also selected it.[18] For the day after burial our testatrix requested three masses of the Trinity, five low masses in honor of the wounds of Christ, and a high mass of Notre Dame. She asked that her "principal service" be held on the next Sunday, if possible, with all six of Saint Peter's canons participating in the vigils, the usual three high masses—of the Holy Spirit, Notre Dame, and Requiem—the *grande recommandise,* and thirty low masses. The laymen at church would receive four sols, the women three, and the canons two sols six deniers.[19] Thirteen poor people were each to offer a candle and receive two sols. Their number, as another testator pointed out, symbolized God and the twelve apostles.[20]

From the day following her death, a daily low mass would be said at Saint Peter's for a year's duration, for the remedy of her soul and those of her late relatives and friends. After each mass the priest would recite Psalm 129, the *de profundis,* while standing on her grave. She ordered one high and thirty low requiem masses for her "anniversary and end of the year." Other services were to be performed at Saint James's, the four mendicant orders, the Hôtel-Dieu (a hospital and home for the poor), the Church of Hernonville on the cuesta's edge north of the city, where her family had property, and at the convent in Reims where her daughter was a nun. She also instructed the officers of the thirteen confraternities to which she belonged "to do their duty towards her soul" — in other words, to hold a service.

The form for such occasions had been codified over the previous century by the Burgundian court. Georges Chastellain bombastically chronicled the funeral of his patron Duke Philip the Good in 1467. Fifteen hundred robes were cut from black cloth for the members of the ducal household, "so many that there was an infinite number of people to be seen wearing mourning, and in black robes, throughout Bruges, . . . given what the town did on its own account, as much by the guilds and confraternities as by the nations [of resident foreigners] who also showed themselves in strength, and by those of the legal professions and the great of the city." Together with the duke's own men, the townspeople were marking the culmination rather

---

18. Jehanne Noel, wife of the *grenetier* (judge of salt-tax matters) Jehan Coquillart, was the sister-in-law. AD, Marne, 4E 16692 (1536).

19. 1 livre = 20 sols; 1 sol = 12 deniers.

20. Pierre Pirche, merchant of Reims: AD, Marne, 4E 16696 (1540).

than merely the expiration of Philip's ceremonious life. "Then," Chastellain continues, "came the day of his burial, which was a Sunday, when the ceremonies were great, great in cost and expense, great in singular grandeur of display, and great in singular prayers and devotions among all the private individuals and the foreigners, with crying and weeping," and even more demonstratively by the duke's son and servants. The leaden pace of the prose, which at times scarcely seems to move at all, apes the burial procession itself, an event whose importance could be measured by the degree to which it was drawn out. Time almost stood still to permit the accumulation of prayers to the credit of Philip the Good's soul.[21]

Damoiselle Coquillart of Reims planned in her will to seize as much of the city's stage as she could, for a long moment, and then to continue the performance in the wings with daily masses. Some of the townspeople who knew the lady may have considered her a bigot, to use a term current in her time as in Philip's for people who practiced their religion incessantly. Other wills, nevertheless, differ from hers in degree rather than in kind.[22] In 1577 for example, Thiebault Cambron of Reims, whose occupation the notary did not state, but who lived in the poor parish of Saint Maurice on the outskirts of town, ordered a more modest though equally pious funeral.[23] He convoked to the procession his curé, the other permanent priest of the parish, six more secular clerics, and the Carmelites. Cambron wanted six three-quarter pound torches carried. He left two of them for the parish after the completion of his services, and one to each mendicant order, which suggests that only the necessity to choose among alternatives kept him from inviting them all. Rather than make a total donation of 40 to 100 sols for their appearance, he preferred to have a set of fifty low masses said, at a probable cost of 100 sols. These masses were in addition to his three customary services at Saint Maurice's: the first to be performed soon after his death, the second, principal service following his burial in the parish churchyard, and the third on the next day.

The 249 Rémois wills in our sample, which begins with the first

21. Georges Chastellain, *Oeuvres*, ed. Kervyn de Lettenhove (8 vols., 1863–1866; reprint ed., Geneva, 1971), V, 232–233. For an appreciation of Chastellain's style, see Huizinga, *Waning of the Middle Ages*, pp. 262–266.

22. Ibid., p. 42. A *bigote*, depicted with her hands joined in prayer, is among the figures in a dance of death that appears in *Ces présentes heures à l'usage de Châlons* . . . (Paris, 1512), sig. ii.

23. AD, Marne, 4E 16745.

extant notarial register in 1525, were drawn for men and women from the families of artisans, merchants, legal practitioners, bourgeois landlords, *anoblis* or men in the process of becoming noble, canons of the cathedral and collegial churches, as well as *laboureurs* or prosperous peasants, vine-growers, and their wives, from villages in the region. About half of the resident testators, 120 to be precise, invited all four orders, and the Minims too, after their arrival in 1572. But numerical statements from the notarial archives are apt to be misleading because it is impossible to know to what degree the clientele of a notary whose records have survived is representative of the whole. One man, the Hon. Jehan Audry, requested the Carmelites to act as his pallbearers.[24] Four people besides Damoiselle Coquillart asked that novice friars, who obviously represented innocence, carry the lights.[25] Pierre Natier, one of these testators, not only wanted four novices around his bier but also thirteen little children in the procession, each holding a small pot of incense and a candle.

Châlons, lacking the Carmelites, had three mendicant orders; the run of wills begins in 1558. Our sample of Catholic Châlonnais is smaller and also probably less pious than that of Reims, since by design nearly half the sixty-five wills come from three Protestant notaries, who had mixed clienteles.[26] As at Reims, however, virtually every other Catholic testator — twenty-one of the forty-four who were clearly orthodox — invited the mendicants. At Troyes only the Franciscans and Dominicans had founded churches. Sixteenth-century wills in the notarial archives here are few, and with one excep-

24. AD, Marne, 4E 16750 (1582).
25. Jehanne, wife of the carter Didier Clermont: AD, Marne, 4E 16692 (1533); Nicolas Goujon: 4E 16707 (1552); Pierre Natier: ibid.; and Thomasse de Laplace: 4E 16753 (1584).
26. The notary Depinteville, whose own records (AD, Marne, 4E 6361–87) begin in 1558 and end in 1605, wrote in his colleague Jehan Collin's register (4E 8063) that he was expelled from Châlons by the governor of Champagne in October 1567 and remained absent until April 1568, and was away again from September 1568 to September 1570 because of the "troubles." The registers of Jacques Roussel I cover the years from 1554 to 1603, with one gap between the beginning of intense persecution in 1559 and the end of the first religious war in 1563, and a second gap in 1589 when the Catholic League was in power, but none in 1572, the year of the Saint Bartholomew Massacre, which did not have repercussions in Châlons (4E 8824–28 and 9765–68). His family was later prominent in the Reformed church of Châlons, which existed openly from 1591. The notary Jacob Debezanson, whose registers from 1596 to 1604 survive (4E 8759–60), was married within the Reformed church (AD, Marne, Châlons, Protestants, Registre de l'état civil, marriages, 18 Jan. 1595). These three notaries provide the only sixteenth-century Protestant wills that, to my knowledge, survive in the archives of Champagne. Of the 65 Châlonnais wills, they furnish 30, of which 16 are Catholic, and 11 Protestant. Three mention neither church.

tion date only from 1580, making it possible to read them all. The notaries in question served a milieu composed in large part of clergymen and their domestics, who invited the mendicants to participate in thirty-seven of the sixty funerals.

During the sixteenth century, the friars were the butt of satire, a weapon that is directed only against men and institutions enjoying at least some, and usually much, popular credit. Their invitation to funerals is our first indication that they continued to serve the religious needs of a good number of the Catholics of Champagne.

Testators did not slight the secular clergy for the friars. In 1594 Damoiselle Suzanne de Noirfontaine, who lived in the market village of Saint-Martin-d'Ablois, south of Epernay, directed that her two services in the nearby church of Vauciennes, where she would be buried, be held "with as many priests as will be found in the said place." A second will from Saint-Martin-d'Ablois, drawn in the next year for one Estienne Vauldeier, uses similar language, suggesting a formula. The point of inviting a phalanx of priests was to multiply the number of prayers. In the countryside this was a common practice for testators of mark or means. Dame Jacquelyne de Laignes, widow of the late captain of Chaource, ordered "thirteen psalms by thirteen priests" around her body on the day of death, and left three sols "to each priest, up to the number of fifty, who will say a mass in her intention." Nicole Coquebert, widow of Nicolas Forest, merchant of Reims, stipulated that the curé or chaplain of Merfy, northeast of the city, announce during his prone on the Sunday before her service in that church, "If there is at Merfy any priest who will be disposed to say Mass, then all can do so."[27]

It would seem that a similar offer at Reims might convoke a synod of the ragamuffin clergy, but Damoiselle Margueritte Cuissotte, a resident of Châlons who had her will drawn in Reims, Nicole Coquebert and her daughter-in-law Barbe Fort, the merchant Nicolas Ribaille, and Nicolas Goujon, an *escuyer* or true nobleman, seneschal of Reims and seigneur of Tours-sur-Marne, all extended the invitation.[28] Damoiselle Claude Godet, widow of an *eschevin* (alderman) of Châlons, wanted "all the masses that will present themselves on the day of her said burial to be paid" — a revealing phrase that stresses the task at hand and slights the men who would

27. Noirfontaine: AD, Marne, 4E 10648; Vauldeier: ibid.; Laignes: AD, Aube, 108G 29 (1527) ; Coquebert: n. 17, above.

28. Cuissotte: AD, Marne, 4E 16695 (1539) ; Coquebert: n. 17, above; Fort: AD, Marne, 4E 16700 (1545) ; Ribaille, ibid.; Goujon: n. 25, above.

perform it. More charitably, Dean Jehan Clement of the cathedral chapter of Châlons, left the sum of five sols to "each priest who will appear and who will not have an ordinary mass." Well-off artisans and peasants, who had to be more prudent, stipulated a specific, moderate number of masses. Baudinet Bonhomme, pewterer of Reims, wanted ten for his first and third services, and twenty for the principal one. Jehan Boursin, vine-grower of Prouilly, a village on a tributary of the Vesle, ordered six high and twenty-four low masses for each of his three services.[29]

In making provisions for funerals most testators were concerned, in part, to offer a retrospective demonstration of social position. But it was possible to be both pious and humble. The cardinal of Givry, bishop of Langres, stipulated that his body be buried in his cathedral chapter at night, without any pomp, accompanied only by thirteen torch-bearing poor people. For the day of his burial and the ones to follow he also ordered twelve hundred low masses.[30]

To serve such needs, and those of the more ordinary testator, the secular clergy had to be numerous. It was not limited to the holders of benefices, who were supported by endowed property. Rather it included "the stipended habitués who continually serve in divinis or who are necessarily required to perform the divine service" in a particular church. Mary Magdalene's parish of Troyes had twenty of them in 1549. But even the stipendiaries were insufficient in number to meet the laypeople's periodic but insistent religious needs. This task fell to the clerical supernumeraries "who are not stipended but who frequent [the church] and go to the divine service performed there when it suits them, without constraint."[31] The laity, and priests of means acting as individuals, provided much if not most of the work for these day laborers, in the form of funeral services and anniversary masses. In England they were called masspriests, a term that the Reformation made pejorative.[32]

29. Godet: AD, Marne, 4E 6366 (1574); Clement: 4E 885 (1597); Bonhomme: 4E 16707 (1552); Boursin: 4E 16673 (1561).

30. Louis Marcel, Le Cardinal de Givry, évêque de Langres (1529–1561) (2 vols., Dijon, 1926), II, 489.

31. AD, Aube, 10G layette, carton 2 (1507), a case of disputed authority between a bishop and a member of the familia of one of Saint Urban's churchwardens. For Mary Magdalene's, see AD, Aube, G 1345, f. 110.

32. Oxford English Dictionary, s.v. "Mass-priest." For a contemporary's illustration of and comment on the term, see John Vowell, otherwise Hooker, The Description of the Citie of Excester (3 pts., Devon and Cornwall Record Society, 1919–1944), pt. 2, pp. 34–35.

The demand for numbers precluded highly selective standards for the recruitment of clergy. Many testators insisted that every priest who participated in their funeral be dressed "in a decent garb," for fear that shabby-looking clerics would mar the solemnity of the occasion and cast a shadow on the social importance of the deceased. Only two made specific reference to the qualities they wanted in a priest. Monseigneur Charles de Roye, who was a great lord of France as well as the count of Roucy, northeast of Reims, directed in 1543 that a perpetual daily mass for his parents' souls be said "by churchmen of good and honest life, whom his heirs and successors will elect." But then Roye lived in a Reformed household. His wife raised their daughter Eleanor, who would marry the prince of Condé in 1551, as a Protestant.[33] The request of Canon Nicole Moyen of Reims was more restrained. He asked in 1546 that the two hundred masses he commissioned be said "by churchmen not suspect of bad life, if possible."[34] The personal failings of the clergy were not of crucial importance, however, to a people who expected ritual action rather than moral example or intellectual leadership from their priests. When he envisioned a utopia staffed "by priests of exceeding holiness, and therefore very few," Thomas More had an entirely different idea of the clergy.[35]

Testators in Champagne wanted the laity as well as the clergy to be present at their funerals in force. The vine-grower Jehan Boursin directed that 2 sols be given to each man, and 20 deniers to each woman who came to his principal service. The wife of Aubry Dorigny, *élu* (judge of tax matters) of Brimont, near Reims, left six sols to each of her relatives, friends, and neighbors in attendance.[36] What seems to have been an occasional practice in Reims and its region was more common at Châlons, where seven of our testators set aside a sum for neighbors who paid their last respects. Messire Guillaume de Sainct Michel, vicar of Saint Nicaise's parish, explained why. He did so "for the prayers that they will present to God for my soul."[37]

---

33. Jules Delaborde, *Eléonore de Roye, princesse de Condé (1535-1564)* (Paris, 1876), ch. 1; AD, Marne, 4E 16698 (1543).
34. AD, Marne, 4E 16701.
35. *Utopia*, ed. Edward Surtz, S.J., and J.H. Hexter, in *The Complete Works of St. Thomas More*, IV (New Haven, 1965), 226–227.
36. Boursin: n. 29, above; Dorigny: 4E 16759 (1590).
37. AD, Marne, 4E 6230 (1577).

Burial within a church was another frequent request or demand, depending on the testator's social condition. Dame Jacquelyne de Laignes had a chantry built for her family's remains in the parish church of Chaource, which was being reconstructed during the sixteenth century. She directed in 1527 that two weekly masses be said there after her death, in perpetuity, for her parents, first husband, friends, and herself. A quarter-century later the anobli Vincent David, sieur of the nearby hamlet of Bruyères, accomplished his late mother's testament by founding a daily mass in their chantry at Chaource. He also endowed annual services in the chapel for both of his parents, and for his paternal grandparents, who unfortunately lay elsewhere in the church. Assuming that his own will, which has not survived, included perpetual services for his wife and himself, then he would have made provision for the souls of three generations of Davids. The chantry was not merely one vehicle among many which a prestige-conscious society had invented to affirm social rank, but also a means of facilitating prayer for the family dead, who lay together right below the chapel's paving stones. Living members could assemble there for memorial services. A contract of 1561 between the Franciscans of Troyes and the notary Jehan Chevrier and his wife, who had founded a chapel in the friars' church, obliged the syndic of the order, after the couple's death, to notify their relatives and friends each time a service would be held in the chapel. The wife of the anobli Sebastien Mauroy of Troyes acquired the right for herself and her heirs to erect benches or seats, and bury whomever they pleased, within the chapel she had acquired in Saint John's parish church, which was the fourth chantry there.[38]

Prayer said for family members was only the first circle in a set which expanded progressively outward until it encompassed the whole community of the faithful. During this period, an extraordinary effort was made to cultivate reciprocal aid among Christians. No man stood alone before the Divine.

Bourgeois landlords, merchants, lawyers, and their wives were commonly buried in church, though not in a private chapel, unless they had less affluent parents whose remains lay in a churchyard, and whom they desired to join. Artisans in the towns and vinegrowers in the countryside occasionally stipulated church burial

38. Laignes: n. 27, above; David: AD, Aube, 108G 43 (1553); Chevrier: ibid., nouvelles acquisitions, 189; Mauroy: E 947 (1556).

too.[39] To put the matter in numerical terms, payment was received during the parish fiscal year 1521-22 for 57 new graves which had been dug within the church, and 103 in the churchyard of Mary Magdalene's Church of Troyes.[40]

Not all testators were scrupulously concerned about their place of burial or about their last rites in general. Maistre Garlache Sonyn, *enquesteur* or investigator for the king at his court in Reims, asked that he be buried in whatever place and church may seem suitable to his wife; that as many priests and other persons attend, and as many torches be carried for the reverence of the crosses that will be there, and as many services, prayers, and orisons said for the remedy and salvation of his soul, as will seem good to his said wife, praying and bidding her to do her duty, as she would wish him to do for her in like circumstances.[41] A small proportion of the Rémois testators (28 out of the 249) used variations on this formula. They chose a means of expression that gently masked their disinterest while it saved the appearances, explicitly recognizing and paying proper lip service to the norms of the community. One exceptional case by a man calling himself Catholic classes the others as conventional. The anobli Denis Grossaine asked his brother to do his duty in having services performed, but stated that he intended no "solemnity" during his burial, near his uncle's grave in the cemetery of Saint Hilary's parish at Reims, and only a small lantern and a candle for light.[42]

The Part of the Poor in the Economy of Salvation

Charity, the supreme theological virtue, is the love of God because of his infinite mercy, and of our fellow men out of the love for God.

39. Barbe Serval, wife of the Hon. Homme Henry Ponleurant, wanted burial close to her late mother in Saint Peter's cemetery in Reims: AD, Marne, 4E 16754 (1585). Church burial was stipulated by Jehanne Philippe, wife of Jehan Varin, carpenter of Châlons: ibid., 4E 6370 (1578); Jehan Boursin, vine-grower: n. 29, above; André Leschorcher, vine-grower of Troyes: AD, Aube, 2E 3/111 (1587).

40. Ibid., 16G 50, ff. 89 and 116v-117.

41. AD, Marne, 4E 16704 (1549).

42. Maistre Denis Grossaine, seigneur of Yrnal and Vendeul, near the Vesle, east of Reims: AD, Marne, 4E 16671 (1556). Canon Regnault Grossaine was later forced by the cathedral chapter of Reims to resign; the wife of Jérôme Grossaine, lieutenant of the bailiff of Vermandois, was included in a list of the municipality of Reims of those suspected of heresy: M.E. Henry, *La Réforme et la Ligue en Champagne et à Reims* (Saint-Nicolas, Meurthe, 1867), pp. 38 and 429, gives neither precise sources nor dates.

It transcends mundane affection or compassion, qualities of which all men are capable. The Catholic who aids his neighbor does so, first and foremost, for God's sake, even though he may have other motives, including the wish to merit salvation.[43] Testators like Person Le Fas, pewter-merchant of Reims, who instructed his executors to distribute alms "for the honor of God," were expressing a theological truth, not merely a pious sentiment.[44] Those who truly love God, conversely, love all his creatures, and in particular the poor among them. But despite the simplicity and clarity of this doctrine, attitudes of the well-to-do toward the poor were complex, if not ambiguous.

The difficulties of the late Middle Ages had drawn many peasants to the cities of Europe, in search of work that was not always there. These migrants exacerbated the unrest of impoverished townsmen. Together, both groups taxed the patience as they threatened the security of men of property. Some of the more prosperous townsmen began to regard the poor with a new harshness.[45] Although there were no risings in the Champagne towns at the end of the Middle Ages, there were plenty of poor — more than 2,000 indigents among the 12,000-odd residents of Reims alone in the famine year of 1482.[46] The sixteenth-century demographic boom only increased their number. In the course of the century, as we shall later see, municipal authorities in the province founded new institutions to aid and contain the poor.

Our present task, however, is to probe the attitudes of individuals. Given both the preeminence of charity in the Catholic hierarchy of values, and the acuteness of the problem of poverty, a discussion of the ways in which the people of Champagne practiced the charitable gesture should touch the quick of their religiosity.

The basic evidence comes from the bequests in wills. It is true that a man may have left different forms of alms to be distributed after his death from those that he was accustomed to give — if he

43. *Dictionnaire de théologie catholique*, s.v. "Charité."

44. AD, Marne, 4E 16700 (1540). This phrase was apparently not a formula, since it recurs in only seven other wills.

45. Michel Mollat and Philippe Wolff, *Ongles bleus, Jacques et Ciompi* . . . (Paris, 1971), pp. 177–179 and 303, offer suggestive thoughts on this as yet underexplored subject. Georges Duby, "Les sociétés médiévales: une approche d'ensemble," *Annales: E. S. C.*, 26 (1971), 12, calls for studies to determine whether social tensions and popular revolts may not have been as prevalent in the twelfth and thirteenth, as in the fourteenth and fifteenth centuries.

46. Desportes, "La population de Reims," p. 467, n. 23.

gave — from day to day. A more serious difficulty lies in the necessity to infer the testator's assumptions about charity and his attitudes
toward the poor, of which he himself may or may not have been
conscious, from the bequests he made. Such inferences are sensed,
they cannot be proven. And even if the individual will is read correctly, there is still the problem of oversimplification in searching
for regularities, or clear differences, among them all. For to reduce
complex personal feelings to a few well-defined categories risks con-
cealing the very ambiguities we want to uncover. Given these hazards, we can only seek the range of gestures then current, but not
the frequency with which they were practiced.

Damoiselle Remyette Chardon had survived her husband, the
Hon. Philippe Frizon, merchant of Reims. She instructed her executors to dole out 10 livres, in 3-denier portions, on the day she died.
This would have meant eight hundred recipients. The threepenny
figure was crossed out, however, and quadrupled, by the hand of
the original notary. Her future executors may well have insisted on
this change, to lighten their own burden. For the day of her burial,
the widow left 20 livres to the inmates of the Hôtel Dieu, or charity
hospital, and to the town poor, again at the rate of 3 d., corrected to
12 d. She wanted twenty setiers of rye, moreover, to be divided
among eighty poor householders (pauvres mesnagers). Every poor
person in the city who came for it, finally, was to receive a loaf
worth sixpence. The widow obviously intended that her alms reach
as many people as possible. Aside from the householders, whom she
singled out for special attention, she made no distinctions among
the poor, according to either need or merit. She may well have believed that, as a woman of means, she had an obligation to every
one of the indigent which made it impossible for her to give meaningful aid to any of them. This was an old-fashioned pattern. But
then a person who belonged as she did to the Confraternity of Saint
Nicholas of Tolentino, patron of the souls in purgatory, at the
Augustinian church, as well as to three confraternities elsewhere,
was certainly pious in the traditional sense.[47]

To support the point we can turn to the will of Pierre Pirche,
which is dated 1540. He styled himself an "honneste homme," a
vague term that indicates social aspirations rather than an estab-

47. AD, Marne, 4E 16753 (1584); the will of Nicolas Frizon, an in-law, identifies
the church at which the confraternity met: 4E 16749 (1581).

lished position, and places him a notch below the Hon. Philippe Frizon.[48] Among his bequests are 40-sol grants, in twopenny coins, for the "indigent and needy poor," on the days of his death and principal service. Needy implies a certain selection: in theory, at least, his executors would have to verify that the 240 recipients on each day were in actual want. A difficult task, given their number, and an unprofitable one, since only a pittance was at stake. The other provisions in Pirche's will suggest a man of traditional leanings. He was a member of two confraternities. In the event of his premature death, he wanted others to fulfill the vows of pilgrimage he had made: three trips to both Saint-Lié's and Notre-Dame-de-Liesse, in the region, and single journeys to Saint Barbara's and Saint Nicholas's in Lorraine. For his bastard son John, he reserved 25 livres. Should the boy die before marrying or taking holy orders, the money was to be divided into thirds: one for prayers, one for the poor, and one for the testator's relatives. Pierre Pirche was a sixteenth-century merchant, but hardly in the Erasmian — or Weberian — mold.

Others practiced a similar style of giving. In 1575 Gaulchier Chaussart of Reims, whose occupation is not stated, set aside 100 sols, in threepenny coins, for the day of his principal service. Catherine Quentin of Troyes, wife of a royal sergeant-at-law for the countryside, left twopence, up to a total of 40 sols, to the poor beggars in 1540, "as soon after her burial as possible." Pierre Ozanne, merchant and resident of Troyes, who in his first will chose the church of the adjacent village of Saint-Lyé for a burial place, left a sol in 1587 to every widow who would attend the service. This is certainly a larger sum than those cited earlier, and the widows are a well-defined and limited group. Still, Ozanne's intent to treat them all equally tentatively suggests that he may fit the pattern we have been sketching. He also endowed, in perpetuity, a distribution of a setier of rye and one of barley in small loaves for the poor beggars after High Mass on four Sundays from April to June. His executors, and ultimately his heirs, would administer the grant, which would help to tide over the poor at a particularly critical time, when grain prices were rising to their annual heights, as the harvest of the pre-

48. N. 20, above. Marcel Couturier, *Recherches sur les structures sociales de Châteaudun, 1525–1789* (Paris, 1969), pp. 216–222, places honorific prefixes in their social context.

vious summer was being progressively consumed and the present
crop was still on the ground. Ozanne was making provision for the
future in a way that our other testators did not. His intended recipients were, nevertheless, the beggars. When he decided shortly afterwards to be buried in the Dominican church of Troyes, he replaced
the bequest to the widows of Saint Lye with three bushels (a quarter-setier in all) of rye, again in small loaves, for the poor of
Troyes.[49]

Bishop Gilles de Luxembourg, of Châlons, displayed his charity
on a much grander scale. In 1532 he provided 50 livres, in threepenny coins, for distribution on his death. Although he may not
have taken the trouble to calculate that he would be reaching four
thousand people, the bishop surely knew that he was providing for
all the poor of Châlons, and more. At the same time, twenty-five
setiers of wheat were to be milled into threepenny loaves. After ar-
ranging for a lavish funeral and making generous donations to several churches, Luxembourg left the remainder of the estate to the
poor, specifically naming them as his heirs. He wanted all the funds
spent to convert an abandoned, or perhaps little used, building in
Châlons into a shelter for the homeless poor, with a coal fire every
evening from All Saints' to Christmas. One such shelter already existed, in the parvis of Notre-Dame-en-Vaux. The bishop's solicitude
for the most abject, and his treatment of them equally, is clear.[50]

The giving of a pittance to as many recipients as possible may
have been the city dweller's version of a traditional rural practice.
The seigneurs in our sample of testators, whether noble or bourgeois, commonly provided for a distribution of bread or money to all
the village poor. Charles de Behan, squire and seigneur of Hagni-
court, north of the Aisne, wanted them to receive the bread from
six setiers of wheat. The Hon. Jehan Audry, seigneur of La Lesne,
but living in Reims, made an identical bequest. Pierre Le Caussonnier, squire and seigneur of Ystres and part of Bury, where he lived,
on the plain below the Mountain of Vertus, left 60 livres for the
needy poor among his villagers, to be brought to their homes by
persons whom his executors would select, and an equal sum for
those of the surrounding villages, to be distributed in front of his

49. Chaussart: AD, Marne, 4E 16743; Quentin: AD, Aube, 2E 1/1; Ozanne: AD, Aube,
375G 5.
50. AC, Châlons, GG 215 (1532).

house.[51] Seigneurs were responding to a moral obligation to relieve, at the time of their death, the needy among their peasants, who expected the distribution as a matter of custom. It formed one link in the complex network of exchanges — asymmetrical exchanges, to be sure — between the two.

Our urban testators may have been playing the part of seigneur vis-à-vis the urban poor. This makes good sense in the bishop's case, for he held the title of count and was seigneurial judge in a large part of Châlons. In general, as Bernhard Groethuysen maintained, the great needed the poor to reflect their own eminence. Grandeur is but relative, he pointed out, and can manifest itself only through contrast. Why, after all, did God create the rich in the first place, if not to relieve the poor — all the poor, in fact. At the same time, since the great had the opportunity to sin on a wholly different scale from their inferiors, they felt obliged to expiate their wrongs in a grandiose manner, and relied on the existence of the poor for this purpose, too.[52] Liberality in almsgiving, then, was one of the attributes of the nobility. But how can this analysis apply to the generality of our testators? No merchant, however honorable, much less a sergeant's wife, could pretend to be among the great. Certainly there was no lack of complaints in sixteenth-century France from the authentic greats against the sons of shopkeepers who were aping their ways. On the village level everyone knew who the seigneur was. In the urban setting, however, with its complex social structure, the prestige of an individual was often much less clear-cut. What more striking indication of a person's status could there be than the capability to assemble the poor on his death, en masse, to receive his alms? Here was a strong incentive to magnify the gesture of giving.

The motives of most people were no doubt mixed. An individual testator may have meant to use the poor for his own purposes, without really being aware of this intention. Of greater significance is the style of giving: a feeling of responsibility to all the poor, a lack of discrimination among them, and an insignificant handout to everyone who could be reached, with possible overtones of a search to acquire or to demonstrate social prestige.

Groethuysen distinguished sharply between the way in which the

51. Behan: AD, Marne, 4E 16745 (1577); Audry: n. 24, above; Le Caussonnier: 4E 6377 (1585).

52. *Origines de l'esprit bourgeois en France* (1927; reprint ed., Paris, 1956), pp. 176 and 190.

nobility and the bourgeoisie regarded charity. The latter may have given alms, but they did not need the poor as a negative complement. They were confident in their ability to please God by manifesting the virtues proper to their own estate — work, order, and tranquility — and they blamed the poor for not being more like themselves.[53] In our period, however, one would have had to look hard to find good bourgeois, even acquisitive merchants, who were willing to rest their case for salvation on a life of bourgeois virtue alone. Certainly every testator cited thus far acknowledged some dependence on the poor, by making his almsgiving an integral part of the funeral cycle. And taken together, roughly a quarter of those in our sample who gave alms stipulated that at least part of them be distributed at a time between their death and the day after burial. In this way the testator complemented the religious ritual with a demonstration of his piety, at the crucial moment when the church, his family, and friends were pleading for mercy on his soul.

A smaller but still significant number went further, and incorporated the poor into their services, following the example of the great of sixteenth-century France. Five hundred torch-bearing poor marched at the head of Francis I's burial procession. In Champagne, the cardinal of Lorraine provided in his will for four hundred, all to be clothed in black robes and hoods. Bishop Gilles de Luxembourg contented himself with fifty; the torches they would carry would be decorated with his arms.[54] When the body of the wife of the bailiff of Troyes, Anne de Vauldrey, seigneur of Saint Phal, passed through the city on its way to burial, the inmates of the hospitals, fifty of the town poor, and another fifty from Saint Phal followed it.[55] Arnold de Cadennet, a Provençal squire who fell sick in Châlons and had his will drawn there, also considered himself important enough to have fifty marchers. But since he was not certain that his executors could assemble that number from among his own villagers, he instructed them to gather neighboring ones as necessary.[56]

The number of poor mourners was a measure of the social gulf

53. Ibid., p. 191.

54. Ralph Giesey, *The Royal Funeral Ceremony in Renaissance France* (Geneva, 1960), p. 9; BN, Fonds français, 4507, ff. 167–174; n. 50, above.

55. *Mémoires et livre de famille de Nicolas Dare* (Troyes, 1886), pp. 29–30. Dare, a merchant of Troyes, belonged to an old family and took an active part in municipal affairs during the last two decades of the sixteenth century. His chronicle of births, marriages, and deaths may be of interest to historical demographers.

56. AD, Marne, 4E 838 (1570).

that separated them from the deceased. By convoking the poor to march, moreover, and dressing them with dignity for the occasion, the testator made them momentarily respectable, and gave them a social purpose — that of honoring his memory. To what extent had this practice become generalized in the cities of Champagne, among men and women of less lofty social condition, and what additional motives might they have had in adopting it?

Among the Catholic residents of Châlons in our sample who gave to the poor, seven testators out of thirty-six directed that poor people participate in their funeral, or else invited them to witness their services. Three of them were women of noble family, at least by marriage (one squire and two anoblis); one, the widow of a bourgeois seigneur; two canons; and the last — to break the pattern — a priest's housekeeper. The evidence is too limited to be conclusive by itself. Still, Damoiselle Loyse Bijet, wife of the Hon. Charles François, sieur of Chaufour, referred to the compensation of "the thirty poor who carry the torches and candles" in a tone that assumed that this was a customary practice for a person of her condition, and did not need to be spelled out in detail. She left each marcher an ell of white cloth worth 25 sols. Marie Haale, an anobli's daughter, wanted an unspecified number of poor dressed in black, and paid "as honorably as possible." Maistre Jean Viart, canon of Notre-Dame-en-Vaux, did not include the poor in his procession, but offered twopence, instead, to all those who attended his services, up to a total of 20 sols each time. He anticipated, or at least hoped for, 120 people in church.[57]

In Reims, sixteen of the seventy-three resident charitable testators, a roughly similar proportion, were involved. But only two of them were nobles, out of ten in the sample, eight of whom gave to the poor. And one of the two was a woman who came from a Châlonnais family. Most of the rest were bourgeois notables, save for an archer, a cooper's widow, and a concierge. The testator in every case but one did not try to pack the church or greatly lengthen the procession. Rather he directed that a symbolic number of poor people be present — twelve or thirteen, to represent the apostles. Nicolas Frizon the elder, merchant and late in-law of the widow

57. Bijet: AD, Marne, 4E 8759 (1598) ; Marie, daughter of the late Noble Homme Jehan Haale, procureur royal of the Presidial Court of Vitry: 4E 886 (1598) ; Viart: 4E 837 (1569) .

with whom we began this discussion, convoked thirteen of them to march in his procession and attend his services. Lacking in worldly goods, like the apostles, they were innocent in the sight of God, at least much more innocent than a heavily laden merchant like Frizon. And so it was very fitting — perhaps it would even be advantageous — that they walk before his coffin, candle in hand. At the very least, they would endow his last rites with a certain nobility and grace. Frizon made provision, in advance, to display his love of God at his final hour. He left each marcher five sols, the only mention he made of the poor in his will. This was one of the few charitable gestures then current that the widow of Philippe Frizon did not later make. But even if he was a much less generous person than she, still they both acknowledged, in separate but complementary ways, the spiritual significance of the poor.[58]

For Troyes, the evidence available is limited to the clergy and common people, for no nobles are represented in the few extant sixteenth-century wills. Testators seem to have brought the poor into their funerals frequently — in seventeen out of the twenty-eight wills that mention them at all. The testators, who were merchants, artisans, and priests, typify the Troyen group as a whole, which, as I noted earlier, was perhaps more pious than the community at large. Their resources, generally speaking, were limited, and the scale on which they involved the poor, modest. In several instances, the intent was to use them to carry the torches and candles that accompanied every funeral procession, rather than to supply additional sources of light. The widow of Jacques Passot, painter, wanted six of each borne by poor people who were to be given three deniers; this would cost her estate but three sols. More affluent, and much more pretentious, the merchant-furrier Philippe Larbalestrier's widow ordered twelve and twelve, every one to be decorated with her arms. Others provided for thirteen symbolic marchers instead of, or in addition to, the torch-bearing poor. Two suburban innkeepers, curiously, stand out from the rest of the testators. François Herluyson of Saint-Jacques-les-Troyes, and Guyon Chartres

---

58. Anne Coquault, wife of the Hon. Jehan Bennart, was the testator concerned to have a numerous contingent of the poor and convoked thirty of them — ten poor men, ten children, and ten women (listed in that order) : AD, Marne, 4E, 16743 (1575) . Catherine, widow of the cooper Nicolas Laloudre: 4E 16695 (1539) ; Jehan Oudinet, king's archer, living at Verzy: 4E 16700 (1545) ; Batiste Gaillart, concierge of the abbot's residence at Saint Remy's Monastery: 4E 16757 (1588) ; and Nicolas Frizon: n. 47, above.

of Pont-Hubert, each stipulated that four poor men act as pallbearers. This was a layman's variation on the occasional practice
followed by clerics of asking the friars, who lived by the rule of
poverty, to carry the coffin.[59]

The part played by the poor in the funeral ceremony varied, then,
from place to place. Whether we have correctly captured the individuality of each town in this respect may be open to question, given
the nature of the evidence. What matters more is that, in different
ways, men and women of means — sometimes of very limited means
— were able to mimic portions of the dialogue between the great
and the poor. They had two possible reasons for doing so. Either
they were acting out of pride, and mustering the poor to demonstrate their importance, or in modesty, giving God's unfortunate,
but favored, creatures the respect due them at so solemn a moment.
In logic, either motive might preclude the other, but not necessarily
in the minds of individual testators.

A handful of them asked the poor, explicitly, for spiritual aid.
Jean Nicot of La Chapelle Saint-Luc, a village on the outskirts of
Troyes, wanted twenty poor men clothed in doublets after his death,
so that they would have occasion to pray for his soul. Nicole Coquebert, widow of the Hon. Gerard Moet of Reims, left a quarter-setier
of rye, and the money to mill it, to each of a hundred poor widows
with children, in order that they recommend her in their prayers.
Another widow of Reims, Collette Le Gros, whose late husband had
been a merchant-apothecary, ordered that thirteen poor widows, including a few whom she cited by name, receive five sols for the same
purpose. Nicolas Goujon, seigneur of Tours-sur-Marne and seneschal of Reims, directed that thirteen poor men, known to be of good
character, attend his funeral services. His executors would give them
their dinner, a setier of wheat and five sols, with the injunction to
remember and to have pity on Goujon's soul. And finally, one of
his descendants, Hierosme Goujon, left 18 livres to the municipal

---

59. Anaintare Maillet, the widow Passot: AD, Aube, 2E 7/144 (1596) ; Margueritte La
Croix, the widow Larbalestrier: ibid. (1604) ; François Herluyson, merchant-innkeeper:
2E 3/111 (1587) ; and Guyon Chartres: 2E 3/110 (1585) . Other Troyens who asked
that the friars carry their coffins were Canon Nicole Bourguignard of Saint Stephen's:
ibid. (1584) ; Claude, daughter of Nicolas Arnoul (no profession stated) : ibid. (1584) ;
Canon Lazare Pouville of Saint Stephen's: 2E 3/111 (1595) ; and Denis Boyvin, vicar of
Saint Urban's: 2E 7/144 (1602) .

bureau of poor relief of Châlons (of which more in a subsequent chapter) to buy meat for the homeless poor, who were then lodged in a barn, so that they would pray for him.[60]

These five donors seem as interested in what the poor can do for them as in what they can do for the poor. Their egoism, nevertheless, is predicated on humility. For to them the poor are not merely incidental, the passive objects of a gesture they are making toward God. Rather the donors are dependent upon the recipients of their own alms, who act as mediators on their behalf. This position gives them a special kind of power which, like all power, endows them with a measure of dignity and entitles them to some respect. The exchange of alms for prayers, moreover, creates a personal relationship between donor and recipient. The secret charity that Jesus enjoined in the Sermon on the Mount becomes irrelevant. To pray for their benefactors, the poor must know who they are. No other testator openly stated the intention to exchange alms for prayers. But some of them must have shared the idea, to a greater or lesser degree, without caring or taking the trouble to express it.

Of the five, the elder Goujon alone stipulated that only the virtuous be chosen. Their intercession, he must have reasoned, would have special value. Nicot and the widow Coquebert, in calling upon thirty and one hundred poor people, respectively, showed that they measured prayers quantitatively. Not surprisingly, their other bequests fall into the pattern of testators like the widow Frizon. Nicot intended that small breads, from two bushels of wheat, be distributed to those poor people who attended his service and that each of the village widows receive 2 s. 6 d. The Damoiselle Coquebert left 10 livres to be divided equally among the inmates of the Hôtel-Dieu. On the day of her death, moreover, the poor (in general) were to receive four setiers of rye, in bread, and a puncheon of wine. Nicolas Goujon, on the other hand, limited his additional alms to thirteen poor housewives — probably to complement the thirteen men of the funeral ceremony. He left each of them significant quantities of grain and wine, permitting the women to come three or four times for the wine, so that they could make the best use of it. Goujon's criterion of virtue implies that not all the poor were de-

60. Nicot: AD, Aube, 110G 9 (1602); Coquebert: AD, Marne, 4E 16706 (1551); Le Gros: 4E 16696 (1540); N. Goujon: n. 25, above; H. Goujon: 4E 6230 (1595).

serving. This point is made with equal clarity in the will of Damoiselle Claude Lois of Châlons.[61] She followed the local aristocratic
practice of including poor people in her funeral procession, and yet
left four setiers of rye and two of wheat "to the poor who will merit
it." Respect for the principle of poverty did not prevent either her
or Goujon from distinguishing carefully among the poor.

Like Nicolas Goujon, testators who gave selectively favored the
poor housewives or often, more precisely, the poor, hidden housewives. Hidden, or *honteux,* if taken literally, referred exclusively to
members of noble or at least notable families who had become im-
pecunious, yet tried to conceal their distress.[62] In sixteenth-century
French parlance the category was extended to include "people who
did not come to poverty by wickedness, but by adversity and fortune."[63] Even more broadly, and as used by our testators, the term
simply meant those who kept their misery to themselves, rather
than displaying it publicly by begging in the streets. The widow of
Jehan Godignon of Châlons provided for a distribution of grain to
the "poor, hidden housewives, not beggars." Alpin Desaulx of the
same city set aside 30 livres for "hidden people not daring to demand
alms."[64] He did want three dozen small breads handed out as well,
once his services were completed, but this was to be done in secret.
The testators discussed earlier had welcomed the very beggars whom
the widow Godignon and Desaulx shunned. Clearly begging evoked
strong, and contradictory, responses in sixteenth-century Champagne. For some, it was an inevitable aspect of the human condition, and those who were reduced to it had to be helped, without
any real hope, however, of improving their lot or reducing their
number. For others, the fact that poverty may have been blameless
in theory did not give the poor license to beg. They were expected
to live docilely, in a fixed residence, striving their utmost to make
do on what they had. The poor could only hope to benefit from
the generosity of their betters as long as they made no overt demands
on them.

The donor who thought this way recognized no responsibility to

61. AD, Marne, 4E 8760 (1601).

62. Emile Léonard, *Histoire générale du protestantisme,* I (Paris, 1961), 296. Cf. Brian
Pullan, *Rich and Poor in Renaissance Venice* (Cambridge, Mass., 1971), p. 231, on
the *poveri vergognosi.*

63. Françoys Bellemère, *Directoire de la vie humaine,* . . . (Troyes, n.d.), sig. Aiii.

64. Godignon: AD, Marne, 4E 8824 (1559); Desaulx: 4E 885 (1597).

all the poor of his community. He was not obliged to spread his alms thinly. And in fact, bequests to the hidden poor rarely stipulated the number of recipients or insisted that they be treated alike. This made it possible for an executor, within the limits of the funds provided him, to offer something more meaningful than a handful of pennies or a small loaf of bread. The Hon. Hillebert Bouchier, merchant of Reims, left 40, which he later changed to 60, livres for the poor, hidden housewives, and for poor girls who would be married at Reims. The housewives were also to receive sixteen setiers of rye. He gave his executors complete freedom in allocating the money and grain, advising them simply to act "as they would see best." Another Rémoise, Marie Grant Jehan, the widow Loreignol, whose social status is not given, made somewhat similar provisions: fifty livres to "poor, hidden housewives, poor widows, orphans, poor marriageable girls, and other needy persons," again at the executors' discretion. One more testator, and he of exalted rank, linked the housewives and single girls. The cardinal of Lorraine left 500 livres to the poor of Reims during his services, half of which would go to these two groups.[65] The association is consistent. In the first place, the executors, in awarding a dowry, would most probably look to the hidden poor, preferring a girl of known family and established residence to one who lived from the streets. More importantly, she received, not fleeting help, but the kind of assistance whose effects would last a lifetime.

Other testators were concerned with young men. Nicolas Dare, a prominent merchant of Troyes, endowed a foundation to yield 50 livres annually, for a duration of sixty years, to aid the needy poor, and to permit children to learn a trade. Anne Coquault, wife of the Hon. Jehan Bennart, bourgeois of Reims, left a lump sum of 12 livres to apprentice the impoverished.[66] Whichever sex they were partial to, these testators had a common intent. They meant to enable a poor boy or girl to acquire, in the language of the sixteenth century, an estate, whether that of a skilled craftsman or of a respectable married woman, and take a recognized, if still humble, place in the social order.

Nine testators of Reims, out of the seventy residents who gave

65. Bouchier: AD, Marne, 4E 16706 (1551); Marie Grant Jehan: 4E 16744 (1575); the cardinal: n. 54, above.

66. Dare: *Mémoires de Nicolas Dare*, p. 133; Coquault: n. 58, above.

alms, and four out of the twenty-six Catholics in Châlons, mentioned the hidden poor in their wills.[67] In Troyes the term was not
used. The Rémois testators included three merchants and the wives
of a noble who held a *licence* in law, of an eminent attorney, and of
a notary. The status of the remaining three is not given. Once again
we are dealing, generally speaking, with bourgeois notables, but this
is more a reflection of our sample, and of those who had the means
to give distinctively, rather than of the specific style with which they
gave. My instinct is that, even if figures were available in sufficient
depth, they would not allow clear shadings — much less divisions —
in attitudes toward charity among people of different estates and
professions in sixteenth-century Champagne. This was a matter of
personal feelings, not of class-bound judgments.

We cannot separate the two styles of giving with precision, for
some testators could be supple enough to practice both. The sieur
de Chaufour's widow, who, it may be remembered, took the presence of thirty poor people at the funeral virtually for granted,
wanted the criterion of merit used in awarding bushels of rye to
twenty poor widows. On the other hand, she also made a general distribution of three setiers of rye and twelve bushels of wheat to all
comers, on the day of her principal service. Anne Coquault summoned thirty marchers to her funeral, and also provided funds for
apprenticeship. Even the widow Frizon, archetype of the undis-
criminating donor, remembered the poor householders in her will,
though her intention, here as everywhere, was to reach them in
numbers.[68]

A balance between unguarded and selective almsgiving may well
have been the most traditional practice, for it reflects the church's
own attitude toward poor relief, as it was developed by the canon-

67. *Reims:* Jehanne, wife of Guillaume Baalain (occupation no longer legible) : AD,
Marne, 4E 16696 (1540) ; Damoiselle G. Coquillart: n. 15, above; N. Ribaille, merchant: n. 28, above; Guillemette Hoquart, wife of Hon. Homme Jehan de Brissault le
jeune, licen. en loix: AD, Marne, 4E 16700 (1545) ; the widow of Colynet Dorigny,
merchant: 4E 16703 (1548) ; Hon. H. Bouchier: n. 65, above; Marie Grant Jehan:
n. 65, above; Perette Jaquart, wife of Jehan Olivier (occupation not stated) : AD,
Marne, 4E 16744 (1576) ; Jabin Rogier, wife of Nicolas Mercier, notary: 4E 16753
(1584) .

Châlons: The widow Godignon and Alpin Desaulx: n. 64, above; Hon. Jacques
Henrey, master-painter: AD, Marne, 4E 8230 (1581) ; Jehan Clement, dean of the
cathedral: ibid., 4E 885 (1597) .

68. Damoiselle Loyse Bijet, widow of the sieur de Chaufour: n. 57, above; Anne
Coquault: n. 58, above; Damoiselle Remyette Chardon, the widow Frizon: n. 47, above.

ists of the high Middle Ages, and handed down intact to the sixteenth century. The canonists did not hesitate to draw distinctions
among the poor, but they regarded the unworthy — the sturdy,
professional beggars — "as abnormalities, associated with a special
type of moral perversity. They taught that it was proper to deny
alms to such individuals when they were known, but not that all
charitable activity should be regulated as though its principal purpose was to exclude the undeserving rather than to help the deserving.
They deprecated the squandering of large sums in 'indiscriminate
charity,' but countenanced a certain openhandedness in day-to-day
almsgiving." By the end of the Middle Ages, however, as Brian
Tierney observes, such an attitude offered no practical guide for
dealing with the great number of poor.[69] It is hardly surprising, under the circumstances, that some of the more prosperous townsmen
blamed the beggars for their own plight. In direct opposition to the
canonists they considered a poor man guilty until he could prove
himself innocent, by showing that he was making at least a partially
successful effort to survive on his own. Men who thought this way
must have found it difficult to see the spiritual value of poverty.

The Strong Carry the Weak

Catholics approached the saints, those exemplars of humanity, in
the same way that the poor approached their betters. They offered
prayer in exchange for patronage and favor. But unlike the poor
man in the face of the rich, the loyal Catholic did not have to fear
ambivalence or latent hostility from the saints. Charles Wagley, in
his study of an Amazon town, makes a point that holds for Catholicism generally: the saints protect, yet never punish, as long as they
are shown proper respect.[70] The saints' superabundance of merit enabled them to intercede with God for the living and the dead, and
filled the treasury from which the pope drew indulgences — a clas-
sic case of the strong carrying the weak.

A person's Christian name governed his initial allegiance. The
choice depended most often not on the parents' preferences, but on
the names of the sponsors at baptism, one of whom passed down his

69. *Medieval Poor Law: A Sketch of Canonical Theory and Its Application in
England* (Berkeley and Los Angeles, 1959), p. 62, and ch. 6.
70. *Amazon Town* (New York, 1953), p. 220.

saint to the infant. The godparents of the first-born, ideally, were a
set of grandparents. Jehan Pussot, carpenter of Reims, recorded in
1570 that his eldest daughter "was named Perette, by my father[-in-
law] Pierre Pinchart and his wife." Twenty-one years later Pussot
and his wife sponsored Perette's eldest, Jehan. Nicolas Dare, mer-
chant-clothier of Troyes, called his first child Anne, after his mother
and a cousin, who served as godparents together. In all, at least
three and perhaps four of Dare's six children by his first wife were
given a godparent's name. One of the others, a girl, received the
name of her sister who died in infancy.[71]

The Protestants furnish proof that Catholics were called after
godparents. The baptismal register of the Reformed Church of
Châlons, which opens in August 1591, shows 105 female births for
the first nine years. Thirty girls were named Marie. Of their 23 god-
mothers listed, 15 were Maries, too. Even the most reformed parents
generally followed traditional usage, especially for the girls. Helye
(Eli) Thelisson, the Protestant schoolteacher, named one of his
Marie, after her godmother, instead of, say, Suzanne or Sara. (He
followed a pattern, not a rule; otherwise there would have been no
Suzannes, Saras, or Helyes.) Using his own, Old Testament, name,
Abel Brichot sponsored his nephew and a kinsman of his wife, the
only two sixteenth-century Abels in the register.[72] This practice emphasized continuity within the family. It also permitted a Catholic
to consider his saint as a more distant but more powerful godparent,
and even to address him as such. Claude Enfer, merchant of Chaource, invoked "Monsieur Saint Claude, my godfather," in his will.

71. Jean Pussot, "Journalier ou mémoires," *Travaux de l'Académie nationale de
Reims*, 23, no. 1 (1855–1856), 154; 25, no. 1 (1856–1857), 15; *Mémoires de Nicolas
Dare*, pp. 111–114. Pussot, a carpenter of Reims, stuffed his "Journalier" full of the
details of family life, meteorology, and great occasions in town. His adult life covered
the half-century from the 1570s to the 1620s. An ardent churchgoer, Pussot both
listened attentively to sermons and had a meticulous knowledge of ritual. He was a bit
of a prude, and can be quite a bore, but the reader who picks his way through the
memoirs will find, after 1600, some information on the Jesuits and on the incipient
Catholic Reformation. The memoirs are most interesting when, as a great-grand-
father and an octogenarian, Pussot became reflective. He gathered his resentments
against individual clerics into a general skepticism about the clergy, praised the
Venetians for dominating the church in their lands, and, finally, rehabilitated Erasmus,
who was guilty only of mixing a few attacks against some monks into his writings.

72. AD, Marne, Châlons, Protestants, Registre de l'état civil; Thelisson: 8 Nov. 1592;
Brichot sponsored Abel, son of Loys Bezanson and Rachelle Billet (9 Nov. 1597) and
Abel, son of Jacques Brichot (21 July 1599).

Michel Noel, curé of Saint Aventin's parish of Troyes, used the same phrase for the archangel Saint Michael.[73]

The surviving evidence does not make clear what responsibilities human godparents undertook. They often left small sums of money to godchildren. Clerics complained, as was their wont, that godparents neglected their religious duties. Canon Gentien Hervet, in his catechism for the diocese of Reims, berated them for considering their obligations fulfilled once they had charged the parents with teaching the child his beliefs.[74] The criticism suggests that godparents were not totally unconcerned.

What men and women expected of their saintly godparents, on the other hand, is very clear indeed. In 1561 the vine-grower Jehan Boursin chose burial in front of the statue of Saint John the Baptist in the Church of Prouilly. At Ervy, southwest of Troyes, an elderly donor had himself represented in a stained-glass window depicting the baptism of Christ, which he gave to the parish church about 1510. Drawn to half the scale of the biblical figures, he kneels before a prayer bench, his hands piously joined. Three even smaller figures, his adult sons, kneel behind him. Next to them stands a massive and majestic Saint James, the donor's name-saint, who visually dominates and visibly protects the group. The saint has his hand on the old man's shoulder and his eye on someone in front and above him whom the window does not show. In the corresponding panel on the right, Saint Anne presents Anne the donor's wife to the unseen figure, while the woman's five daughters look on.[75]

This pattern recurs throughout Champagne, and continues until the religious wars interrupted window-making. In other provinces Emile Mâle found more complete illustrations, which identify the unseen figure as the Madonna with the Christ Child in her arms. She is a middle link in the chain of prayer that leads from man to God. The essential function of the name-saint, then, was to protect his dependents beyond the grave, and to intercede for them with the powers above. For this reason, donors who died after commissioning

73. Enfer: AD, Aube, 108G 29 (1557); Noel: ibid., 2E 3/110 (1584).

74. Margueritte Hurtault and Alpin Desaulx of Châlons left 10 s. and 5 s., respectively, to each of their godchildren: AD, Marne, 4E 6374 (1582) and n. 64, above. Other testators named godchildren individually, without indicating whether they were making bequests to all. Hervet, Catéchisme, f. 9.

75. Boursin: n. 29, above; the Ervy donor: Biver, L'école troyenne, p. 156, fig. 156.

a window, but before it was completed, were nevertheless shown with their saint.[76]

People in Champagne did not, however, call their name-saint a patron. This term was reserved to the responsibilities of saints to groups, as opposed to individuals. The merchant Claude Enfer distinguished between "Monsieur Saint John [the Baptist] my patron" to whom the parish church of Chaource was dedicated, and "Monsieur Saint Claude my godfather." The Church of Nogent-sur-Seine was named for Saint Laurence, whom a priest identified in his memoirs as the "patron and godfather" of one Laurent Gravier.[77] Men and women, in their wills, were much more likely to commend their souls to the parish patron than to their name-saint. Half the testators of Reims and Troyes did so, enough to indicate a common practice that stopped short of being a formula.[78] By contrast only one Rémois, the pious nobleman Nicolas Goujon, and three Troyens — a priest attached to a parish, a canon, and a canon's servant — invoked name-saints.[79] The difference between the will and the window was that the testator was appealing to the community for support immediately after his death, while the donor was thinking of the long run, when his neighbors and priests would themselves be gone, and the parish patron's attention focused on other, living persons. Only the name-saint could offer permanent support. The window, as Mâle pointed out, would serve as a perpetual reminder to him.[80]

The intensity and joy with which parishioners celebrated the fes-

76. Mâle, *L'art religieux de la fin du Moyen Age*, pp. 162–163. Three of the Cathedral of Troyes's nave windows, erected at the turn of the sixteenth century, furnish examples of the depiction of deceased donors. The Daniel window, given by the merchant Jehan Corart — who was deceased, as the cross in his hands indicates — and his wife (Biver, *L'école troyenne*, pp. 67–69, fig. 40) ; the Job window, given by Jehanne de Mesgriny, widow of the écuyer Jehan Molé, and depicting both of them (ibid., pp. 71–72, fig. 42) ; and the Tobias window, given by the merchant Jehan Festuot the elder — whom Biver identifies as deceased at the time the window was made — and his wife (ibid., pp. 73–75, fig. 44) .

77. Enfer: n. 73, above; Claude Haton, *Mémoires*, ed. F. Bourquelot (2 vols., Paris, 1857) , I, 341.

78. Of our 249 wills from Reims, 121 call on the saint of the testator's church. 81 of these identify him as their patron. For the 60 wills from Troyes, the corresponding figures are 28 and 13. Only 6 Châlonnais invoked the patron, either because of a difference in local custom, or more plausibly because Protestant notaries writing Catholic wills did not suggest the possibility to their clients.

79. *Reims:* Goujon: n. 25, above. *Troyes:* Martine Collot, servante: AD, Aube, 2E 3/110 (1583) ; Canon Nicole Bourguignard: n. 59, above; and Guillaume Bendot of Saint James's: AD, Aube, 2E 7/144 (1603) .

80. *L'art religieux de la fin du Moyen Age*, p. 162.

tival of their patron provides a further indication of his importance. The churchwardens of Saint James in Troyes ordered the portal and treasure of the church covered with tapestries. They had the floor strewn with rushes, and gave flowered hats to the girls who solicited donations for the vestry. A friar came to deliver a sermon, for this was one of the four holidays on which the vestry was obliged to pay a preacher, in addition to the five sermons that the Abbey of Saint-Jacques-aux-Nonnains, whose church the parish shared, was supposed to provide. The abbey rarely met its obligations, and in the second half of the century the parish grew lax, too. By 1578 the churchwardens were no longer inviting a friar on the feast of the Nativity of the Virgin, nor after 1578 on the Annunciation. They continued, however, the sermons on Saint James's Day and on the Sunday following the anniversary of the dedication of their church to him. When Mass was over, if not while it was still being celebrated, the time came for play outside, which took the form of street dances. Ecclesiastical officials, towards the end of the century, were becoming concerned about such carousing. The cathedral chapter of Troyes admonished Saint Aventin's parishioners, who were under its judicial authority, to stop dancing while services were being held.[81] This secular aspect of the festival was as important as the religious side, for it gave men and women the opportunity to show conviviality toward one another while they honored the saint whose patronage they all shared.

On the day following the patron's holiday, as well as after Corpus Christi and one or two other festivals, the vestry of Saint Giles's Church of Montreuil-sur-Barse, a populous and rich village east of Troyes, paid for elaborate and expensive sets of services for the parish dead. When during the religious wars troops of soldiers began to cross their fields, they omitted the sets after the other festivals as luxuries, but maintained those of the patron and Corpus Christi.[82]

In evil times Catholics appealed beyond their parish to the patrons of towns and regions. To quell a fire in 1530 the clergy of Troyes carried in procession the relics of three protectors of the dio-

---

81. The festivals at Saint James's: AD, Aube, 14G 16 (1503), f. 15; 14G 18, cahier no. 2 (1526), f. 75; 14G 28 (1578–1580), f. 11. The list of the sermons to be delivered is in 14G 18, cahier no. 3 (1527), f. 112, and 14G 20 (1530), f. 25; those actually delivered were noted annually, e.g., 14G 16 (1503), f. 12, and 14G 52 (1598), ff. 17–18. For the cathedral and Saint Aventin's, see G 1292, f. 218 (1599).

82. Ibid., 279G 1 (1564) – 279G 3 (1585).

cese: Saint Loup, Saint Helen, and Saint Hoylde. The bones of Saint Loup, who was credited with having preserved Troyes from Attila, lay in the abbey that bore his name. Saint Helen's relics, which were believed to be of Greek origin, were one of the treasures of the cathedral. The remains of Saint Hoylde, a Champenois virgin, graced Saint Stephen's Collegial Church. During a severe drought in 1556, the peasants of the surrounding countryside marched village by village to the Cathedral of Troyes, in hopes that Saint Mathie, another local virgin, whose relics were housed there, and Saint Helen, would intercede with God for rain.[83]

Relics of the saints also served to cure personal ills. One layer of sixteenth-century Champagne's religious topography was a fine mesh of pilgrimage sites. The people of Reims had a healing saint within a few miles, at Saint Brice's village church on the plain. Or they could climb to the point where the Mountain of Reims approaches the city most closely and faces it directly, to reach Saint Lié's relics, in his chapel near the market village of Ville-Dommange. The bones of Saint Fery at the Church of Verneuil-sur-Aisne, which today's maps show as Moussy-Verneuil, were twenty-six miles away, almost a full day's journey down the valley of the Vesle, and then north at Fismes to the Aisne. Saint Bertaud's Abbey was northeast of Reims, sixty kilometers to Chaumont-Porcien across the plain. He at least was known to history. Fifteenth-century popes had granted indulgences to his pilgrims for the purpose of rebuilding the hospital attached to the abbey. Paul II, issuing one of them in 1466, noted that innumerable poor, sick, and especially mad people *(phreneticos)* were the saint's clients.[84] To the south lay the relics of Saint Bertha at Saint Peter's Abbey in Avenay, where the Mountain faces the Marne, those of Saint Radegonde at the Church of Mareuil-sous-Aÿ in the valley below, and of Saint Gond at his abbey in the marshes at the foot of the Mountain of Vertus. Beyond the province, Rémois

83. Giles Constable, "Troyes, Constantinople, and the Relics of St Helen in the Thirteenth Century," in *Mélanges offerts à René Crozet*, II (Poitiers, 1966), 1035–1042. For the fire of 1530 and the drought of 1556 see, respectively, Marie-Nicolas Des Guerrois, *La saincteté chrestienne . . .* (Troyes, 1637), f. 419, and Nicolas Pithou, "Histoire ecclésiastique de l'église de la ville de Troyes . . . de la restauration du pur service de Dieu et de l'ancien ministère en la dicte église . . . ," BN, Collection Dupuy, MS 698, ff. 88–89v.

84. *Acta sanctorum* (Antwerp, 1643–1883; reprint, Brussels, Culture et Civilisation, 1966–1971), p. 102: 16–19 June.

went to Saint Claude in Franche-Comté, known for his help to the crippled and the maimed, and to Saint Fiacre, near Meaux in Brie, who aided those afflicted with hemorrhoids and other rectal complaints.[85]

These shrines and others are identified for us by the instructions of sixteen female and three male testators that either professional palmers or relatives make the pilgrimages which they themselves had vowed but could not expect to accomplish.[86] Since the saints in question were not specialists in women's ills, the sexual imbalance may in part reflect the opportunity of a mature woman to go on pilgrimage, in prayer and recreation, while her husband was at work. A younger wife, conversely, constrained by yet another pregnancy or child at the breast, might have found it more difficult than her husband to carry out a vow that she had made. By sending another, in any event, the testator would be "discharged towards God and the blessed saint," as Damoiselle Coquillart phrased it, after citing her promise to Saint Claude. Our list, of course, only suggests the density of the network. Village priests, in response to a bishop's questionnaire of 1727, reported many more shrines, while noting that a good

85. The saints' curative functions and their shrines are catalogued in Louis Réau's magisterial *Iconographie de l'art chrétien* (3 vols., Paris, 1955–1959), vol. III. See also Paul Pedrizet, *Le calendrier parisien à la fin du Moyen Age* (Paris, 1933), and A. Poulin, *Les pèlerinages du diocèse de Reims* (Charleville, 1927).

86. Jehanne, wife of the linen-worker Jehan Bendet: pilgrimages to N.-D.-de-Liesse, Saint Fiacre in Brie, Saint Gond, and Saint Lié, AD, Marne, 4E 16668 (1525); Jehanne, wife of Jehan Grant Jehan: Saint Sebastian at Soissons, n. 65, above; Ysabeau, wife of the dyer Robert Charlier: Saint-Nicolas-de-Rangouille, AD, Marne, 4E 16691 (1528); the merchant-apothecary Jehan Courtin: Saint Claude, 4E 16668 (1529); Marit Rogier, a tanner's wife: Liesse, Saint Bertha, and Saint Lié, 4E 16691 (1529); Jehanne, wife of the carter Didier Clermont: Saint Claude, n. 25, above; the sword-cutler Pierre Langlet: Liesse, 4E 16692 (1536); Jehanne Noel: Saint Léger at Soissons, and Saint Bertault, n. 18, above; Margueritte Parisot, a cooper's wife: Liesse, AD, Marne, 4E 16694 (1538); Jehannette de Launoy: Liesse, 4E 16695 (1539); Pierre Pirche: Saint Nicolas-de-Rangouille, Saint Barbe, Saint Lié thrice, and Liesse thrice, n. 20, above; the widow of Augustin Delospital: Saint Claude, AD, Marne, 4E 16696 (1540); Jehanne, wife of Guillaume Baalain: Liesse, Saint Ch[Catherine?], Saint Fery, Saint Radegonde, and Saint Brice, n. 67, above; Gerarde, wife of Jehan Mery of Janvry: Saint Restitute, AD, Marne, 4E 16696 (1540); Damoiselle G. Coquillart: Saint Claude, and Saint Arnoul in Lorraine, n. 15, above; Anne, wife of the shoemaker Gerardin Martin: Liesse and Saint Amand, AD, Marne, 4E 16703 (1548); Henriette Party, wife of Jehan Coeur of Reims: Saint Fiacre, Liesse, Saint Catherine, Saint Fery, Saint Lié, and Saint Brice, 4E 16704 (1549); Alipson Maisalte [?]: Saint Fery (to which she wanted her daughter taken by "un autre personne esraige"), 4E 16707 (1552); the wife of the tavern-keeper Guillaume de Larcher: Saint Venise (Veronica) near Lagny-sur-Marne, Saint Fiacre, N.-D.-de-Recommandise at the Carmelites of Paris, N.-D.-de-Lorette at Paris, N.-D.-les-Vertus near Paris, and Saint Fery, ibid. (1552).

portion of them no longer attracted anyone. Sixteenth-century ecclesiastical visitations, which could have had much more to report, are mute on the subject.[87]

The eighteenth-century priests, as professionals, were quite specific concerning the ills that a given saint could cure. It would be difficult to establish, however, the degree to which sixteenth-century lay people had a clear understanding of the division of labor among the locally-known healing saints. Their reputation, especially when it was not buttressed by indulgences, depended on the word-of-mouth advertising that followed successful cures. Then, too, time, money, and the distance that one wanted to travel were important criteria in choosing among shrines.

Peasants threatened by agricultural crises sought aid from the saints in town, while city dwellers went to the countryside for relief from individual problems. The principle of reciprocity appears once again as a crucial element in sixteenth-century religion.

The wonder-working relics were the cutting edge of a massive physical presence of the supernatural in Champagne. An inventory of the Cathedral of Reims in 1622 lists a piece of the true cross, a vial of the holy milk, an arm of Saint Andrew the Apostle, as well as the head of Reims's own Saint Nicaise, and much more.[88] Even the parish church of Chaource claimed in 1502 a piece of the true cross and some bones of Saint Eloy.[89] Such inventories were comprehensive statements of all that a church might claim as its relics, rather than a short list of those that common belief had authenticated. We need not assume that the canons of Reims or the parishioners of Chaource gave full credence to their respective holdings. Opinions must have differed from one person to another. The presence of many putative relics must nevertheless have been a necessary condition for the efficacy of some of them.

All the attributes of the saints were united in the person of the Virgin. Every testator invoked her by formula, as "the glorious Virgin Mary," but some were more precise and more intimate. To the

87. See A. Poulin, "Les pèlerinages du diocèse de Reims à la fin de l'Ancien Régime," *Nouvelle Revue de Champagne et de Brie*, 10 (1932), 152–185. Neither AD, Marne, Reims depot, G 254, Visitations of the deanery of the Mountain, nor G 286, of Epernay, mentions pilgrimages.

88. BN, Fonds français, 11,576. See also Albert Cerf, "Notice sur la relique du saint-laict conservée autrefois dans la cathédrale de Reims," *Bulletin monumental*, 5th ser., 6 (1878), 5–23.

89. AD, Aube, 108G 27.

squire Nicolas Goujon, who used the chivalric idiom, she was "his well-beloved mother Mary dame and mistress." More simply, Adam Maure, merchant of Bar-sur-Aube, and four other testators addressed her as "the glorious Virgin Mary his mother." Another merchant, Robert Gillet of Reims, explained the theological basis for this parentage by recommending his soul to the "saintly prayer of the glorious Virgin Mary Mother of God and of all the saints of paradise."[90] But even if a Christian could not be certain of an immediate welcome to the community of saints on high, he could have faith that Mary's gentle hand would guide him through purgatory and toward that ultimate goal.

The Virgin was also the patron of churches, not merely of cathedrals like Notre-Dame of Reims and collegial churches like Notre-Dame-en-Vaux of Châlons, but of simple villages like Pont-Sainte-Marie outside of Troyes, which celebrated its annual festival with gusto on Assumption Day. Marian shrines did not require relics to draw the faithful. The churches of Notre-Dame-de-l'Epine, to which nearly every Catholic of Châlons left a few sols, and of Notre-Dame-de-Liesse, a day's ride from Reims to the Laonnais in Picardy, enjoyed a national reputation. While the peasants around Troyes were marching to the city's cathedral in 1556, those farther down the Seine Valley went to the Belle-Dame of Nogent-sur-Seine, a miracle-working statue around which a chapel had been built. The village church of Notre-Dame-de-Voulton near Provins in the same region, attracted worshippers from the Brie champenoise. A company of men who had gone on pilgrimage to the Holy Land in 1532 made their last stop of the return trip at Voulton, fulfilling a vow. Everywhere townspeople venerated small statues of the Virgin in the niches of buildings and on street corners. One Pietà stood at the end of the alley in Troyes known as the rue de la Chausson. According to a Protestant observer the statue was ordinarily dressed in silk clothes. Especially on Sundays, a lamp burned before it. "Great and enormous idolatries were committed there daily."[91] Truly every Catholic was a ward of the Virgin.

90. Goujon: n. 25, above; Maure: AD, Aube, 330G 6 (1530); Gillet: AD, Marne, 4E 16749 (1569).

91. Pithou, "Histoire ecclésiastique," ff. 168 and 318; Robert Mandrou, *Introduction à la France moderne (1500–1640)* (Paris, 1961), p. 285; Haton, *Mémoires*, I, 31; André Richard, *La Belle-Dame de Nogent-sur-Seine* (Nogent, 1943); Denis Possot, *Trèsample et abondante description du voyage en la terre saincte . . . depuis la ville de Nogeant sur Sene . . .* (Paris, 1536), sig. Pi.

Soul-brothers and Sisters

The Catholics of Champagne had the opportunity to enlist supernatural patronage by participating in confraternities. This form of association has been defined by a modern scholar as "a spiritual and charitable union with the purpose of support during life and aid after death."[92] Sixteenth-century parlance was a good deal less precise. Any group that had religious objectives and included laypeople could be styled a confraternity. A definition this broad allowed room for associations that differed widely from one another. At a time when politics meant religion, political factions qualified. Catholic ultras in Champagne and elsewhere formed armed confraternities or leagues during the Wars of Religion. The Parisian group performing mystery plays called itself the Confraternity of the Passion. A confraternity existed in the diocese of Troyes to aid in the completion of the cathedral.[93] Every guild of artisans or professional men, moreover, formed a confraternity in which membership was compulsory. Here the religious unity reinforced a solidarity that already existed at the same time that it placed the members under the protection of the patron saint of their craft. So, for example, all those professionally associated with the royal courts of Troyes belonged to the Confraternity of Saint Louis and Saint Yves.[94] Yves was a renowned thirteenth-century canon lawyer, Louis IX of France the model of a just king and judge. In the sixteenth century, though such a group met for religious services, offered works of art to the church at which it met, and may have taken on obligations of charity toward its less fortunate members, it was essentially the religious adjunct of a secular organization. We shall be concerned chiefly with the pious confraternity, a voluntary association with no outside ties. Like the guild confraternity, it honored a specific devotion and met in a particular church. The surviving records indicate that every parish had at least one such group, and that most had several. Townsmen were not limited to parish confraternities. They could

92. *Dictionnaire de spiritualité ascétique et mystique, doctrine et histoire*, s.v. "Confréries." See also, by the same author, J. Duhr, "La confrérie dans la vie de l'église," *Revue d'histoire ecclésiastique*, 35 (1939), 437–478.

93. J.H. Mariéjol, *La Réforme et la Ligue, l'édit de Nantes*, in Lavisse, *Histoire de France*, vol. VI, pt. 1 (Paris, 1911), p. 174; Louis Petit de Julleville, *Les mystères* (2 vols., Paris, 1880), I, ch. 12; BN, Collection Dupuy, 231, ff. 33, 176–177; AD, Aube, G 1573 (1501–1502), f. 31v.

94. A copy of its charter of 1510 is given in BN, Collection Dupuy, 228, ff. 85–89. See also BN, Collection de Champagne, 50, ff. 75–78.

also participate in others at collegial churches, monasteries, and hospitals, which were directed by the clergy but drew members from the community at large.

During the early part of the century, many parishioners honored their patron saint by attending his association. At almost every parish church in Troyes the patron's was one of the most popular confraternities. Throughout Champagne urban churches also offered a set of confraternities in the Virgin's name. For more than two centuries the mendicant orders had been propagating her cult. Pope Urban VI established, and the Council of Basel in 1441 confirmed, the Visitation as a festival day. The Franciscan Sixtus IV (1471-1484) promoted the doctrine of her Immaculate Conception. During the same period the Annunciation emerged from obscurity to an important place in the festival cycle.[95] Each of these devotions, as well as that of the Virgin's mother, Saint Anne, was honored by numerous confraternities in Champagne. An especially famous Marian association was that of Notre Dame of Loreto, at Saint Nicholas's Church in Troyes. After a fire that devastated Troyes in 1524, the Loreto chapel, to which the bishop awarded indulgences, was the first part of the church to be rebuilt. In 1533 some of those who came to the chapel were favored by miraculous cures. A year later the bishop founded the confraternity, which had 150 members in 1544, when their number is first given in the churchwardens' accounts.[96] Few Champenois had the time, inclination, or resources to go to Jerusalem or Rome, and make a side trip to Loreto on the way.[97] Confraternities like the one at Saint Nicholas's Church offered townsmen the chance to receive the spiritual benefits of long and costly pilgrimages to far-flung shrines without ever leaving home.

Attention to the Virgin and parish patrons did not necessarily deflect Christians from the worship of Christ. A few of the associations that celebrated his mysteries must have been among the most popular in Champagne. Saint Remy's was but a modest parish of Troyes,

95. E. Delaruelle, E.-R. Labande, and Paul Ourliac, *L'église au temps du grand schisme et de la crise conciliare (1378–1449)* (2 vols., Paris, 1964), II, 777–779; Pedrizet, *Le calendrier parisien*, pp. 113–114.

96. AD, Aube, 17G 7, f. 19, makes reference to one of the miracles. E. Poulle, "Eglise Saint-Nicolas de Troyes," Société française d'archéologie, *Congrès archéologique de France*, 113e session, Troyes 1955 (Orléans, 1957), p. 74. The 9 l. 7 s. 6 d. received by the confraternity in 1544 indicates the number of members, since each paid 15 d. Numerical statements on confraternity membership are summarized in the appendix.

97. Possot (*Trèsample description*, sig. Oi) mentions such a side trip.

yet 337 men and women participated in its Confraternity of the
Cross in 1555. They came from the town as a whole, since in 1517,
by way of rough comparison, the church's most popular local confraternity, that of Saint Remy himself, had only 68 members. (Unfortunately it is impossible to estimate what percentage of the parishioners this figure might represent, since the Troyen tax rolls,
which list the inhabitants, are organized by quarter rather than by
parish.) At Saint Ayoul's parish in Provins, the Confraternity of the
Name of Jesus had 427 members in 1555, leaving Saint Loup's Confraternity, with 56 participants, far behind. The Protestant Nicolas
Pithou mentions a holy name confraternity at Saint Bernard's Hospital in Troyes. It brought in so much revenue, according to him,
that the Franciscans founded a similar one in order to fill their
coffers, too. We might observe, rather, that the Franciscans were active promoters of this devotion, which had been growing in importance since the fifteenth century, when Joan of Arc placed the holy
name on her standard.[98] On Corpus Christi Day, moreover, which
the French called *la fête Dieu*, confraternities in rural as well as urban churches honored the Holy Sacrament.

Together these devotions — patron, Virgin, Savior, and Corpus
Christi — comprised about one-half of the confraternities at urban
parishes. Almost all of the rest were devoted to the healing saints. In
Troyes this was true for seven of the fourteen associations at Saint
John's Church in 1527, five of the eleven at Saint James's in 1563,
and seven of the fourteen at Mary Magdalene's in 1599. Sebastian
and Roche, the two healing saints who protected against the plague,
were worshipped throughout Latin Christendom. The saints invoked
against other major ills of the century were less universal. Relics like
those of Claude, in Franche-Comté, and of Fiacre, in Brie, drew pilgrims in search of renewed health. At Paris Saint Maur aided those
with gout and rheumatic disease. Each of these five saints seems to
have had a following in most large urban parishes. The fact that
some were also patrons of important guilds — Claude of the tanners
and Sebastian of the archers — is but a further indication of their
popularity. Other saints were commemorated less frequently. Edmund of Canterbury, a twelfth-century archbishop who had come
to Pontigny, south of Troyes in Burgundy, to die, was invoked by

98. BC, Provins, MS 258; Pithou, "Histoire ecclésiastique," f. 39; E. Delaruelle, "La
spiritualité de Jeanne d'Arc," *Bulletin de littérature ecclésiastique*, 1964, pp. 24–25.

pregnant women. Marcou, at Corbeny near the city of Laon, helped those suffering from scrofula. The kings of France, on their way back to Paris after coronation at Reims, paid him an obligatory visit. Saint Syre, a legendary sister of Saint Fiacre, who lies buried in the village outside Troyes that bears her name, helped to cure hernias and the gravel. Her relics were the object of a local pilgrimage.[99]

A few confraternities were dedicated to saints who were neither parish patrons nor directly linked to the cure of physical ills. The most important was Saint Barbara, to whom one prayed to avoid a sudden death, which would preclude the reception of the last rites. The Augustinians of Reims maintained a confraternity in honor of Saint Nicholas of Tolentino, the protector of souls in purgatory.

In general the friars of Champagne were particularly active and successful in promoting confraternities at their monasteries. The discussion that follows will not give them sufficient credit, since the necessary records have not survived. But the testaments from Reims remind us of the importance of the mendicant orders. To cite a striking example, the merchant Nicolas Frizon patronized confraternities at all four orders: Saint Barbara's at the Franciscans, Saint Nicholas of Tolentino's at the Augustinians, the Trinity at the Dominicans, and the Assumption and the Blessed Sacrament at the Carmelites.[100]

Regardless of the devotion it honored and the church where it met, festivals and funerals were the concerns of the pious confraternity, which celebrated its saint's day or other holiday to a greater degree than the ordinary ceremonies of the church provided. For the festival, members purchased a candle either in church or from the pious women who solicited memberships from door to door.[101] The members designated one of their number, either in turn or by auction, for the honor of guarding the baton, or ceremonial staff, during the year to come. As the standard-bearer he or she was expected to make a special offering to the association. The members, carrying their candles and accompanied by the torches of the confraternity,

99. Possot, *Trèsample description*, sig. Pi.

100. See note 47, above, and Marlot, *Histoire de Reims*, IV, 29 and 616, for Saint Nicholas's Confraternity.

101. Pithou ("Histoire ecclésiastique," f. 117v) refers to "plusieurs bigottes de celles qui faisoient mestier de quester les confraries, les messes des trespasses, et bailler a loiage leurs oraisons."

conducted the new standard-bearer, in procession, to his home to deposit the staff. They returned to the church for the celebration of a high mass. On the following day Requiem Mass was sung for the benefit of the souls of deceased members.

This basic pattern was frequently embellished. Several confraternities commissioned sermons at their churches for the Sunday before the festival. The Confraternity of the Cross at Saint Remy's Church in Troyes preferred to hear its preachers in the open air, in front of an imposing calvary on the main square known as the Beautiful Cross. The accounts for 1592 include a payment for transporting a pulpit there from the church. On the day of the holiday, Saint Peter and Saint Paul's Confraternity at the Cathedral of Troyes placed flowered hats on statues of the choir screen. The Confraternity of the Cross hung a tapestry, and set flowered hats on an image of the cross. The Holy Sacrament Confraternity of Saint Urban's strewed rushes on the church floor to create a festive air.[102]

The processions, too, could become elaborate affairs. The lower panels of an early sixteenth-century stained-glass window given by the Holy Sacrament Confraternity to Saint Alpin's parish church of Châlons depict twelve members acting out the Last Supper. They receive communion from a priest, as the apostles received it from Christ. In the next panel their costumes are visible. Dressed as the apostles, they march behind a canopy sheltering the Holy Sacrament. The twelve were in the vanguard of the confraternity's actual procession on Corpus Christi Day. As the inscription on the window read:

DOUZE CONFRERES GENS DE BIEN
EN DOUZE APOSTRES REVESTUS
SONT ACCOUSTRES PAR BON MOIEN
POUR DECORER LE DOULX JHESUS

EN CESTE EGLISE ET EN CE LIEU
DOUZE HOMMES EN LA PROCESSION

102. The Confraternity of the Cross: AD, Aube, 20G 135, f. 5, and 20G 140, f. 2v; the Holy Sacrament Confraternity: ibid., 10G 757, f. 9 (1534), and Saint Peter and Paul's: G 1573, f. 31v (1502), all of which heard sermons, as did Saint Savinian's of the Cathedral of Troyes: ibid., f. 30, and Saint Gibrian's of Saint Remy's Monastery at Reims: AD, Marne (Reims depot), H 1308, f. 12 (1546–1549).

LE JOUR DIST DE LA FETE DIEU
DENOTENT L'IMITATION[103]

A century earlier the Burgundian sculptor Claus Sluter and the Flemish painters Robert Campin and the Van Eycks had succeeded in integrating donors and saints into the same pictorial space. These artists gratified their patrons' desire to draw as close as possible to the holy figures. The confraternity members of Châlons entered this field, and also participated in sacred drama.

The pilgrims of Saint James's Confraternity at Reims celebrated their holiday with equal verve. The cooper Jehan Gaulteron left them the three silver scallop shells that he wore in the procession; the widow Pynart, her pilgrim's staff.[104] Scallop shell and staff were the attributes of Saint James, whose relics at Santiago de Compostela in northern Spain were the most famous pilgrimage of the West, and the one that conferred most prestige on those who accomplished it. In 1686 Archbishop Le Tellier of Reims found it necessary to restrain the participants. He had learned that "all those confrères and pilgrims attend with their staffs, and several among them are dressed in special costumes representing apostles, . . . and one among all the others, under the pretext that the feast of Saint Christopher falls on the same day as Saint James's, carries a child on his shoulders, and attends the procession in this way, proclaiming these words from time to time: 'Child, how heavy you are.'" The archbishop complained that such ceremonies, instead of increasing devotion, only excited the curiosity of a crowd of children, who tagged after the procession irreverently. He ordered the suppression of all the paraphernalia, save for the pilgrims' staffs.[105]

Membership in this confraternity at Reims was almost certainly not limited to the saint's bona fide pilgrims, since he was the patron of the parish church where the confraternity met. Even at Paris the famous confraternity at Saint James's Hospital admitted those who had not made the pilgrimage if they had traveled to the shrines of Saint Claude, and Saint Nicholas in Lorraine, or if they paid the

---

103. The inscription, lost during the restoration of the window, is quoted by Hurault, *Les vitraux anciens*, p. 7. See also Mâle, *L'art religieux de la fin du Moyen Age*, pp. 177–178.

104. AD, Marne, 4E 16671 (1552), and 4E 16705 (1550).

105. Quoted by Louis Paris, *Remensiana* (Reims, 1845), pp. 298–302.

confraternity a sum equivalent to the cost of a trip to Santiago.[106]
The Parisian association is interesting in another respect. The clergy
of the hospital sued the lay officers of the confraternity before Parlement in 1584 to halt the diversion of the confraternity's resources
to the annual banquet. Counsel for the defense informed the court
of the custom, from time immemorial, of a procession by the clergy
through the banquet rooms while the members were at table, as a
sign of devotion and a means of uplifting one and all to devout
thoughts.[107] This practice kept the clergy exactly at arm's length, far
enough away to allow the members to dine in a relaxed manner,
sufficiently close at hand to symbolize the religious significance of
their dinner. The confrères of Saint James at Reims took a further
symbolic step in reducing the importance of the clergy to the occasion. By costuming themselves as supernatural beings, and reenact-
ing the central event in the life of their saint, they established a
form of communication with him that obviated the need for clerical
mediation. It was even possible for confrères to represent themselves
as clergy. The sixteenth-century statutes establishing Saint Stephen's
Confraternity at his abbey in Dijon, which were approved by the
cardinal-abbot, Bishop Givry of Langres, allowed the standard-
bearer to lead the procession to church wearing the clerical vest-
ments. Michel Mollat made an acute observation when he maintained that during the late Middle Ages priests joined confraternities to neutralize possible competition. In a well-staffed church like
Mary Magdalene's of Troyes, conversely, the clergy, as one métier
among others, had its own occupational confraternity.[108]

Clerics were essential to the laity for remembering the dead. The
requiem mass performed on the day after confraternity festivals
sometimes took on major proportions. At Chaource the Holy Sacrament Confraternity paid forty-three priests to say Mass in 1521, and
thirty the next year. Thirty-four, including several canons who were
members, officiated at the confraternity of the same name at Saint
Urban's collegial church of Troyes.[109]

106. Pedrizet, Le calendrier parisien, p. 183.

107. Henri Bordier, "La confrérie des pèlerins de Saint-Jacques et ses archives," in
Société de l'histoire de Paris et de l'Ile-de-France: Mémoires, 2 (1876), 382.

108. Marcel, Le Cardinal de Givry, I, 491; Michel Mollat, La vie et la pratique religieuses au XIVe siècle et dans la première partie du XVe, principalement en France
(2 pts., Paris, 1966), pt. 1, p. 96. The clerical confraternity met on Corpus Christi
Day: AD, Aube, 16G 47 (1511–1512).

109. AD, Aube, 108G 45, and 10G 757.4, cahier 4, f. 11.

The pious confraternity could carry on activities throughout the year, not merely during its own holiday period. In Troyes, for example, masses were sung in honor of the Eucharist every Thursday by Holy Sacrament confraternities at Saint Urban's, and at Saint John's, where all eight non-beneficed priests officiated. The Confraternity of the Cross celebrated its weekly mass, appropriately, on Fridays.[110]

Rural confraternities may have participated rather extensively in the ordinary responsibilities of the parish, and have been more an adjunct of the vestry than a wholly separate entity. The chaplain of the Holy Sacrament Confraternity at Montreuil-sur-Barse said four weekly masses, and the confraternity paid the vicar for matins on the four great holidays and five Marian festivals, and for vigils at the ember times. At the village of Courtauld, near Ervy, each testator who mentioned the confraternities in his will left a sum to be divided among all of them at the church, without mentioning any by name. It may well have been common practice here for the pious parishioner of means to belong as a matter of course to every association, or at least to have them all participate in his funeral. A ledger from Pel, in the upper Aube Valley, lists some twenty-seven confraternities. By "confraternity," these villagers must have meant the celebration of the holiday in the accustomed way.[111]

Confraternities also played an important part in the permanent decoration of the church. Occupational confraternities often, perhaps commonly, commissioned an image of their patron. The vine-growers honored Saint Vincent, whose name was similar to their own. Those of the village of Creney offered a window in his honor. At Bouilly they placed a statue of the saint in the confraternity's own chapel.[112] The goldsmiths of Troyes told the legend of Saint Eloy, who had been a goldsmith himself, in their window at Mary Magdalene's Church, where the guild met. An inscription beneath the window expresses their desire "to obtain remission of their sins and full grace . . . and that the peace of God be given them for this good deed, in paradise." Their claim on plenary grace may seem presumptuous. One suspects that, in decorating its chapel, the typi-

110. Ibid., 10G 757, ff. 5–6; 15G 405, f. 55; 20G 135, f. 4.
111. Montreuil: ibid., 279G 2; Courtauld: ibid., 139G 5; Pel: ibid., 307G 2.
112. Creney: Mâle, *L'art religieux de la fin du Moyen Age*, p. 171; Bouilly: Société française d'archéologie, *Congrès archéologique*, 113e session, Troyes 1955 (Orléans, 1957), p. 386.

cal urban professional confraternity was acting out of mixed motives. For the guild was demonstrating not merely piety to its patron and to God, but civic spirit and wealth to the other guilds and to the town as a whole. This was one of the ways in which it could hope to maintain or increase the prestige of its members as individuals and the part that they might play as a group, vis-à-vis the other guilds, in municipal affairs.

Pious confraternities were even more important as donors than the guilds. Mâle was prepared to conjecture that any otherwise un-attributed stained-glass window had probably been donated by one of them.[113] Clearly they were among the most important patrons of late-medieval art. The Holy Sacrament window at Châlons, whose lower panels portray confraternity members as apostles, is in honor of the Eucharist. The first of its upper panels depicts the Hebrews receiving manna in the desert. "Manna," an inscription informs the faithful, "signifies Saint Jesus our savior. By means of his purified blood, all salvation rests in him alone."[114] The second panel is a representation of the Last Supper. At the Cathedral of Troyes Saint Sebastian's Confraternity took on the major task of subsidizing one of the nave's windows, which was being erected at the turn of the sixteenth century. In twenty-four panels the window recounts the saint's legend. A second set of panels in the triforium below shows a crowd of people, who are identified as the members by an inscrip-tion reading, "The Confraternity of Saint Sebastian have given this window in the year 1501. May God keep them."[115] The crowd is composed of both sexes, since the pious confraternity was an asso-ciation for women and men together. It is true that, save for the widows, the persons on a popular confraternity's list of paid mem-bers are mostly male. But the fact that Troyen churchwardens re-corded the name of the man of the house does not imply that the woman was left out.[116]

A confraternity not only enabled its members to benefit from the protection of a saint like Sebastian during their lifetime, but also

---

113. *L'art religieux de la fin du Moyen Age,* p. 176.

114. See n. 103, above.

115. Biver, *L'école troyenne,* pp. 65–67, fig. 39.

116. Natalie Davis, "City Women and Religious Change," *Society and Culture in Early Modern France* (Stanford, 1975), p. 75, suggests, in contradistinction, that women did not play an important part in confraternity life. For the predominance of women in confraternities that declined, towards the century's end, see below, ch. 6.

provided them with aid after death. Every confraternity paid its last respects to its members, at least in the annual requiem mass. Some ordinary parish confraternities must have gone beyond this basic effort, for three testators of Troyes, early in the seventeenth century, convoked to their funerals the crosses and processions of the confraternities to which they belonged.[117] The evidence is more satisfying for the larger associations that were accustomed to transcend parish lines. At Saint John's Church of Troyes in 1575 the confrères of the Holy Sacrament unanimously decided that when any one of them died the news would be published throughout the town. Their clerk, dressed in his official tunic and red hat, holding his staff of office in one hand and ringing a bell in the other, would call out at all the principal intersections the name of the deceased and the hour and place of his burial, in order to invite the members to attend his services and pray for his soul.[118] The pilgrims of Saint James, at Reims, were expected to accompany the corpse of a member to his grave, and seem to have performed the same office for others at a price.[119] The Confraternity of the Cross was obligated to insure that twenty low masses were said for each member, and maintained a wardrobe so that mass-priests who lacked suitable habits could be appropriately dressed.[120] At Saint Urban's members were entitled to even more. When Jehanne Terret died in 1534, a high mass was sung. Three canons, nine vicars, and the two bell ringers and four choir boys attended. Eleven low masses were also said. Surely there would have been no other way in sixteenth-century Champagne for the candlemaker Jehan de France or the shoemaker's wife Jehanne Lizarde to have canons attend a funeral mass said in their intention.[121] Judging from those members whose profession is cited, however, most were people of substance.

117. The merchant-furrier P. Larbalestrier's widow: n. 59, above; the leather-worker Simon Fournier's wife: AD, Aube, 2E 7/144 (1604); the fishmonger Jean Quinost's wife: ibid. (1605).

118. AD, Aube, 15G 405, ff. 87v–88.

119. Jacques Roland, legal practitioner of Reims, convoked the pilgrims to his burial, asked each to pray for him, and left the confraternity 30 s.: AD, Marne, 4E 6703 (1548). The widow Pynart, who gave the confraternity her pilgrim's staff, and therefore was a member, also convoked them, but without payment: n. 104, above. The tailor Etienne Laignier also convoked them without payment: 4E 273* (1555).

120. AD, Aube, 20G 135, ff. 2–3. Apparently the confraternity paid for the difference between twenty masses and those that the member himself provided for in his will.

121. AD, Aube, 10G 757, f. 15; 10G 757.4, cahier 3 (1541–1542), f. 10, and cahier 7 (1545–1546), f. 16.

For the confraternities of Champagne as a whole, it is difficult to determine the degree to which men and women from the various estates participated, since the occupations of only relatively few are given. The range of membership at the small town of Chaource was wide. In 1513 Nicolas de Moustier, the most important seigneur of the immediate environs and the captain of the town, took the baton. Sebastian David, the bailiff's lieutenant, and nineteen clergymen were among the members. The standard-bearer in 1521 was the cabinetmaker Guillaume du Proux. Other participants included three members of the Jamyn family, which later in the century would give a poet to the Pléiade. Etienne Jamyn was a *laboureur* or substantial peasant in 1521, Jacquot a butcher, and a second Etienne a weaver. A carder and an oil-seller were also members. The participants in the confraternities of the Holy Sacrament and of Saint Quirin at the saint's collegial church in Provins over the course of the century included anoblis, canons, a notary, merchants, an archer, a barber-surgeon, a baker, a mason, a weaver, shoemakers, wheelwrights, an oil-vendor and laboureur, and vine-growers. At Saint James's Church of Troyes, the wife of the merchant Louis Merat was standard-bearer of Saint Roche's Confraternity in 1578. That same year a servant of her husband was kidnapped somewhere between Lyons and Troyes. The chronicler Claude Haton of Provins, who describes Merat as one of the richest merchants of Troyes, heard that the man was carrying perhaps 20,000 livres in notes, and that notes and bearer were together ransomed for 1,000 livres.[122] Did people like Merat's wife mix with the artisan's wives among the confraternity members? The documents left for historians to ponder offer no response. They do allow us to say that men and women met in a pious confraternity who did not often meet elsewhere. And they met, one might say, as soul-brothers and sisters *(confrères et consoeurs)*. There was an opportunity for human contact, for elbow rubbing and conversation, between artisans and cultivators of substance on the one hand, and merchants and notables on the other.

The possibilities of fraternization should not however be exaggerated. The practices of some confraternities effectively limited participation. The members of Saint Gibrian's Confraternity at Saint Remy's Monastery of Reims, who dined together on the festival

122. AD, Aube, 108G 45; BC, Provins, MS 221; AD, Aube, 14G 28, f. 7; Haton, *Mémoires,* II, 933.

day, imposed a 30-sol entry fee, which kept out undesirables while
it helped to pay expenses. More significantly, the poor probably did
not have the resources to participate in any confraternity. The Holy
Sacrament Confraternity of Chaource was entitled to the best robe
of the deceased, which was then sold at auction to the next of kin.
An estate lacking a suitable robe paid in coin: a minimum of one
livre in 1521.[123] Confraternity candles at the parishes of Troyes cost
1 s. 3 d. during the first half of the century — a good portion of a
day's wage for a *manouvrier* (day laborer), when he worked.[124] In
the countryside the term "manouvrier" referred to the poorer peasant. There is no mention anywhere in Champagne, town or country,
of a manouvrier as a confraternity participant.

Toward people too poor to join, the pious confraternity usually
assumed no special responsibilities. Chaource's Holy Sacrament Confraternity, in performing an annual act of charity, was most unusual.
During the first half of the century the association bought "little
loaves for God" (*michettes pour Dieu*) and distributed them with
lentil soup to the parish poor at festival time. In 1521 and 1547 the
confraternity spent some 9 livres for this purpose, out of total ex-
penditures of approximately 136 and 194 livres respectively. It also
made a token gift of 10 deniers to each of the hermits of the town,
for there was a perpetual endowment in Chaource to maintain two
men in seclusion. The next extant ledger, for 1588, shows the confraternity tailoring its generosity to a declining membership. This
time it simply gave 4 deniers to each poor person — about 262 of
them, at a time when the confraternity itself had 188 members.[125]

Champagne could boast one truly exceptional confraternity,
whose major function was charity. The Confraternity *dudit denier*
— of the said penny — had been founded "by divine inspiration and
the counsel of Bishop Jehan de Chastelvilain," in the words of the
royal act of recognition of 1379.[126] Each member contributed one
penny a week, hence the name. The association had its seat at the
collegial church of Notre-Dame-en-Vaux. Its major task was to provide a monthly subsidy to seventy of the poor, according to their

123. AD, Marne (Reims depot), H 1306–1308; AD, Aube, 108G 45.
124. AD, Aube, 17G 9, f. 36, supplies the figures of 2 s. 6 d., and 4 d., for manou-
vriers at Saint Nicholas's Church of Troyes in 1534.
125. AD, Aube, 108G 45.
126. Archives nationales, JJ 114, no. 251, ff. 129v–130; reprinted in Siméon Luce,
Histoire du Bertrand du Guesclin et de son époque (Paris, 1876), pp. 611–615.

individual needs. One of the few sources of information for this confraternity is its statutes, as recorded by the crown. The degree to
which they were observed, either at the time of foundation or during the sixteenth century, is a matter of conjecture. They merit a
summary, nevertheless, as an indication of the activities that, ideally,
a confraternity could undertake, for the statutes went beyond the
care of a privileged seventy. They ordered the purchase of a great
quantity of doublets and shoes for the poor at the beginning of winter. Bread was to be given at Christmastime to all who came for it,
since this was the period of greatest need. Throughout the year the
confraternity had to provide ten loaves of white bread a week to
each of the mendicant orders. The statutes also stipulated the distribution of white bread, the rich man's food, to the hospital and
prison poor. The relative abundance of grain during the later fourteenth century, after the onset of plague, may have made these luxuries possible, or at least thinkable. At one of the town's hospitals
the confraternity was to maintain twenty-six sickbeds, furnished
with linen: two for indigent persons near death, and the rest for
women in childbirth and poor schoolboys. It was also to pay for the
treatment of poor orphans and the other sick poor.

Like all confraternities, this one attended to the souls of its own.
The statutes provided for a solemn requiem mass on the death of a
member. For the benefit of the deceased each person in Châlons,
member or not, was to recite the seven penitential psalms, or if he
did not know them, then the Pater Noster and the Ave Maria four
times. The passing of a member's spouse was observed with a simple
mass, since he or she "aided in earning the penny that the other contributed." The confraternity had fifteen masses said every week for
all its members, past, present — and future. On four days of the
year it offered special masses: Ascension Monday, the Sunday following the Assumption, the Sunday before All Saints', and the first
Sunday of Lent, at which sermons were delivered and the statutes
read. Exercises of personal devotion were also prescribed, including
the recitation of seven Pater Nosters and seven Ave Marias daily, in
honor of the seven gifts of the Holy Spirit. At table, before dinner
or supper, members were expected to say grace, or to substitute one
Pater Noster and one Ave Maria, both before and after the meal.
All were to commune three times a year, at Christmas and Pentecost
as well as at Easter.

The Confraternity *dudit denier* was the municipal charitable institution of Châlons. Each parish had collectors who received the weekly pennies of the members and reported monthly to the governors of the confraternity. In order for the pennies to have met the heavy expenses, virtually all who were solvent in the town must have belonged. Everyone in Châlons was obligated, at least in theory, to recognize the benevolence of the confraternity by praying for a member on his death. This fourteenth-century association left enough traces of its activity in sixteenth-century documents to demonstrate its continued vitality. More than half of the Catholic testators in our sample who were residents of Châlons mentioned it in their wills. Bishop Gilles de Luxembourg left the confraternity 30 livres in 1532, the widow Godignon 10 livres in 1559. She also instructed her executors to give 2 s. 6 d. to each of "the seventy poor of the visitation." In 1581 the painter Jacques Henrey wanted the confraternity to distribute his 30-sol legacy to poor people afflicted with the plague. At times of epidemics, in fact, the municipal government directed the confraternity to make substantial contributions to the poor.[127]

If the poor could not participate in confraternities at all, then the artisans did not participate at will. Those who can be identified from the confraternity rolls were usually members of but one association. If we knew the estates of all the members, this statement might have to be modified, but probably not withdrawn. At Saint James's Church of Troyes the saddler Jehan Huon was a member of the Confraternity of the Conception from 1525 to 1532.[128] Blaise Chantefoin, a scabbard-maker, took the baton of the Annunciation in 1554. This act may have been an investment to ward off suspicion about his orthodoxy, since he was attracted to the Reformation by 1556.[129] Or perhaps he was a loyal standard-bearer of the Virgin who soon afterwards experienced a rapid conversion. Finally, one Feli-

127. The bishop: n. 50, above; the widow: n. 64, above; Henrey: n. 67, above. AC, Châlons, GG 216 (7 June 1516), and BB 7, f. 66 (1 Aug. 1531), tax all the confraternities in town; in practice this meant *dudit denier* and the Immaculate Conception Confraternity at Notre-Dame-en-Vaux.

128. 14G 21, f. 26, identifies his craft; 14G 18, cahier no. 1, ff. 22 and 24; cahier no. 2, f. 64; cahier no. 3, f. 103; and 14G 20, f. 21, note his participation.

129. AD, Aube, 14G 26, f. 20. Nicolas Pithou gives his occupation, for Chantefoin "had some entry and knowledge into the true religion" by 1556 ("Histoire ecclésiastique," f. 95). To escape the Saint Bartholomew's Massacre of 1572, Chantefoin fled to Geneva (*Livre des habitants de Genève*, ed. Paul Geisendorf [2 vols., Geneva, 1957 and 1963], II, 9 and 28, which notes that he had previously been an inhabitant).

zon, potter, completed the list of artisans identified as participants in the confraternities of this church when he joined Saint Gond's in 1583.[130]

The ledger from Saint James's for the year 1526 shows that half the participants belonged to but one of the nine confraternities of the church. At the other extreme, a handful of people joined several. They were the ultra-devout, a small minority of the whole, who were distinguished by means as well as motivation. This information cuts two ways. Not many persons in the parish took the trouble to show their special respect to several devotions, though enough did so to indicate that their action was not considered bad form. But if the number of frequent participants, of churchgoers, was limited, then confraternity membership was that much more widespread. It encompassed a greater part of the community than would have been true otherwise, had the confraternities been composed merely of a small knot of people accustomed to seeing one another from festival to festival.[131]

The Champenois who belonged to several associations were people of some means. Thibaut Trumeau, the official printer of the diocese, was a member of seven confraternities at Saint James's in 1532, and of six in 1538.[132] The widow of Denis Clerey, a merchant and at one time mayor of Troyes, belonged to seven in 1578, and also served as a standard-bearer at Saint Nicholas's Church in 1597.[133] Daniel Coulon, the owner of a rotisserie, joined three confraternities in 1552, when he was a churchwarden of the parish. Two years later he belonged to eight, and took the baton of one of them. Nicolas Pithou, the Protestant historian, identifies him as a "good-for-nothing, seditious, and mutinous." For during 1561, when the Protestants were practicing their religion openly, the rotisseur nearly caused a riot. He met a group returning from a Reformed service with a hail of stones as they passed his house. By 1563 Coulon

130. AD, Aube, 14G 37, f. 6.

131. The number of people who participated in the confraternities of Saint James's Church of Troyes during 1526 was 93 (AD, Aube, 14G 18): of these, 46 belonged to 1 confraternity, 14 belonged to 2 confraternities, 17 to 3, 4 to 4, 3 to 5, 3 to 6, 3 to 8, and 3 to 9.

132. AD, Aube, 14G 21 and 14G 24; Alexis Socard and Alexandre Assier, *Livres liturgiques du diocèse de Troyes imprimés au XVe et au XVIe siècle* (Paris, 1863), ch. 3.

133. She is listed as the widow of M. de Vaubercey, since her husband had been seigneur of that village (AD, Aube, 14G 28); see ibid., 17G 31, f. 9, for Saint Nicholas's Church.

had joined all the confraternities of the church. Protestants who had fled during the first religious war were now returning to their homes. Catholic zealots did their best to murder as many of them as possible. Coulon shot at two Huguenots, and brought one to the ground, where a mob dispatched him.[134]

What did a printer commissioned by the church, a mayor's widow, and a rotisseur who hated Huguenots to the death have in common? Perhaps only that all three were persons of reputation within the community. Churchwardens had to be financially solvent. They were not chosen from among the good-for-nothings. Coulon's nine confraternities, at 15 deniers a candle, cost him 11 s. 3 d., and meant that he would have to be a standard-bearer frequently. I would hazard the assumption that this was an indulgence that only a man in comfortable circumstances would allow himself. The testators of Reims who mentioned three or more confraternities in their wills were all at least of this social condition, from the tavernkeeper's wife who left 100 sols to the poor, to the merchant Frizon who belonged to six at the friars', and the Damoiselle Coquillart, our model testatrix.[135] She was a member of the patron's confraternity at Saint Peter's, her own parish, and would be buried in its chapel, beside her relatives. But she also instructed her executors to fulfill her financial obligations to eleven other confraternities at six different churches: Saint Claude's, at Saint James's parish; Mary Magdalene's and Saint Fiacre's, at the Magdalene's Church; Saint Nicholas of Tolentino's at the Augustinians; Saint Apollonia at the Carmelites; the Holy Sacrament, Notre-Dame-de-Pitié, and the Rosary at the Dominicans; and Saint Barbara's, Saint Francis's, and the Immaculate Conception at the Franciscans. If in the course of the year the lady regularly took a candle at each of these confraternities, she succeeded in making the rounds of the churches of Reims.

The artisans and their wives who could not enjoy such luxuries of devotion did not necessarily feel religiously deprived. As a temple official in Taiwan recently told an anthropologist, "if you worship a great host of gods, . . . then when you bring one of them a problem

---

134. AD, Aube, 14G 25–14G 27; Pithou, "Histoire ecclésiastique," ff. 172v and 262v–263v.

135. The wife of the tavernkeeper Guillaume Larcher: n. 86, above; Frizon: n. 47, above; Coquillart: n. 15, above. The other testators in this group are Honneste personne Colleson Doynet, a merchant-carpenter: 4E 16694 (1538); and the legal practitioner Jacques Roland: n. 119, above.

he will just say, 'you often worship old So-and-so; why not bring this problem to him instead of bothering me with it?' But if you worship only one or a few gods, it is harder for them to shift the responsibility for helping you to their codivinities, and it is easier for you to get action."[136] One saint may have been enough. Well-to-do people like Damoiselle Coquillart, nevertheless, were the ones who maintained the tone of conventional piety, with their chantries and anniversary masses, frequent pilgrimages, and plural membership in confraternities. "Folk religion" in sixteenth-century Champagne was sustained and embellished by an elite.

136. David Jordan, *Gods, Ghosts, and Ancestors: The Folk Religion of a Taiwanese Village* (Berkeley and Los Angeles, University of California Press, 1972), p. 103.

3 / Secular Crisis and Religious Solidarity

As small groups offering benefits to people who acted in common, the confraternities of Champagne exemplify the principle of association that had characterized the late Middle Ages. Georges de Lagarde points to the cellular construction of society during this period. Both state and church were weak and disorganized, compelled to acquiesce in the partition of their authority if they were to govern at all. This was the age of the estates, not merely (and in France not mainly) the representative assemblies, but "the social and political groups that shared the effective domination of a country." The estates were mutually hostile, for as soon as one of them gained an advantage it was challenged by another, which claimed a share in the newly won privileges and prerogatives.[1] Cities enjoyed a greater or lesser measure of autonomy; within them guilds jostled one another for position, but joined together to question the direction of municipal life by the upper crust of urban society. The villages in Western Europe strengthened their community organization. During the early stages of the long-term depression they were forced to defend themselves against the expedients of their seigneurs, who were in economic difficulties. If a seigneur became a rentier, after conceding defeat, then his peasants had to take a more active part in managing their own affairs.[2] And what was true of the temporal world holds for the spiritual. The schism "tore to shreds the seamless robe" of the church.[3] Competing popes hurled bulls at one another, while they attempted to contain the pretensions of the cardinals and keep the conciliar movement at bay. Franciscans and Dominicans could not amicably divide the spoils they had won from the secular clergy.

1. Georges de Lagarde, "La structure politique et sociale de l'Europe au XIVe siècle," *L'organisation corporative du Moyen Age à la fin de l'Ancien Régime*, Etudes presentés à la Commission internationale pour l'histoire des assemblées d'états, III (Louvain, 1939), 104; Lagarde, *La naissance de l'esprit laique*, vol. I: *Bilan du XIIIème siècle* (3rd ed., Louvain, 1956), ch. 7.
2. Léopold Genicot, "Crisis: From the Middle Ages to Modern Times," in *Cambridge Economic History of Europe*, 2nd ed. rev., I (Cambridge, At the University Press, 1966), 733–734.
3. Delaruelle et al., *L'église au temps du grand schisme*, I, 19.

It is typical, moreover, of times of depression, when men are pre-occupied with security, for them to gather together in associations that protect the members, rather than to act boldly as individuals, taking the greater risks that promise greater gains. The conviction that there is only a limited amount of wealth (and power, and prestige), which cannot be increased but only wrested from the grasp of others, dominated the late Middle Ages.

In their religious behavior as well, people leaned on one another, and joined together. "The relationships between human beings and religious objects," Robin Horton observes, "can be [in part] defined as governed by certain ideas of patterning and obligation such as characterize relationships among human beings. In short, Religion can be looked upon as an extension of the field of people's social relationships beyond the confines of purely human society."[4] In the late Middle Ages this meant that Christians emphasized the ties that bind the dead in the church expectant together with the living in the church militant. It also meant that access to the benefits that religion could offer, whether in this world or in the next, was open to people only if they acted within and through small groups: the family, the guild, the parish or urban community, and the confraternity. "Never had man been less isolated," wrote Emile Mâle with reference to the fourteenth and fifteenth centuries. "Divided into small groups, the faithful formed innumerable confraternities. It was always a saint who brought them together, for the saints were then the bonds that united men."[5]

The great emphasis on the Virgin and on the multiplicity of saints may also in part be understood with reference to the political situation. The fragmentation of authority, and the interposition of corporations as mediators between sovereign and subjects, clouded people's understanding of divine power. For the never-ending tug of war within both church and state made it difficult to know just how much authority the ruler had relinquished. Under these circumstances men could not clearly perceive the relationships within the celestial hierarchy.[6] A crucial and unresolved religious question of the late Mid-

---

4. Robin Horton, "A Definition of Religion and Its Uses," *Journal of the Royal Anthropological Institute,* 90 (1960), 211.

5. Mâle, *L'art religieux de la fin du Moyen Age,* p. 167.

6. The concordance between the polity of a society and its conception of the supernatural is the brilliant starting point for what proves to be a disappointing book: Guy Swanson, *Religion and Regime* (Ann Arbor, 1967). Unfortunately Swanson

dle Ages was the degree of responsibility and independent initiative that God had devolved on the Virgin — and on the saints, those independent power brokers in an age of bastard feudalism.

But were people satisfied with the religious efficacy of their petty groups, particularly since they were well aware of the tremendous hostility between the corporations into which they were organized? Fifteenth- and sixteenth-century preachers were continually harping on the characteristic vices of each estate. In theory they were encouraging their listeners to reform; in practice they were reflecting the tensions that charged social relations. Claude Haton observed, with reference to the Franciscans and Dominicans, that "commonly among people of the same estate there is a certain envy that turns them one against the other."[7] Surely people knew that the boons for which they asked would be granted them only as Christians united in true fellowship.

Annual ceremonies like Corpus Christi, and occasional events like the performance of mystery plays, served as attempts to neutralize the animosities that made harmony so difficult to achieve. Corpus Christi was celebrated on the Thursday following Trinity Sunday. The idea of the festival had been initiated early in the thirteenth century by a nun from the diocese of Liège, who had had a vision that she interpreted as a call for a feast day to honor the Holy Sacrament. The holiday was first observed in Liège, and then introduced later in the century to the universal church, when the bishop, who had been born Jacques Pantaléon of Troyes, became Pope Urban IV. During the late Middle Ages and the sixteenth century, Corpus Christi, as an aspect of the growing devotion to the Eucharist, was enthusiastically observed.[8] The city of Angers staged the most pompous procession in France, which was led by the crier of Pater Nosters, whose regular occupation it was to announce deaths and call for prayers.[9] The residents of Besançon marched to the tomb of the city's patrons, saints

---

arbitrarily defines and rigidly compartmentalizes the various forms of religious thought and of government in Reformation Europe.

7. Haton, *Mémoires*, I, 12.

8. *New Catholic Encyclopedia*, s.v. "Corpus Christi"; *Lexikon für Theologie und Kirche*, s.v. "Fronleichnam"; Gerhard Matern, *Zur Vorgeschichte und Geschichte der Fronleichnamsfeier besonders in Spanien* (Münster, 1962).

9. Lebrun, *Les hommes et la mort en Anjou*, pp. 487–488. Georges Espinas, *Les origines du droit d'association dans les villes de l'Artois et de la Flandre française jusqu'au début du XVIe siècle* (2 vols., Lille, 1941–1942), I, 468, 812–813, and 1034, points out that the purpose stated by local town governments and seigneurs for per-

Ferréol and Fergeux.[10] This was a holiday for everyone. At the turn of the fifteenth century, Parisian prostitutes went to the town of Senlis to attend the religious celebration, not merely to take the air, but presumably because they could not comfortably participate at home.[11]

Solidarity was the theme of Corpus Christi, the day on which all Catholics participated, and on which people reaffirmed the unity of the groups to which they belonged. In Champagne, the guildsmen of Reims marched together. Once the general procession, at Troyes and no doubt elsewhere, had returned to the cathedral, the marchers from each parish and clerical corporation began processions of their own.[12] The churchwardens of Montreuil-sur-Barse observed in 1549 that the inhabitants followed "the good custom" of accompanying the Holy Sacrament to the end of the village. They demarcated its limits, and so defined its territory, in the process.[13] Claude Haton noted that on the octave of the main festival, for *la petite fête Dieu*, the parishioners of Provins organized confraternities of the Holy Sacrament, "to which up to this day they have shown great devotion, faith, and honor, for which they are greatly to be praised." As on Corpus Christi Day itself, the residents of the streets along which the procession passed decorated the fronts of their houses with linens and tapestries. After the procession, mass, and family dinner, "the neighbors of each street and canton assemble, through their mutual friendship, up to twelve, fifteen, or twenty, more or less, depending on the number of residents who are in each canton of the street, to play and take recreation together, men on one side and women on the other, each with his companion. . . . While some play, others obtain the meat for supper, which is prepared at one of their houses, where men and

---

mitting the formation of guilds was to allow or require the members to participate as a corporation in the Corpus Christi procession. See his documentary evidence in ibid., II, 189–193, 281, 397, 482, 520.

10. Fohlen, *Histoire de Besançon*, I, 604.

11. Roger Vaultier, *Le folklore pendant la guerre de Cent Ans d'après les lettres de rémission du Trésor des Chartes* (Paris, 1965), p. 121.

12. AD, Aube, 10G layette, carton 3: a case between the bishop and Saint Urban's Collegial Chapter, heard by Parlement in 1655 and 1659, which refers to this practice as traditional.

13. AD, Aube, 279G (1564): inventory of the *objets de culte*. Adrien Friedmann, *Paris, ses rues, ses paroisses, du Moyen Age à la Révolution* (Paris, 1959), pp. 328–329, makes the point that processions which followed parish boundaries inculcated the sense of solidarity.

women join to sup, each paying his own way as at a tavern." Any newly married man or woman was required to pay the company for his welcome, according to his means; in other words he had to be accepted by the neighborhood. Weather permitting, the tables were set up in the street, in view of all the passers-by who wanted to watch. "By this means they maintain peace, concord, and amity with one another, a matter truly to be praised, since at the said assemblies the poor as well as the rich are received, if it pleases them to come." After supper the festivities took on an increasingly joyous tone, much to Haton's displeasure.[14]

This description, recorded in 1570, may perhaps reflect an attempt to revive a spirit of community that sixteenth-century social changes were progressively undermining.[15] If so, then the people of Provins were drawing on a meaning that the holiday had long held. When Henry VIII and Francis I decided in 1520 to exhibit friendship, they took advantage of the time of the English king's arrival on the continent to meet on Corpus Christi Day. Henry set out from within the enclave of Calais, then an English possession, with a fully armed escort, while Francis and his retinue crossed the frontier. In his chronicle Edward Hall offers a faithful image of how the events of the day were remembered in retrospect, which is more useful than what precisely may have happened. He indicates that men in both parties had doubts about the motives of their late hereditary enemies. The English were unsettled because they were outnumbered, and the French because, one may assume, strength in numbers had not helped them in the past. But after pausing on opposing hillocks, the kings, according to a contemporary French pamphlet, spurred their horses and galloped to the valley bottom. They embraced in the saddle, dismounted, took each other's hand, and entered the gilded tent that gave its name to the Field of the Cloth of Gold. The great lords of both kingdoms then joined them and participated in a toast, repeated several times, to "Good friends, French and English." During the days that followed, revelry mixed with affairs of state. The two Renaissance monarchs, like the inhabitants of Provins, vowed at Corpus

14. *Mémoires*, II, 611–612.
15. Alan Macfarlane, *Witchcraft in Tudor and Stuart England* (New York, 1970), p. 197, and Keith Thomas, *Religion and the Decline of Magic* (New York, 1971), pp. 560–567, comment on the loosening of communal bonds in later sixteenth-century England, with reference to the multiplication of accusations of witchcraft.

Christi time to forget old grievances, showed their neighborliness, and tied the knots of sociability in more or less honest pleasure.[16]

Although the kings had not originally intended to meet on the festival of the Holy Sacrament, their reunion conformed to the pattern of the holiday. The arrangements that governed the emperor Charles V's visit to England two years later show that this conformity was not accidental. Charles entered London just before Pentecost, and joined Henry in pageantry until Trinity Monday, when they turned to business. King and emperor sat in council from Monday to Wednesday, negotiating a treaty. On Thursday, Corpus Christi Day, they marched together from Windsor Chapel in solemn procession, returned to swear on the altar fidelity to their league, and then went out to feast.[17]

During a holiday period when the members of village communities, town parishes, and guilds were about to express their solidarity, they were easily roused against enemies who were outsiders: landlords, clerics doubling as officers of state, and the king's evil councilors. "It was before daybreak on Monday, the first day of the week of the Sacrament in the year 1381," wrote the chronicler Froissart, an intelligent as well as vivid collector of reminiscences, that the villagers of Kent who had been wrought up by the itinerant preacher John Ball "issued from their homes to come towards London and speak to the king, and become wholly free, for they wanted no one to be a serf in England." They pillaged the churches of Canterbury, whose archbishop was lord chancellor, and sent messages beyond the Thames, so that London would be surrounded. "In this way the king could not escape them, and their intention was to come together on the day of the Sacrament or the next." Their movement was joined by the residents of Canterbury, and as they advanced on the capital, "they drew along all the people of the villages to the right and to the left, and on their way

16. Edward Hall, *The Union of the Two Noble and Illustre Famelies of Lancastre & Yorke . . .* (1809), pp. 608–610; "L'ordre de l'entrevue et visitation des rois de France et d'Angleterre," in Bernard de Montfaucon, *Les monumens de la monarchie françoise,* IV (Paris, 1729–1733), 164–181. Other accounts include *The Chronicle of Calais in the Reigns of Henry VII. and Henry VIII. to the year 1540,* ed. J. G. Nichols, Camden Society, 35 (London, 1846), 28; *Journal de Jean Barrillon, secrétaire du chancelier Duprat, 1515–1521,* ed. Pierre de Vaissière (2 vols., Paris, 1897–1899), II, 169–170; and Robert de La Marck, *Mémoires du maréchal de Florange, dit le Jeune Adventureux,* ed. Robert Goubaix and P.-A. Lemoisne (2 vols., Paris, 1913 and 1924), I, 263–271. J. J. Scarisbrick, *Henry VIII* (Berkeley and Los Angeles, 1968), pp. 74–80, provides background, and Joycelyne Russell, *The Field of the Cloth of Gold* (London, 1969), offers detail.

17. Alonso de Santa Cruz, *Crónica del emperador Carlos V* (5 vols., Madrid, 1920–1925), I, 515–516; cf. *Hall's Chronicle,* pp. 640–641.

they stoned and battered down, as though they were a tempest, the houses of the lawyers of the courts of the king and archbishop, and had no mercy on them."[18] By Wednesday evening they had arrived on the right bank of the Thames. Then, as the poet John Gower wrote, "behold, it was Thursday, the festival of Corpus Christi, when frenzy seized every part of the city." The insurgents forced their way across London Bridge while, according to a London chronicler, "the monks and parsons and vicars were devoutly marching in procession to pray God for peace." Richard II courageously met and dispersed the Kentishmen and Londoners in the next two days, but meanwhile there were risings to the north and east of the capital. Thomas Walsingham, the chronicler of Saint Alban's Monastery, which was the object of one of the risings, noted that "all these evils occurred in the various provinces at one and the same time, and almost on the same days, within the octave, namely the feast of Corpus Christi, even though long journeys separated the places."[19] In form, the English peasant revolt was a wave of Corpus Christi processions.

It was also on the Monday before Corpus Christi that the Jacquerie, the great French peasant rising of 1358, which lasted a fortnight, began in the Beauvaisis, north of Paris.[20] At the end of May and into June the days are long and the grain was in short supply. If people were to revolt, then this was a likely moment of the year. I cannot

18. *Chroniques de J. Froissart*, vol. X, ed. Gaston Raynaud (Paris, 1897), pp. 100–102, 331. For appreciations of Froissart, see André Réville, *Le soulèvement des travailleurs d'Angleterre en 1381* (Paris, 1898), p. xi, n. 2; Heers, *L'Occident*, p. 253; Mollat and Wolff, *Ongles bleus*, pp. 116 and 188. May McKisack, *The Fourteenth Century, 1307-1399*, Oxford History of England, V (Oxford, At the Clarendon Press, 1959), ch. xiii, places the revolt in the context of English politics.

19. *Vox clamantis*, bk. 1, lines 919–920, *The Complete Works of John Gower*, ed. G.C. Macaulay (4 vols., Oxford, 1899–1902), IV, 47–48; *The Anonimalle Chronicle, 1333 to 1381*, ed. V.H. Galbraith (Manchester, 1927), p. 141 (for the ascription of this part of the chronicle to the under-clerk in Parliament John Scardeburgh, see A.F. Pollard, "The Authorship and Value of the 'Anonimalle' Chronicle," *English Historical Review*, 53 (1938), 577–605); Thomas Walsingham, *Historia Anglicana*, ed. H.T. Riley, Rolls Series (2 vols., London, 1863–1864), II, 11.

20. *Les grandes chroniques de France; chronique des règnes de Jean II et de Charles V*, ed. Roland Delachenal (4 vols., Paris, 1910–1920), I, 177, states that the rising began on 28 May, which was the day after Trinity Sunday. J. Flammeront, "La Jacquerie en Beauvaisis," *Revue historique*, 4 (1879), 125–126, confirms this date, refuting Siméon Luce, *Histoire de la Jacquerie*, 2nd rev. ed. (Paris, 1894), p. 53, n. 2, who proposed 21 May. See also Jacques d'Avout, *31 juillet 1358, le meurtre d'Etienne Marcel* (Paris, 1960), ch. 9: "La quinzaine des Jacques." Guy Fourquin, *Les campagnes de la région parisienne à la fin du Moyen Age* (Paris, 1964), pp. 232–234, explains the Jacquerie as the response of peasants in a rich agricultural area to the fall in grain prices that accompanied the decline in population.

therefore insist with equal emphasis on each of the risings at Corpus Christi time. It is probably no more than a coincidence that the Norfolk men who adumbrated Kett's Rebellion by throwing down enclosures on June 20, 1549, would also have been celebrating Corpus Christi Day, had England still been merry.[21] More to my point is the action of the Catholics in the province of Maine, who in 1562 at the height of the first French civil war massacred Protestants on the holiday, and in this way expelled the foreign body.[22]

Of much greater significance for general European history was the day at Barcelona that has come to be called *el Corpus de sang*. The efforts of the Count-Duke Olivares in the 1620s and 1630s to mobilize the resources of the Iberian peninsula for the needs of the Spanish monarchy had threatened the liberties of the principality of Catalonia. When the theatre of war with France moved from the plains of Picardy to the gates of the Pyrenees and required the Catalans' grudging participation, they became even more hostile to the central government at Madrid. In May of 1640 local risings in Catalonia were widespread. Then on June 7, Corpus Christi Day, the agricultural laborers who normally came to Barcelona on the holiday in order to hire themselves out for the harvest, and the rebels who mingled with them, rioted in the city and murdered the viceroy. The revolt of the Catalans was now fully underway.[23] In ordinary years Corpus Christi Day at Barcelona was a splendid occasion, and the standard by which other religious processions were measured. When the riots annulled the festival of 1640, the town staged a belated celebration in November, lest God be slighted. Barcelona, moreover, was the capital of a peo-

---

21. S.T. Bindoff's pithy essay *Ket's Rebellion, 1549* (London, 1949), is a model study of the step-by-step escalation of a riot into a rising. See also Frederic Russell, *Kett's Rebellion in Norfolk* (London, 1859). The *Chronicle of the Grey Friars of London (1189–1556)*, in *Monumenta Franciscana*, II, ed. Richard Howlett (London, 1882), 220, notes that on June 20, 1549, "in diverse places in London [the holiday] was kept holy day, and many kept none, such was the division." Sir John Arundell, a leader of the Western Rising of 1549, which was a religious revolt, had the holiday celebrated with a procession: *Troubles Connected with the Prayer Book of 1549*, ed. Nicholas Pocock, Camden Society, n.s. 37 (London, 1884), 38–39.

22. *Histoire ecclésiastique des églises réformées au royaume de France*, ed. G. Baum and E. Cunitz (3 vols., Paris, 1883–1889), II, 635.

23. Miguel Parets, *De los muchos sucesos dignos de memoria que han ocurrido en Barcelona y otros lugares de Cataluña*, ed. Celestino Pujol y Campos, Memorial histórico español (vols. XX–XXV, Madrid, 1888–1893), XX, 161–175; M. Batllori, "Un nuevo testimonio del 'Corpus de sang,'" *Analecta sacra Tarraconensia*, 22 (1949), 51–53; A. Rovira i Virgili, *El Corpus de sang* (Barcelona, 1932); J.H. Elliott, *The Revolt of the Catalans* (Cambridge, 1963), ch. 15.

ple who claimed to venerate the Sacrament more than any other Christians, and who used this claim to magnify their horror at the destruction of churches by troops in Spanish pay and more generally to justify their grievances against the Castilians and Madrid.[24] In a struggle that pitted the sense of community of a principality against the pressure to meld into a modern state, el Corpus de sang had a special meaning.

The Venetians, self-conscious practitioners of the art of politics, recognized and broadcast meanings that elsewhere were implicit. In 1606 Paul V imposed an interdict on the proud and recalcitrant city, which had refused to repeal laws that the Counter-Reformation pope considered anticlerical. Venice mobilized its people, and impressed on them the rationale for civic solidarity during the Feast of Corpus Christi. It was celebrated, as Henry Wotton, the English ambassador, wrote, "by express commandment of the State (which goeth farther than devotion, with the most sumptuous procession that ever had been seen here, wherein the very basins and ewers were valued in common judgment at 200,000 pound sterling, besides many costly and curious pageants, adorned with sentences of Scripture fit for the present," such as "my kingdom is not of this world."[25] Much could be made of Corpus Christi in times of crisis because even under normal circumstances it was a high point of popular religious feelings and expression.

In France the formal name for the holiday was *la fête Dieu*, the festival of God. Colloquially, the people referred to the procession in particular, and the holiday in general, as *le sacre*, which is best rendered as the anointment or consecration of the Holy Sacrament.[26] In practice, they used a holiday officially devoted to celebrating communion with their Maker to manifest a sense of community among themselves. Ideally, this end was served throughout the year by the very act of taking communion. The evangelical humanist

24. Corpus Christi as the standard: Parets, *De los muchos sucesos*, XX, 13, 23, 45, 145, and XXV, 262; the November celebration: XXI, 35–39; the Catalans and the Sacrament: XXI, 52–55 (letter of the "captain-general of the Christian army"), and [Gaspar Sala], *Proclamación católica a la magestad piadosa de Felipe el Grande . . .* (Barcelona, 1641), pp. 12–14, on the Catalans and Corpus Christi.

25. *The Life and Letters of Sir Henry Wotton*, ed. L. P. Smith (2 vols., Oxford, 1907), I, 350; William Bouwsma, *Venice and the Defense of Republican Liberty* (Berkeley and Los Angeles, 1968), pp. 389–390.

26. *Dictionnaire de la langue française* (Paris, 1863–1872; reprint ed., 1956–1958), s.v. "sacre." For further examples of this usage, see the *Histoire ecclésiastique*, I, 345: "le grand sacre d'Angers," and II, 634: "le jour qu'ils [Catholics] appellent leur Sacre."

Marguerite de Navarre, sister of King Francis I, has her party of
travelers in the *Heptaméron*, published in 1558–59, "hear the Mass
and receive the Holy Sacrament of union, at which all Christians
are made one . . . ." [27] In the sixteenth century most men and women
received the Sacrament a few times a year at best.[28] But people craved
a sense of unity, and derived great satisfaction from proving to themselves that they had achieved it. They celebrated Corpus Christi as
exuberantly as the festival of their parish patrons — and for much
the same reasons.

The mystery plays, which became an important aspect of French
religious life toward the end of the fifteenth century, also helped to
enhance solidarity. The plays fully realized the latent theatrical possibilities in mimed confraternity processions. Whereas in England
performances were often given at Corpus Christi, in France Pentecost was the common time.[29] A life of Saint Maclou, played at Bar-sur-
Aube in 1408, during a quiescent moment in the Hundred Years'
War, was the first documented open-air performance in Champagne
by a mixed company of laymen and clerics — as opposed to the
dramatization of a part of the liturgy by priests in church.[30] The
difficult times that followed precluded extensive productions. The
town council of Châlons, significantly, had refused subsidies in 1467
and 1469 to groups of players, for fear of establishing a precedent.
Unambiguous records of plays recur only in 1482 at Langres, 1483
at Troyes, 1484 at Reims as part of the festivities for Charles VIII's
coronation, and in 1486 at Châlons, where the councilors were now
willing to help to underwrite a performance.[31] More than twenty
plays were staged in seven towns of Champagne from the 1480s to

27. Marguerite de Navarre, *Nouvelles,* ed. Yves Le Hir (Paris, 1967), p. 15.
28. H. O. Evennett, *The Spirit of the Counter-Reformation* (Cambridge, 1968), p.
38. Scattered evidence of the amount of wine for ablution purchased by churchwardens does exist, e.g. in AD, Aube, 18G 11, f. 31 (1584–85), but despite the valiant
attempt of Jacques Toussaert, *Le sentiment religieux en Flandre à la fin du Moyen
Age* (Paris, 1963), pp. 161–175, it would be hazardous to infer from such figures the
number of people who communed on a given holiday.
29. E. K. Chambers, *English Literature at the Close of the Middle Ages,* Oxford History of English Literature, II, pt. 2 (Oxford, 1945), 18. For the evolution of the religious theatre, see O. B. Hardison, *Christian Rite and Christian Drama* . . . (Baltimore,
1965), and more specifically, V. A. Kolve, *The Play Called Corpus Christi* (Stanford,
1966). Petit de Julleville, *Les mystères,* is the standard French study, and Delaruelle
et al., *L'église au temps du grand schisme,* II, 605–624, an excellent recent discussion.
30. A. Vallet de Viriville, "Notice d'un mystère par personnages représenté à Troyes
vers la fin du XVe siècle," *Bibliothèque de l'Ecole des chartes,* 3 (1841–1842), 450,
n. 4.
31. Maurice Poinsignon, *Histoire générale de la Champagne et de la Brie,* 2nd ed.
(3 vols., Châlons, 1896–1898), II, 32–33.

the 1540s, though as we shall later see this was a terminal date only for preplanned, formal productions.[32] Some of these were prodigious efforts. Scores of players performed before most of their fellow towns-people, many visitors from the surrounding countryside, and tourists from other parts of the province, during three or four days — or sometimes eight, as at Châlons in 1531, when the players gave one instead of two acts a day.[33]

Ninety-five actors were required on the first day at Troyes in 1490 to represent episodes from the Creation to the death of Adam, which were taken from the *Mystery of the Old Testament,* a cycle of plays then current in France. The following three days, devoted to the New Testament and based on the *Passion* by the Parisian cleric Arnold de Greban, provided more than two hundred additional parts. Apparently this did not satisfy all the would-be players of the next performance, for marginal notations in a hand different from the original copyists' include bit parts for two more shepherds, seven more subjects of Herod, and two more ladies-in-waiting, played by men, of Mary Magdalene. Several additional speeches, moreover, were given to one of the Pharisees.[34] Canon Guillaume Flamang wrote 115 parts into his *Life and Passion of Monseigneur Saint Didier, Martyr and Bishop of Langres,* the only surviving wholly Champenois script, which the saint's confraternity commissioned from him and produced in 1482.[35] As for the size of audiences, the town council of Châlons provided a hint by its efforts at play time in 1531 to secure 300 setiers of grain in addition to the 170 normally needed for eight days.[36]

Parisian actors were organized into a confraternity of the Passion.

32. Performances are listed in Petit de Julleville, *Les mystères,* II, 175–185, and Octave Beuve, *Le théâtre à Troyes aux quinzième et seizième siècles* (Paris, 1913). In addition, I have found mention of a Passion play at Troyes in 1530 (AD, Aube, 14G 20, f. 25), and of one at Châlons in 1531 (AC, Châlons, BB 7, f. 258).

33. AC, Châlons, BB 7, f. 258.

34. The players deposited the text for the first, second, and fourth days with the town council for safekeeping. The council never received the third day, covering Christ's life from the preaching of John the Baptist to the introduction to the Passion. For the relationship with the two other plays, see Petit de Julleville, *Les mystères,* II, 411–413; for the supplementary parts, see the text of the play, BC, Troyes, MS 2282: I, ff. 126 and 139; II, ff. 13v, 48, 51, 53v, 67, 86, 129, and 136.

35. Guillaume Flamang, *La vie et passion de Mgr. sainct Didier, martir et évesque de Lengres* (Paris, 1855). André Rémond ("Quelques aspects de la vie sociale dans le théâtre, à Langres, vers la fin du Moyen Age," *Revue d'histoire économique et sociale,* 33 [1955], 19–76) emphasizes the relationship between the political sentiments in the text and loyalty to the French monarchy.

36. AC, Châlons, BB 7, f. 258.

In Champagne, with the exception of the single performance by Saint Didier's Confraternity, which was apparently never repeated, men formed temporary companies on the occasion of each play. Fifteen "bourgeois, legal practitioners, and merchants" of Reims, for example, petitioned the town council in 1530 to allow them to stage the Passion and charge admission to recover a portion of their expenses. Some artisans with means, and others without, took parts. Soon afterwards the municipal magistracy of Mézières, a town on the fringes of the Ardennes, allocated funds for the poor players.[37] By contrast the Troyen carpenter Jehan Carbonnier and the shoemaker Huguenin Raguin were men of sufficient standing to sign a receipt in the name of all the players in 1490, acknowledging a fifty-livre subsidy from the municipal government. The clergy were essential as star performers. That same year friar Nicole Molu of the Dominicans requested and received a grant from the town council because the time he had spent studying and playing the role of Christ over the past seven years and more "at the request of several bourgeois" had compelled him "to foresake and abandon his vocation and practice of preaching and other [matters]."[38] The phrasing makes it clear that here, as at Reims, lay notables took the initiative in producing plays. Town councils were mindful of the money non-resident spectators would spend and of the prestige a play would bring, as well as conscious of their religious obligations. They gave the notables, who were their relatives, cooperation and sometimes financial aid. Clerical corporations offered good will. Saint Stephen's Chapter of Troyes agreed in 1531 to a performance in front of its cloister and within the jurisdiction of its court, on condition that each of the seventy-two canons be allotted three complimentary seats.[39]

The Champenois notables were sponsoring a genuinely popular art form, which could satisfy the tastes of men and women of all social ranks without exceeding the capacities of any. Prices of admission at Reims in 1531, significantly, were set for two extremes of purses. A seat in the stands cost three deniers (for a single act, morning or after-

---

37. Pierre Varin, *Archives législatives de la ville de Reims* (4 vols., Paris, 1840–1852), pt. 2 (Statuts), I, 870–871; Petit de Julleville, *Les mystères*, II, 122. See also Charles Gailly de Taurines, "Une représentation du mystère de la Passion à Mézières, en 1531," *Revue historique ardennaise*, 10 (1903), 65–77.

38. Petit de Julleville, *Les mystères*, II, 58–59; AC, Troyes, Fonds Boutiot, AA, carton 60.

39. Beuve, *Le théâtre*, p. 21.

noon, presumably). Each window in a *chambre*, or temporary loge, was two livres for the full performance.[40] Assume that a poor artisan sacrificed half a day's work to take his wife and two older children to the play at a cost of one sol. The man of means and leisure paid at least forty times that amount for his family.

The plays themselves could hardly have been easier to follow. The set was composed of a station for each of the locales at which action took place: a scaffold for heaven, a mouth opening into the pit of hell, a Garden of Eden on ground level, and several more. Actors stood at their stations until the time came for them to play. With every scene and every actor visible throughout the perfomance, the spectator did not have to tax his memory. The plot unfolded as the players moved from one station to another. The rebellious angels, for example, were hurled from heaven to hell. A spectator unable to hear clearly over the crowd noise, or to comprehend all that he did hear, could still follow what was happening. The stage effects left little to his imagination. A fire from heaven consumed Abel's sacrifice in the Troyes play. Idols tottered on their pedestals when the Holy Family arrived in Egypt. During the Transfiguration, Jesus' clothing shone like gold.[41]

In their range from pathos to burlesque, the plays had something for everyone. Jesus endured a rude whipping, staggered under the burden of the cross, and hung from it while he delivered his lines. No wonder friar Nicole felt that he merited the town council's generosity. *The Vengeance of Christ,* a play that culminates in the destruction of Jerusalem, must have relaxed the tension of the audience by providing it with a more comfortable outlet for the impulse of cruelty. It followed the Rémois Passion in 1531, and was produced independently in Troyes in 1540.[42] The devils, important figures in both the Troyen *Passion* and *Saint Didier,* offered comic relief, as they brayed their plots against men and fought with one another if a scheme failed. The fool, a character in the *Saint Didier* text and a later addition to the Troyes play, helped as well, with his obtuse and

40. Varin, *Archives législatives,* pt. 2 (Statuts), I, 875.

41. BC, Troyes, MS 1282: I, ff. 59v and 162; II, f. 15v.

42. Raymond Lebègue, *La tragédie religieuse en France; les débuts (1514–1573)* (Paris, 1929), p. 6, states that Christ was whipped "with incredible realism," thereby satisfying the cruel instincts of the crowd. Petit de Julleville (*Les mystères,* I, 375) maintained that the beatings were feigned. A synopsis of the *Vengeance* is in ibid., II, 451–460.

occasionally scatalogical remarks on the action and on the spectators. Canon Flamang has him swear by the death of God — one of those blasphemous oaths that royal decrees, municipal ordinances, and church councils were interminably reproving, and the people forever mouthing.[43] The spectator who saw a little of himself in the fool hardly suffered from the shock of recognition. But he could also identify with more ennobling figures. On stage the Virgin conceived, and Jesus lived and died, just as they had fifteen hundred years ago. The audience flinched under the whip with its Savior, and helped him to carry his cross. They experienced the biblical drama as if they themselves had been in the Holy Land.

Art historians have noted the affinities between the religious theatre and the iconography of stained-glass windows. Both related biblical episodes and saints' lives with vigor and intensity. The scenes of the Champenois windows, easily readable, are so large that they fill several panes of glass and force the observer to disregard the lead supports that cut through them. Brutal color characterizes the windows of Troyes and its region — to borrow an image from Paul Biver that suits the general tenor of the plays as well as their costumes. Inscriptions flow through the Troyen windows — gleaming letters on white, yellow, or blue streamers of glass, which heighten the effect of color and add decorative qualities rather than identify the scene. At times they make no sense, especially in the rural windows, which were executed summarily from designs already used in town, because illiterate painters were not interested in carefully copying what they did not understand.[44] By contrast, the exhortations at the bottom to pray for the donors are comprehensible and legible. With this exception the textual element served the visual, here as in the plays. The glass-painters who worked at Châlons had a more refined touch, but all things considered used only slightly cooler tones to narrate the same subjects.

This exuberance contrasts sharply with the French windows of the fourteenth and earlier centuries, which have left scarcely a trace in Champagne. Clear glass had been used, to let in the light that would

---

43. Flamang, *La vie et passion*, p. 61. On oaths see Rapp, *L'église et la vie religieuse*, p. 160.

44. Réau (*Iconographie*, I, 258–266) provides a judicious discussion and a bibliography of art and theatre; on the scale of the Champenois windows, see Emile Mâle, "Le vitrail français au XVe et au XVIe siècle," *Histoire de l'art*, ed. André Michel (8 vols. in 17, Paris, 1905–1929), IV, pt. 2, 789–795; Biver, *L'école troyenne*, p. 63 on color, and p. 108 on the illiterate painters; Jean Lafond, "La Renaissance," in Marcel Aubert et al., *Le vitrail français* (Paris, 1958), p. 217, on decorative inscriptions.

call attention to the elegance of Flamboyant Gothic ribs. Grave, elongated, sculptural figures of saints were depicted, standing on pedestals, beneath canopies, to reinforce the architectural mode.[45] To look at the subsequent style, however, is to lose track of the architecture as one becomes engrossed in the window. "The last Gothic age was dominated by a pictorial vision" to the extent that the most important and costly step in sculpture was not chiseling the raw stone, but polychroming the finished statue. A talented and prudent sculptor, around 1500, was a painter as well.[46]

The highly colored windows became dominant in Troyes by 1490, at the same time that plays were being staged in all the major towns. The style persisted until the 1530s because the painter-glassmakers, at least those of Troyes, whose work Biver studied exhaustively, preferred retouching old cartoons to making new ones. The producers of plays were meanwhile adding marginal notes to old texts. In many cases they were also donating windows, to the town churches where they lived and to the village churches where they were seigneurs. Guillaume Huyard, the king's attorney at Troyes and *grand maire* of the cathedral, to name but one, was a sponsor of the 1497 Passion; probably he also played a role.[47] The next year he and his brother Jehan, a canon, gave the cathedral one of its nave windows. "A handsome page of color, with clumsy, very naive figures who have a rather barbarous air," it portrays several local and universal saints.[48]

A donor gave a window to appeal for prayer and to place himself under the protection of the saint whose name he bore. But one also gave a window for the same reasons that he participated in a play. These included, according to the municipal account books of Mézières, the desire "to instruct the poor people of the town and its countryside" and, in the words of the Troyen sponsors of 1531, "to incite and move the hearts of the people to devotion."[49]

45. Mâle, "Le vitrail," p. 774; Marcel Aubert, *Le vitrail en France* (Paris, 1946), ch. 3.

46. Henri Zanettacci, *Les ateliers picards de sculptures à la fin du Moyen Age* (Paris, 1954), p. 97, a precise and sensitive study.

47. Biver, *L'école troyenne,* p. 6, and ch. 4. For Huyard as avocat du roi and sponsor: AC, Troyes, A 2, f. 147. A co-sponsor, Simon Liboron, soon to be the procureur royal, gave the Church of the Magdalene a window depicting Saint Louis for the confraternity chapel of the king's officers (Boutiot, *Histoire de la ville de Troyes,* III, 263). The sponsors of 1531 include members of the Marisy, Menisson, and Dorigny families, all previous donors of nave windows to the cathedral (Beuve, *Le théâtre,* p. 21; Biver, *L'école troyenne,* ch. 6).

48. Ibid., p. 58.

49. Petit de Julleville, *Les mystères,* II, 122; cf. Beuve, *Le théâtre,* p. 21.

A century later, in 1644, the English clergyman John Shaw was preaching in Lancashire among "a people . . . who were exceeding ignorant and blind as to religion." On encountering a man about sixty, who was "sensible enough in other things," Shaw asked him about Christ. " 'O Sir,' said he, 'I think I heard of that man you spake of, once in a play at Kendall, called Corpus Christi play, where there was a man on a tree, and blood ran down,' &c. And after that he professed that tho' he was a good churchman, that is, he constantly went to Common-Prayer at their chappel, yet he could not remember that ever he heard of salvation by Jesus Christ, but in that play." Christopher Hill cites Shaw's story as an example of the puritan preachers' conviction that the masses were still ignorant.[50] But the anecdote also demonstrates that such plays had taught illiterate people a good part of what they knew about Christianity.

The plays did have another purpose beyond edification, which a window could not easily convey. The subject of Canon Flamang's *Saint Didier* was the glory of the town and the reasons that all of its inhabitants had to be proud. All the noble characters, from the Roman emperor to the archbishop of Lyons and the four barons of France, laud Langres whenever they speak of it. The three privileged orders represented, moreover — the canons of the cathedral, the four barons of the duchy of Langres, and the bourgeois of the town — are forever complementing one another on their spirit of mutual cooperation and their zeal for the interest of Langres. The author was writing, the confraternity acting, and the residents of the city observing, a play in praise of themselves. No doubt the other two plays about patrons — *Saint Maclou* of Bar, whose tooth the collegial chapter possessed, and *Saint Loup* of Troyes, which was performed in 1485 and 1540 — stressed the same theme.

When Didier becomes bishop of Langres his first words are that God has inspired him to maintain everyone, great and small, in unity. The devils in the play, by contrast, seek to divide. Satan addresses his chief, Lucifer, as "prince of disordered hell." In the final act he plans, unsuccessfully, to prevent the translation of the saint's bones to a new reliquary by turning the bishop then in office and the monks

---

50. "The Life of Master John Shaw," *Yorkshire Diaries and Autobiographies in the Seventeenth and Eighteenth Centuries,* Surtees Society, 65 (London, 1875), 137–139; Christopher Hill, *Society and Puritanism in Pre-Revolutionary England* (New York, 1964), pp. 250–251.

who have come to participate in the ceremony against one another. The Troyen Passion play echoes this theme. The main attribute of the devils is their lack of order, which is what makes them ridiculous. Thrown to hell, they bray the refrain, "devils, let's hurl and cry, that is the best we can do." According to the noted historian of drama Raymond Lebègue, almost all the characters in the mystery plays are insipid, save for the Virgin, tender and sad. But perhaps the real exception is Satan, willful and resourceful, alert to seize opportunities, and loyal to Lucifer though at the same time scornful of him. Fortunately Satan is wholly subject to the power of God. Certainly he is the only individualist, as well as the strongest character, in both parts of the Troyen play. In obvious contrast to the cacophony of hell, the angels at happy moments like the Nativity chant together in unison "as melodiously as possible."[51]

The Rémois sponsors of 1530 recalled that the purpose of playing the Passion was "in order to have a good and true commemoration for the honor of God, and for the salvation of the soul of each and every one."[52] There could be no better way to please Him and benefit man than to encourage a spirit of harmony among the spectators, who in effect represented an entire region. Manifestations of harmony were even more important during times of agricultural crisis. At such moments all those who were affected had to join together in demonstrating the good will that was a necessary condition for the recovery of divine favor. We have already noted the march of the peasants on Troyes during the famine of 1556. In 1573, the worst agricultural year of the century, Claude Haton observed that in Provins

on Saint George's Day, April 23, the parishes of the Holy Cross and Saint Ayoul, the Franciscans and Dominicans, went all together in procession to the churches of the town of Nogent[-sur-Seine], and on their return passed by the town or market village of Chalautre-la-Grande, in honor of Mons. Saint George, patron of Chalautre. At both places they were honorably and devoutly received by the priests and people, in honor of God and of the holy relics and bones that those of Provins carried with them, including the head of Mons. Saint Ayoul.[53]

In this case the people seem to be saying that God is angry with us because we are not in harmony with one another; let us recultivate

---

51. Flamang, *La vie et passion*, pp. 106, 25, and 343; BC, Troyes, MS 1282, I, ff. 14v, 113v–114; Lebègue, *La tragédie religieuse*, pp. 22–23.
52. Varin, *Archives législatives*, pt. 2 (Statuts), I, 870–871.
53. Haton, *Mémoires*, II, 715.

that harmony, by fraternizing as we worship each other's saints, in order to dissipate his wrath.

Such processions must have been responses to deeply felt emotions. In 1579, a year of spring frosts,

on the Sunday after Easter the parishioners of the market town of Courlons [Courlon-sur-Yonne] called on their curé to go in procession, after vespers, to a neighboring church or chapel, to pray God to preserve the fruits of the earth. The curé granted them the procession, to a certain place that he chose, closer than the one to which their devotion inclined, and vespers said, he began the procession, with his vicar and the parishioners. But when they were outside the village, the parishioners turned and took the road to the place on which they had decided, and not the one the curé wanted. The latter, seeing himself disdained and held in contempt, stopped short and began to argue with his parishioners, saying that it wasn't up to them to lead him where it seemed good to them, but rather that he should lead them where he wanted. At this there arose a great argument and commotion; the said curé was alone on his side, and no one (or very few) were in agreement with him. After some words, several particularly agitated parishioners picked him up bodily and threw him into the Yonne, where he nearly drowned, and would have if other parishioners hadn't pulled him out. While the argument was proceeding, and the curé was being drawn out, the other parishioners with the vicar were continuing along the way that they had decided to go. [54]

The farther they went the more favorably God would look on their plea, because the more they had done to bring villages distant from one another in space, but suffering from a common problem, together in devotion. It is well known that the Catholic clergy occupied the pivotal position of mediators between man and God. I have tried to temper this statement slightly by suggesting that on certain ritual occasions laymen represented themselves as clerics. In the light of the present argument I would further maintain that at the end of the Middle Ages the most salient function of the clergy in the eyes of the laity may have been to act as intermediaries between men, living and dead, and between groups.

A major grievance of the traditionally-minded people who participated fully and vigorously in the kinds of activities we have been considering may have been the awareness that the rituals they valued so highly did not always bring concord. We already have one wet curé as a witness. Corpus Christi, Rabelais commented (and he knew much of France, though admittedly not Champagne, well), was a day for women to dress themselves in splendor — by definition, in competi-

54. Ibid., p. 977.

tion with one another. The processions of 1573, Haton lamented on reflection, after having praised them, "were performed more in pride, curiosity, and worldly honor than in saintly devotion, especially on the part of some clerics more than that of the simple people, and it seemed that the said processions were held at Provins by envy of one church for another."[55] Ideals were tarnished in practice; the clergy did not always do its duty, or act with the appropriate humility, since it was divided by the very kinds of rifts that these rituals were intended to heal. Such failings do not invalidate our case, though they do help to redefine what "the simple people" took the term "clerical abuses" to mean. Men and women realized that their attempts to cultivate harmony were unsuccessful. And whom did they blame but the clerics, those servants of God who could not unite laymen while they were themselves at each other's throats?

This form of anticlericalism by itself could never lead to heresy. Sixteenth-century Protestant reformers quarreled with the church on much more fundamental grounds. They were attacking an institution that had made a genuine and sincere, though flawed, attempt to respond to the needs of the Christian people at a particular period in time. The aspirations of some Christians changed drastically during the sixteenth century, too drastically for the church to respond. For it was both restrained by inertia and committed to the care of the greater number of the faithful, who were letting go of the past much more slowly.

If the inability of the clergy to restore harmony among men disturbed many orthodox Catholics, then the insecurity of their relationship with God must have troubled them even more. No one, as we have observed, stood alone before the Divine. But even with all the human aid they could muster, men and women toward the end of the Middle Ages, like Adam and Eve after the Fall, "hid themselves from the presence of the Lord God." They preferred, rather, to identify as closely as possible with the sacrifice of the Son, who had died to save them from the Father's wrath. Jesus became the symbol of suffering. Christians who empathized with the Passion, and helped him to carry his cross, could expect in return to transfer their burden of sin and guilt onto his shoulders, leaving them with an immense sense of relief, though perhaps not with the feeling that their souls were truly

55. *Pantagruel*, Oeuvres complètes, ed. Jacques Boulenger and Lucien Scheler (Paris, 1955), p. 264; Haton, *Mémoires*, II, 722.

cleansed. The Virgin, mother of them all, but localized and particularized in the shrines and statues that made her accessible to the individual believer, was the symbol of compassion. Tolerant, forgiving, and understanding, she would use her influence to plead the case of souls which would otherwise sink straight to hell of their own dead weight of sin.

Early sixteenth-century media effectively conveyed the late-medieval themes. The Passion play imprinted the full measure of Christ's suffering and the Virgin's sorrows on the minds of spectators, and invited them to share in both. The books called "Hours," compilations of prayers published in Paris for the use of the laity, provided literate men and women with a similar opportunity from day to day. The *Hours according to the Custom of the Diocese of Châlons,* dated 1512, includes a service in honor of Notre-Dame-de-Pitié. At matins the reader is instructed to ask the Virgin "that it may please you to have me, miserable sinner, participate in the merit of the sword of sorrow by which your soul was pierced . . . so that I may entirely accomplish the commandments of God, and that in hope of the general resurrection I may avoid damnation and willingly bear the acts and burdens of our Lord, which he has given me, in order that I may achieve enduring joy. Amen."[56] The Hours enjoyed wide circulation. In 1520 two merchant-booksellers of Châlons ordered eight hundred from a Parisian printer who had supplied them, and Rémois merchants too, in the past.[57] Guides to piety reinforced the Hours. In a Troyen tract entitled *Here begins a Little Instruction and Manner of Living for a Laywoman,* a young matron earns the admiration of a master of theology. She has informed him that, among other practices, "every day I bathe myself in the vermilion wounds of Jesus Christ, with full confidence that he will purify my faults with his Passion." The anonymous author must have been a Franciscan, since he praises "our good saintly father, Brother Olivier Maillard," a fifteenth-century preacher of that order. A supplementary tract bound with the *Little Instruction* offers counsel on the manner of "hearing the Mass devoutly." "You must not read your Hours, nor the Pater Noster or Ave Maria, but only think of our Lord . . . on Sunday, at the Mass, how he was at the Garden of Olives, sweating blood and

---

56. *Ces présentes heures, à l'usage de Châlons, toutes au long, sans rien requerir. . . .*
57. AD, Marne, 4E 6188, f. 210, published in Amédée Lhôte, *Histoire de l'imprimerie à Châlons-sur-Marne, 1488–1894* (Châlons, 1894), p. 169.

water ... on Saturday, how he was taken down [from the cross] and placed on the lap of his gentle mother."[58]

Every person in Champagne, literate or not, could learn from and react to the works of sculpture that individuals and confraternities commissioned from local artists during the opening decades of the sixteenth century. In 1515 Dame Jacquelyne de Laignes had a sculptured entombment of Christ placed in her family chapel within the parish church of Chaource. Two soldiers guard the chapel entrance. Standing six feet tall, they must have appeared larger than life to contemporaries. Their commanding presence at the entry helps to differentiate the chapel space beyond from the rest of the church, while their somber mien establishes an air of utmost seriousness, and suggests that they are themselves aware of the significance of the event. A third soldier sits resting on a stone, nearby. Opposite the three and facing the worshipper, Joseph of Arimathaea and Nicodemus lower Christ's body into the sepulcher, while the Virgin, Saint John, Mary Magdalene, and the two other Marys look on (figure 1). Their contained, silent sorrow is more expressive than lamentation, more realistic than the caricature of grief; it sustains the atmosphere of dignity and momentousness, and invites the visitor to participate in a living scene, instead of keeping him at arm's length from a mere copy in stone. Off to one side, finally, kneel the figures of the donor and her late husband, reduced to a scale that is smaller than life.[59]

This art evoked the pity of the spectator, so that he might experience vicariously the suffering of those whom he worshipped (figure 2). Other subjects for sculpture sought to replicate contemporary life and experience. Mary as the Madonna became progressively less divine in the course of the late Middle Ages. "At Saint Urban's of Troyes, for example [at the beginning of the sixteenth century], the Virgin is a young Champenoise with a high forehead, her eyes slit into a tight smile, candid and yet malicious; as for the Child, chubby-cheeked, curly-haired, smiling, busy with a large grape, he is the

---

58. *Cy commence une petite instruction et manière de vivre pour une femme séculière comme elle se doit conduire en pensées parolles et oeuvres tout au long du iour pour tous les iours de la vie pour plaire à Nostre Seigneur et amasser richesses célestes au proffit et salut de son âme* (Troyes, n.d.), sig. Aii, and *Sensuit cy après une petite manière comment une femme séculière se peult conduire dévotement et vertueusement pour le proffit et salut de son âme.*

59. For a comprehensive discussion of these sculptured groups in Champagne, see William Forsyth, *The Entombment of Christ: French Sculptures of the Fifteenth and Sixteenth Centuries* (Cambridge, Mass., 1970), ch. 4.

Word incarnate in a little Champenois boy" (figure 3). "Nowhere,"
Emile Mâle continues, "were the artists further from respect than in
Champagne." Saint Elizabeth had become a bourgeois matron,
dressed to show off her estate; the male saints were depicted as craftsmen, practicing the trades that they patronized (figure 4).[60] Whether
poignant or realistic, the statues served to bring Jesus, the Virgin,
and the saints as close to the Christian people as possible, and helped
to compensate for the distance that they felt separated them from God
the Father.

For Europe as a whole there is substantial evidence of an Indian
summer of late-medieval piety in the decades around 1500. The printing press multiplied the books of Hours, most of which were printed
between 1485 and 1530. Most entombments of Christ were sculptured
in the second half of the fifteenth and the early sixteenth centuries.
Confraternity life in Geneva probably reached its height from 1480 to
the Reformation. In Germany, meanwhile, there was a general intensi-
fication of a piety that included veneration of the saints, the foundation of masses, and the sudden occurrence of mass pilgrimages.[61]

My own marshalling of evidence has taken us from London to Barcelona, from 1381 to 1640. The length of this span of time raises the
impossible and necessary question of when the Middle Ages really
ended. One approach to the answer may be, as William Bouwsma has
shown, that the relationship between cultural modes is as much com-
petitive as sequential.[62] Late Middle Ages, Renaissance, and Reform
were all aspects of European culture from the fourteenth to the first
part of the seventeenth centuries. They competed with one another
for predominance, according to patterns that varied with time and
place, until all three were effectively challenged by a new view of the
world, and a new vision of reality, in the second third of the seventeenth century.

The saccharine and rather self-indulgent religious tendencies that
we have been studying were, then, but one aspect of the cultural life
of a long period in history. I have sought to present them as a continuing response to such difficulties of the fourteenth and fifteenth cen-

60. Emile Mâle, L'art religieux de la fin du Moyen Age, pp. 149–150, 157–161.
61. Dictionnaire de spiritualité ascétique et mystique, doctrine et histoire, s.v.
"Heures"; Jean-François Bergier, Genève et l'économie européenne de la Renaissance
(Paris, 1963), p. 250, n. 3, with reference to both pious and guild confraternities. See
also Henri Naef, Les origines de la Réforme à Genève (2 vols., Geneva, 1968), I, 19;
Bernd Moeller, "Frömmigkeit in Deutschland um 1500," Archiv für Reformationsgeschichte, 56 (1965), 5–15.
62. Bouwsma, Venice, ch. 1, esp. p. 2.

turies as recurrent plague, severe economic dislocation, and domestic political turmoil. Other historians have emphasized instead the living tradition of meditation on the Passion and devotion to the Virgin, which acquired increasing force from the twelfth century onwards. Confraternities were not a creation of the fourteenth century. Nor was the tight bond between the living and the dead entirely new. Masses for souls in purgatory were endowed at monasteries by the nobility throughout the high Middle Ages. What was distinctive about the fourteenth and fifteenth centuries, according to Georges Duby, was the effect of a rapid *vulgarisation* of Christianity, which occurred in the decades around 1300.[63] The late medieval religious climate was, then, primarily a consequence of the diffusion of beliefs and practices from the quiet of the cloister and the relative sobriety of the chateau to the marketplace. "Emotion," R.W. Southern has written, "is the leading characteristic of urban religion."[64] The city crowds, it might be argued, practiced with their own special enthusiasm a religion of which they were for the first time fully aware. We cannot therefore sense without qualification "the mixed smell of blood and of roses" that Huizinga characterized as the "waning of the Middle Ages."[65] But his view should be modified rather than abandoned. The times were excruciatingly difficult in a large part of Europe, which included Champagne. It would have required strong faith and some imagination to have real confidence in God's beneficence. Men and women sought, in view of his ominous attitude, to protect and insulate themselves from his gaze. They used their fuller knowledge of religion to this end.

It is also true that important indicators of what I have called late-medieval piety reached their apogee at the turn of the sixteenth century, when the worst had passed in Champagne and when other, richer provinces were well on the way to economic recovery. Only at this late date can Huizinga's vision of "the extreme saturation of the religious atmosphere, and a marked tendency of thought to embody itself in images" be recognized fully in our province.[66] The Passion play had just recently taken its definitive form, and was now being per-

63. Rapp, *L'église et la vie religieuse*, pp. 128, 146–147; Edouard Perroy, *La vie religieuse au XIIIe siècle*, Les cours de Sorbonne (4 pts., Paris, 1966), pt. 1, pp. 67, 128; cf. Duby, "Les sociétés médiévales," pp. 10–12.

64. R.W. Southern, *Western Society and the Church in the Middle Ages* (Harmondsworth, and Baltimore, Md., Penguin, 1970), p. 48.

65. Huizinga, *Waning of the Middle Ages*, p. 18.

66. Ibid., p. 136.

formed before thousands of spectators in the towns of Champagne. Stained-glass windows incorporating likenesses of their donors into religious scenes, and statues depicting holy figures in the guise of the people of Champagne, were being commissioned in great and increasing numbers. They served to dignify and embellish the churches that were being newly built, enlarged, or completed, from the Cathedral of Troyes which was finally acquiring a western façade, to modest rural parishes.

Popular enthusiasm contributed to and was sustained by the building programs. The town council of Troyes decided in 1474 to replace a dilapidated stone calvary on the main square with a new, beautiful cross. The grandiose structure was melted down for munitions in 1793. Its style, though not its iconography or scale, may be suggested by a beautiful cross in stone from the cemetery of Neuvy-Sautour, southeast of Troyes in Burgundy, which is now in the village church (figure 5). The cross at Troyes rested on a platform of masonry. A stone pedestal, which enclosed the trunk of the cross, stood on the platform. It was decorated with three statues of tempters: Satan, the serpent, and Simon the Magician. Around and above the pedestal, on a series of pilasters and colonnettes, stood statues of Saint Peter, Saint Louis, Saint Loup — and Muhammed. Apples of gilded bronze, containing relics, separated the cross from the crucifix above it. Mary Magdalene clasped the foot of the crucifix, while the Virgin and Saint John rested on two branches, which extended outward in either direction. "The crucifix and all the faces and hands of the images on the said cross" were painted "in beautiful carnation color, as close to life as possible." The monument as a whole stood thirty-six feet high, and was protected by a baldachin.[67]

In early June of 1500 the king's attorney informed the town council that "as a result of the great concourse of people who in the last three weeks have arrived and been attracted to and around the *Beautiful Cross* of Troyes to have health and the cure of certain and diverse maladies of which they are sick, through the prayers and devotions that they perform at the said cross, a people who assemble and sojourn

67. AC, Troyes, Fonds Delion, layette 49; Emmanuel Viollet-le-Duc, *Dictionnaire raisonné de l'architecture française du XIe au XVIe siècle* (10 vols., Paris, 1861–1868), IV, 441–444, fig. 24; A.-S. Det, "La Belle-Croix de Troyes," *Annuaire administratif . . . du département de l'Aube,* 58 (1884), 81–134. Raymond Koechlin and Jean-J. Marquet de Vasselot, *La sculpture à Troyes et dans la Champagne méridionale au seizième siècle* (Paris, 1900), p. 26, reserve judgment on the presence of a statue of Muhammed.

by night and by day, so long and in such great numbers," traffic had become impossible, human waste insufferable, the threat to the good name of the maidens and matrons there acute, and thefts by evil young men rife. The council ordered "all pilgrims, sick people, poor beggars, and others" to vacate the area from 10 P.M. to 3 A.M., and restricted the time that any one person could pray at the cross to "about a half-hour."[68]

While the Beautiful Cross was acquiring its miraculous reputation, Troyen confraternities were flourishing. Previously, as our earliest returns from Mary Magdalene's Church in 1411 and 1412 suggest, the confraternities of the Immaculate Conception and probably of Corpus Christi were already solidly implanted. But participation fell sharply during the next three decades, with the return of the rigors of civil war. From mid-century until the 1510s in Troyes, both the number of associations and the total membership grew, as the patron saints in particular took their place in a denser confraternity network (see tables 3, 5, and 6). By the early sixteenth century it is true that Corpus Christi as a confraternity devotion was already flagging, a trend that we shall want to consider later. Here we must recognize that the growth of population was a necessary condition for the success of the other confraternities. But this is a part of my argument rather than a qualification. Domestic peace and order, greater assurance of life, and the increasing wealth of a more populous society made it easier for people in Champagne to frequent confraternities, stage the plays, and pay for an art that recalled the atmosphere of the difficult and unpleasant past. As the century progressed, other religious tendencies would compete with this late-medieval spirit that refused to die.

68. AC, Troyes, A 3, ff. 24v–25.

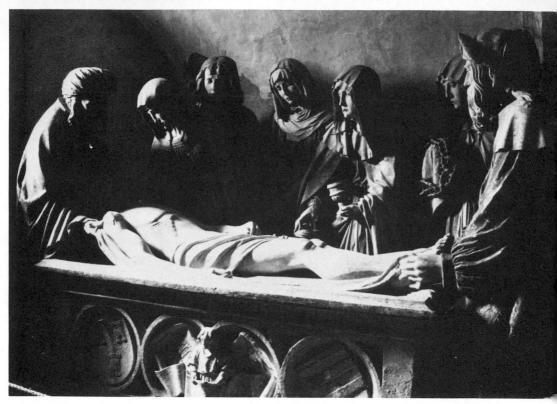

1. *The Entombment of Christ,* at Chaource.

2. *The Pietà* of Bayel.

3. *The Madonna of the Grapes.*

. *The Visitation*. Saint John's Church, Troyes.

5. *The Beautiful Cross of Neuvy-Sautour.*   6. *Saint Agnes.* Saint Nicholas's Chur

yes.

7. *Christ at the Column*. Saint Nicholas's Church, Troyes.

4 / Changing Times

By the turn of the sixteenth century the long period of weakness for the great institutions of Europe, which had fostered late-medieval religiosity, was coming to an end. Confusion over responsibility and authority in the church had abated, as the papal monarchy triumphed over the intermediate orders of the clergy. In the Concordat of 1516, the pope and the king of France resolved the question of who would appoint whom to benefices. The king sat securely on his throne, while his officers in the provinces enforced the public order that had been so noticeably wanting during the Hundred Years' War. Greater clarity in the political and religious hierarchies made it easier to conceptualize the celestial hierarchy, and to assign a more circumscribed position to the Virgin and the saints. If the church had not first achieved a measure of success in putting its own house in order, would the Reformation have been possible?

Demographic and economic expansion were also characteristic of the period. In Champagne as elsewhere, the population was growing, and although the province would never regain the eminence of the days of the great fairs, it was certainly becoming more prosperous. Like most of France, Champagne was at peace, with exceptions made for incursions by imperial armies, in 1521 and again in 1544. Many men looked to the future with confidence, and took the risks that were necessary to ride the crest of inflation. But the rewards of expansion were more selective than the problems of depression had been. For every successful peasant entrepreneur, master craftsman, merchant and bourgeois gentilhomme, there were poor peasants, day laborers, artisans, and petty nobles who were pinched by rising prices, more mouths to feed, and increased competition for land and/or work.[1] Tensions increased within every estate, and became

1. Guy Fourquin (*Les campagnes de la région parisienne*, pp. 446–456) demonstrates that the poorer areas in the Parisian Basin, which would include most of Champagne, experienced an agricultural reconstruction from 1470 to 1520. Febvre and Martin (*L'apparition du livre*, pp. 31 and 41) state that Champenois paper was exported from the mid-fifteenth century, and that in the sixteenth century the paper-

as important as the animosities between estates that had characterized the fourteenth and fifteenth centuries. Inevitably, religious
forms that were based on the organization of people into tightly
knit groups, and that sought to achieve solidarity in society at large,
had become less meaningful — to many of those victims of sixteenth-
century demography and inflation who had fewer illusions about to-
getherness, as well as to many of those victors who had less need for
it.

Works of art offer the most striking evidence of a decline in the
old ideals. The quiet intensity of the *Entombment* at Chaource reflects the calm and measured style known as *détente,* which graced
the sculpture of Champagne during the 1510s and 1520s. The détente was succeeded, first hesitantly and then decisively, by a new
sophistication and affectation.[2] The subjects for sculpture were the
same, but their treatment by the sculptors quite different. The
statue of Saint Agnes at Saint Nicholas's Church of Troyes (figure
6) illustrates the drift toward refined detachment. The hair of this
beautiful woman falls over her shoulders in ringlets whose charm
and fine detail are repeated in the broach on her breast and the
knotted belt at her high waist. The folds of her robe, below the
waist, are tranquil and unpretentious, but they lead to an intricate
fringe at the hem. She extends her rosary, which has been meticu-
lously sculpted, bead by bead, to a lamb of jeweled fleece.

Even the relative restraint of the *Saint Agnes* soon gave way, as
statues no longer stood straight but seemed to sway, off-balance, in
hipshot poses. Exaggerated folds replaced simply-cut garments. The
sculptors of Champagne were achieving technical excellence in the
absence of new spiritual or intellectual stimuli. They were living
on the interest from the emotional capital that had been accumu-
lated in the course of the late Middle Ages.

---

makers of Troyes supplied Flemish and English printers. In the absence of comprehensive social and economic studies of sixteenth-century Champagne, the generaliza-
tions in this paragraph rest on Henri Hauser, *Ouvriers du temps passé (XVe–XVIe
siècles)* (5th ed., Paris, 1927) ; Lucien Febvre, *Philippe II et la Franche-Comté* (Paris,
1911) ; Yvonne Bezard, *La vie rurale dans le sud de la région parisienne de 1450 à 1560*
(Paris, 1929) ; Michel Mollat, *Le commerce maritime normand à la fin du Moyen Age*
(Paris, 1952) ; Emile Coornaert, *Les Français et le commerce international à Anvers,
fin du XVe–XVIe siècle* (2 vols., Paris, 1961) ; Bernard Guenée, *Tribunaux et gens de
justice dans le bailliage de Senlis à la fin du Moyen Age (vers 1380–vers 1550)* (Paris,
1963) , and Fourquin, *Les campagnes.*
    2. Koechlin and Marquet de Vasselot, *La sculpture,* part 2.

Provincial mannerism both adumbrated and facilitated the introduction of the Renaissance from across the Alps, which was itself mannered by this time.[3] After his return in 1526 from captivity in Spain, Francis I began to transform the royal hunting lodge at Fontainebleau, southeast of Paris, into a palace. He called architects, artists, and sculptors from Italy to direct the work. They provided employment for craftsmen from Champagne, who brought what they had learned back to the province. One of the Italian sculptors, Dominique, called le Florentin, who worked under Primaticcio at Fontainebleau in the 1530s, himself came to Champagne. After receiving private commissions from Duke Claude of Guise, governor of Champagne, and from Jean de Dinteville, bailiff of Troyes, he settled permanently in Troyes by 1543. The king awarded him the abbot's revenues of the suburban monastery of Saint-Martin-ès-Aires. Dominique remained in the city until his death, probably in 1564. His work provided a model for local sculptors to emulate.[4]

The statue of *Charity* for the rood screen of Saint Stephen's collegial church is a characteristic example of his art.[5] Charity is depicted as a majestic woman of youthful maturity, with a benign though distant countenance. She holds a *putto* up to her left breast, but pays not the slightest attention to him, while she extends her right hand to steady a second naked, muscular child, who leans against her knee. A third child half hides under her dress — or perhaps toga — and raises it so as to create a sinewy line of folds that curves up from the left toward her right breast, and counterbalances the child nursing on the right.

Such statues neither helped to sustain traditional piety, nor offered anything new, spiritually, to the people of Champagne, except perhaps detachment from the figures they worshipped. *Christ at the Column*, in Saint Nicholas's Church, is an "athlete" of the Renaissance, a god incapable of suffering (figure 7).[6] If he can serve as the norm for physical perfection, then he can hardly evoke the

3. The mannerist tendencies in late Gothic French art are distinguished from Italian Mannerism, which was imported to Northern Europe, in John Shearman's brilliant *Mannerism* (Harmondsworth and Baltimore, 1967), pp. 25–28.

4. Koechlin and Marquet de Vasselot, *La sculpture*, part 3, chs. 2–3.

5. The contract between chapter and sculptor is in AD, Aube, nouvelles acquisitions, no. 1843 (1551). The statue survived the dismantling of the screen during the Revolution, and is now in Saint Pantaleon's Church.

6. Mâle, *L'art religieux de la fin du Moyen Age*, p. 97.

compassion of less well-formed men and women, who look at him in admiration.

By the 1530s statues were no longer polychromed, but simply touched up here and there with gold paint. Murals were no longer painted along the entire surface of the interior walls of churches. Stained-glass windows became more sophisticated, as the painter-glassmakers increasingly turned to neutral tones and to grisaille. "Could one imagine," asks Jean Lafond, "a more complete revolution in a region where the century had opened with a feast of color truly unique in France?"[7] This new art satisfied the more refined tastes of cultivated individuals, but lacked the emotional intensity that could appeal to the people as a whole.

Meanwhile the mystery plays, those stained-glass windows come to life, were performed under municipal auspices for the last time in Champagne in the early 1530s. This was well before the Parlement of Paris, in 1548, prohibited theatrical representations of religious subjects. The municipal officers of Reims, in sanctioning a play in 1529 which would actually be performed in 1531, revealed something of the new attitude. They admonished the players to perform "well and honestly, for the honor of God and the town, as well as for the example of the people, in such a way that scandal cannot come, nor dishonor, to the town."[8] Well-bred people could now be scandalized, not only by the occasional gutter humor or the buffoonery, but also by the very idea of fellow townsmen presuming to act out the Bible. They could question the relationship between the costumes and actions of the players and the actual, historical events of the life of Christ while they asked whether mimicry did any honor to God.

The sixteenth was a more aristocratic as well as a more cultivated century than the fourteenth and fifteenth had been. As the ruling groups of European states, the country nobility, and the patricians of towns recovered their self-confidence, they also recharged their contempt for the "simple people." *The Shepherd's Great Calendar and Compost,* published by Nicolas le Rouge of Troyes in 1529, introduces "a shepherd guarding sheep in the fields, who was not at

7. Jean Lafond, "La Renaissance," in Aubert et al., *Le vitrail français,* p. 219. See also Biver, *L'école troyenne,* p. 6.

8. For the edict of Parlement, see BN, Collection Dupuy, 231, f. 177; Varin, *Archives législatives,* pt. 2 (Statuts), I, 870–871.

all a clerk and had no understanding at all of the written word, but who by means of his great common sense [*sens naturel*] and good understanding alone" offered advice to readers. In the next extant local edition, by Jean Le Coq in 1541, a mutation has occurred, for we meet "a shepherd having sheep and flocks in cities and fields to guard, who was only a small and simple clerk, and had very little understanding of the written word."[9] The ignorant and the uncouth were becoming increasingly contemptible. And the fine arts, which had once served to unify men, now demonstrated the differences among them.

Dominique le Florentin's representation of *Charity* as an impersonal dispenser of aid must have appealed to the city fathers of Troyes because it symbolized the way in which, at least in their public capacity, they were coming to regard the poor. At the beginning of the sixteenth century organized poor relief in Champagne lagged far behind harsh realities, which demographic growth progressively exacerbated. With few exceptions, there is scant evidence of charitable effort at the most immediate level, that of the parish. The churchwardens, judging from the surviving records, neither collected alms from parishioners nor used any of their general revenues for the poor. At Reims (and probably in the surrounding rural parishes) a moribund institution known as the *chartrerie*, which administered charitable donations left to the parish, did survive into mid-century. But the revenues of the chartreries, diverted to other uses, were drying up, and little new money was coming in. Their one service now was to provide bread and lard on Good Friday. Only five of our testators left them anything.[10] As for the parish priests, however generous some of them may have been as individual donors and testators, neither they nor their vicars recognized any precise obligations toward the poor by virtue of their office.

Guild confraternities certainly provided some help to indigent

9. *Le grant calendrier et compost des bergiers avecq leur astrologie et plusieurs autres choses* (Troyes, 1529), sig. Ai; *Le grand calendrier et compost des bergers avec leur astrologie et plusieurs aultres sciences salutaires tant pour les âmes que pour la santé des corps* (Troyes, 1541), sig. Ai.

10. Pierre Varin, *Archives administratives de la ville de Reims* (3 vols. in 4, Paris, 1839–1848), I, 14; Varin, *Archives législatives*, pt. 2 (Statuts), II, 905–906. The testators were Jehanne, wife of Jehan Grant Jehan, 5 sols: AD, Marne, 4E 16668 (1528); Jehanne, wife of Ginot Bennart, 10 sols: 4E 16691; Jehanne Clermont, 5 sols: ch. 2, above, n. 25; the merchant-carpenter Colleson Douynet, 10 sols: 4E 16694 (1538); the cooper Husson Cliquot, 10 sols: 4E 16706 (1551). Pierre Pirche left 15 sols to the charterye of the village of Cernay-les-Reims: ch. 2, above, n. 20.

members, but this was of no benefit to the poor who did not practice a skilled, incorporated trade. The Confraternity *dudit denier* of Châlons was a useful though hardly sufficient organization, and it had no counterpart elsewhere in Champagne.

What of the clerical corporations? The collegial chapters had acquired patronage over many of the almshouses, or Hôtels-Dieu, which had been founded during the high Middle Ages to provide hospitality to pilgrims and poor travelers, or asylum for the orphans, the sick, and the aged. The activity of the patron was usually limited to naming the master, who administered the hospital's property and directed the community of brothers or sisters which actually cared for the inmates. That the hospitals really served a charitable purpose, in spite of the tendency of the personnel to absorb a large part of the income, is shown by the support they received from those testators who made charitable bequests. Thirty-four of seventy-three wills drawn in Reims, thirteen of thirty-six Catholic wills from Châlons, and six of twenty-eight wills from Troyes make small bequests to them. The problem was that the responsibility of any given hospital was limited, either by the founders or by subsequent practice, to a specific group of the sick or the poor. None of them was prepared or equipped to extend itself in the direction of the vast majority of the urban poor, whose chief disability was their difficulty in finding steady work.

Two new hospitals were founded in the sixteenth century, by notables of Troyes. In 1563 Jean Mauroy, sieur de Colvardey, left his house in the city, together with his movable property and the lands that he had acquired during his lifetime, to establish an orphanage at which as many as twelve of the poorest children of Colvardey would be received. Nine years later Gerald de Hault, acting both for himself and as his wife's executor, built a house and chapel next to the old Hôtel-Dieu of Sommevoire, to lodge the hidden poor, present and future, provide them with bread, and give one livre to each of thirty poor people on Holy Thursday.[11]

The problem of poverty, which was clearly too much for the church, increasingly preoccupied the municipalities. They had always been concerned with the poor at times of crisis, perhaps less

11. Colvardey: AD, Aube, E 457 (cited by the inventaire sommaire, but not found by me in the *liasse;* AC, Troyes, A 21, f. 39 (1583), refers to the imminent consecration of the hospital; Sommevoire: AD, Aube, E 202.

out of Christian charity than in the hope of preventing them from
infecting their betters when plague struck, or from raiding stores of
grain during a famine. In 1522, for example, the town council of
Châlons ordered the plague-ridden to shut themselves up in their
lodgings, if they had any, or else to clear out of town ("vuyder hors la
ville"). To provide food for the families of men whom it was pro-
hibiting from working, the council assessed the hospitals and the
Confraternity *dudit denier,* and directed the parishes to ask for alms
during Sunday and holiday services.[12] Such efforts, which in the past
had not outlived temporary crises, developed over the sixteenth century into formal, permanent institutions.[13] In Champagne the city
of Troyes, with its numerous handicraft industries and heavy concentration of artisans and unskilled laborers, acted first. The town
council organized regular collections for the poor in 1530, in private
homes as well as at church. In 1545 it took the decisive step of establishing a bureau of poor relief, the *Aumône général,* following
the example of the great cities of the realm, Lyons, Paris, and Rou-
en. The articles of incorporation, drawn up a year later, make clear,
chapter and verse, the official attitudes toward the poor and the aspirations for the control of poverty on which they depended.[14]

Eight unpaid rectors, two of them clerics and the rest bourgeois,
were to administer the bureau. They had the services of a salaried
general receiver, and of "four servants or beadles, to instill fear in
the poor, and make them keep the necessary order." The rectors' first
task was to draw up a roll of those to be aided. In each parish two
notables and the churchwardens would separate out the healthy
beggars and then list the sick and hidden poor, recording their
birthplace, length of residence in Troyes, number of children, and
estate and craft. After a group of doctors and surgeons had verified
the physical condition of all those on the rolls, the regents were to

12. AC, Châlons, BB 7, ff. 50, 55, 64, and 67.

13. William Courtenay writes of the "laicization of poor relief" in the thirteenth
and fourteenth centuries: "Token Coinage and the Administration of Poor Relief
during the Late Middle Ages," *Journal of Interdisciplinary History,* 3 (1972–1973),
284. Both Pullan (*Rich and Poor in Renaissance Venice,* pp. 197–231 and 279–286)
and Davis (*Society and Culture,* pp. 17–64) make important statements about poor
relief in Europe as a whole.

14. Alphonse Roserot, *Dictionnaire historique de la Champagne méridionale (Aube)
dès origines à 1790* (3 vols., Angers, 1948), III, 1572. See also AC, Troyes, A9, ff. 1v–3
(30 Mar. 1530). The articles are in BC, Troyes, MS 1291, ff. 112–120.

assign an individual pittance to each once. Ten pounds of bread and 12 deniers was considered the normal adult ration.

Since the *Grands jours* of Troyes, a court of visiting judges from Parlement, had ruled in 1534 — and Parlement had confirmed in 1545 — that financial administration of the principal hospitals of Troyes be transferred from the clergy to laymen, the six bourgeois rectors were to assume this responsibility. They would lodge orphans under six years of age in the delivery room of the Hôtel-Dieu-le-Comte, under the supervision of "an honest woman," or elsewhere if a better place could be found. At age six the orphan girls would move to Saint Abraham's Hospital, and the boys to Saint Bernard's, joining street beggars of the same age and sex whose parents were alive. At the two institutions they would learn their religious beliefs (*créance*). Families on the rolls who lodged their own children had to send them as well to the hospitals for "indoctrination and instruction." Notable and bourgeois women were to take the girls into service, and master craftsmen to employ the boys when they reached the age of nine.

Sick men and boys were to be treated at the Hôtel-Dieu-le-Comte, women and girls at the Hôtel-Dieu-Saint-Nicholas, but only until they were cured. "Impotent and decrepit" old people, unable to support themselves, would reside, separated by sex, at the Hôtel-Dieu-Saint-Esprit. The religious personnel of the hospitals, who had the duty of caring for the sick, would be enjoined to confess and console them "as sweetly and humanely as possible." Poor travelers would be suffered the night at Saint Bernard's Hospital, offered 12 deniers (3 d. for a child) the next morning, and forcibly sent on their way. The *michelotz,* pilgrims to Mont-Saint-Michel, would receive bread at the town gates. The bureau was to enlarge the two pesthouses, and appoint a medical staff for them. Those suffering from leprosy, which was a rare disease by the sixteenth century, were to be sent back where they came from.

All of the able-bodied poor who were born in Troyes and had a trade would practice it, for the masters were to be compelled to employ them. The unskilled had to work on the ramparts, earning only the ordinary pittance of the bureau's poor. Outsiders and vagabonds would be expelled. And one of the towers on the town walls would become a prison for the "disobedient and rebel poor." To

beg was forbidden, on pain of the whip or imprisonment. Townsmen were enjoined not to give alms at their doors, on the street, or in
church, nor to rent to or otherwise lodge anyone who lived by begging. They should send him instead to the appropriate hospital or
to the bureau. The rectors or their representatives would visit the
poor on the rolls regularly, as well as collect secret information on
them, to see that they did not "abuse the bureau."

In order to finance these ambitious programs, two parish notables
would call on every householder to learn how much he was willing
to contribute. Then, together with the churchwardens, they would
levy rates on those who had volunteered nothing or made insufficient
offers. Within their own estate, the clerical rectors and two other
notable churchmen would do the same. Charity boxes, moreover,
would be placed in the inns, the shops, and the homes of the bourgeoisie.

Two weeks from the day that the bureau began its work, and annually thereafter, it would stage a general procession of the poor, to
make their number and needs evident, "and give the people a
stronger will to continue the said charity forever." One of the orphans, selected by the beadles, would lead the procession, carrying
a wooden cross from which a crucifix would hang. The rest would
march two by two, the boys led by their schoolmaster, the girls by
the schoolmistress, singing litanies to Jesus and Mary respectively.
The adults, also in pairs, would follow, saying their hours, and Pater
Nosters for their benefactors. Behind them the judicial corps, the
town council, and the bureau's rectors would march. Townsfolk who
wished to participate could bring up the rear. The procession would
conclude with a sermon and high mass, during which the poor
would remain on their knees, caps in hand, as devoutly as possible,
praying God for the prosperity and health of the king and his children, and of all their benefactors.

Despite their reliance on the persuasion of the clergy and the
pageantry of the church, the city fathers who drew up this document
were advocating a wholly secular conception of poor relief, which
was new to Champagne. It had not occurred to the church that
charity might generate social reform in this world, as well as make
the giver more fit for the next one. The bureau on the other hand
promised mundane but extraordinary results: opportunity for the
young, work for every man born in the city, and a steady supply of

bread to all those who, for valid reasons, still could not support themselves. Once the strangers had been flushed out, it would be unnecessary as well as illegal for anyone to live from the streets. The poor, although they might always be with us, need no longer cause annoyance or concern.

The bureau became a permanent Troyen institution, even though it did not solve the problem of poverty.[15] Its very existence, nevertheless, challenged the relationship between rich and poor that guided many men and women as they drew up their wills. No longer could a donor create (or imagine) a moral and spiritual bond with the recipient of his alms, for the bureau was interposing itself between the two. It assembled and paraded the poor, in all their misery, through the city streets precisely to show that their relief was a communal necessity and a matter of public policy, rather than a decision for the individual conscience. Townsmen would contribute to an impersonal, soulless organization, which was to assume complete responsibility for and monopolize contact with the poor. The gesture of giving, while remaining a meritorious act, would inevitably lose the symbolic connotations with which it had once been charged.

Having made his regular contribution, the indulgent donor would have to steel himself against a beggar's pleas, and instead denounce the man to the bureau. But the self-discipline expected of him was as nothing compared to what was imposed on the poor. The lives of those on the rolls became, in return for the weekly pittance, subject to periodic inspection and correction. As for the able-bodied, lately sturdy beggars, the threat of the lash and of prison would prevent them from sliding back into vagrancy. The new order depended on inquisition and regimentation. Together with their place in the moral economy, the poor lost all dignity as well.

The decline of the confraternities provides a further suggestion of a softening in the drive toward solidarity. Membership in the parish confraternities of Troyes shrank noticeably and most often precipitously, although the timing, intensity, and precise form of contraction varied from one church to another. The high point in participation at Mary Magdalene's and at Saint Pantaleon's was achieved in 1519, perhaps in part because this was a plague year when saints Sebastian and Roche were in favor (tables 2 and 3).

15. AC, Troyes, M1–10, are account-books of the bureau from 1547 to 1593.

Total membership at Saint Pantaleon's had decreased by about one-third in 1527, and by two-thirds in 1556. At Saint John's, where the figures are sketchy, the decline was apparently already under way during the 1510s. This parish had a heavy concentration of artisans who were particularly susceptible to innovations in religion. Membership at Saint James's, by contrast, increased until 1525. For both churches, the reduction by the mid-1550s was nevertheless roughly comparable to that at Saint Pantaleon's (tables 4 and 5). The attrition at Mary Magdalene's began in earnest only in the 1540s, but was pronounced during the fifteen years that followed. By 1557 the church's confraternities had lost forty percent of their membership of 1542. Saint Nizier's parish was located in the clerical quarter of the old cité, behind the cathedral, where many poor newcomers to town who worked as weavers or gardeners lived. Those parish confraternities for which we have information in 1524 were well attended. This was still true for some of the confraternities in 1588 and 1599-1600, when the archival evidence resumes. The intervening silence compels me to pass over Saint Nizier's now, while recognizing a dissonant note to which we must return at the century's end (table 7).

At Saint Pantaleon's Church the patron's confraternity weathered the decline better than any of the other devotions, retaining almost half of the number of its members. The membership lists from 1549 to 1557 include more than a score of the notables of Troyes, including eight men who at some point during their lives served as mayor.[16] This vigorous activity by the elite may have sustained the interest of others, and even pressed into participation men who had no great desire to honor a saint. In 1553 Pierre Pithou bore a candle for Saint Pantaleon. Earlier, in 1549 and 1550, he had belonged to the confraternity of Saint Geneviève, the patron saint of Paris, which

16. The mayors, with the dates of their first appearance on the confraternity rolls, were Christophle Angenoust, AD, Aube, 19G 10, f. 30 (1550) ; Pierre Belin, 19G 12, f. 66 (1554) ; Denis Clérey, 19G 10, f. 30 (1550), who had been the confraternity's standard-bearer as a young man, 19G 6, f. 26 (1522) ; Pierre Mauroy, 19G 13, f. 26 (1554) ; Claude II Molé, 19G 10, f. 27v (1549) ; Pierre Nevelet, 19G 12, f. 42 (1553) ; Claude Pinette, 19G 10, f. 30r (1550) ; and Nicolas Riglet, 19G 13, f. 26v (1554). A complete list of the mayors of Troyes during the Old Regime is provided by Roserot (*Dictionnaire historique*, III, 1542–1545). The withdrawal of the notables ruined confraternities "by weakening the community of Christians," according to Pierre Deyon: *Amiens, capitale provinciale* (Paris, 1967), p. 379.

also met at Saint Pantaleon's. Long ago Pithou, as his son Nicolas tells us in the history of the Reformed Church of Troyes, had received "some beginnings and entry" into God's truth from the humanist and biblical scholar Jacques Lefèvre d'Etaples. Since the elder Pithou believed to the time of his death that it was licit to attend the Mass, he could not have seen a threat to his soul in the confraternities. But since he did believe in justification by faith, he could not have found any spiritual benefit in them either.[17] No doubt he participated in order to demonstrate his orthodoxy to neighbors, who could expect him to belong only because they did too.

Such social conformity could not be exercised on behalf of any of the other patrons of churches in Troyes. At Saint James's the patron's following began to slip away after 1520, while the total participation in the confraternities of the church was still rising. The membership rolls do not include a set of distinguished names, nor even by the 1550s very many names at all, since over three decades the confraternity had fallen from the most to the least popular association in the church. There are no lists of individual members at Saint John's. The patron's confraternity remained popular until 1544, but then lost more than half of its strength in the next twelve years. At Mary Magdalene's the translation of the saint's relics, rather than her regular festival day, was the focus of confraternity activity. The translation declined steadily in popularity from the 1520s. Six people joined together in 1531 to form a confraternity for the festival day, and twenty-six revived the confraternity in 1542, but it soon declined and then disappeared.

Most of the Virgin's confraternities fared even worse than those of the parish patrons. Only two of the Troyen associations in her name still drew large numbers of worshippers by mid-century: the Confraternity of Notre-Dame of Loreto at Saint Nicholas's Church, which had the special attraction of indulgences, and the Immaculate Conception at Mary Magdalene's, which may have attracted people from adjoining parishes. Madame de Cernel, for example, a member of the confraternities of the Annunciation and of Saint Pantaleon at the latter's church in 1554, also participated in the Immaculate Conception Confraternity at Mary Magdalene's in 1551, and was its

17. AD, Aube, 19G 12, f. 41v (1553); 19G 10, f. 25 (1549), f. 27v (1550); Pithou, "Histoire ecclésiastique," ff. 37v and 77v–78r.

standard-bearer in 1556.[18] The absence of general membership lists
at Mary Magdalene's precludes further pursuit of this suggestion.
We do, on the other hand, know the names of a good many of the
standard-bearers. The majority were women, in sharp contrast to
the pattern at other Troyen churches.[19] Perhaps women were also
especially numerous as confraternity members at Mary Magdalene's.
If the church's confraternities did in fact enjoy extra-parish support,
of whatever sex, then this would help to explain why their popularity was sustained so long. It would also temper our emphasis on
the decline at Saint John's, Saint Pantaleon's, and Saint James's, all
of which were within strolling distance of the Church of the Magdalene.

The decline of the older Corpus Christi confraternities, some of
which can be traced back far into the fifteenth century, was especially sharp. A number of new Holy Sacrament confraternities were
founded, as we shall later see, in response to the Protestant movement.

More and more, people were using the confraternity as a means
to serve their need, as individuals, for the preservation or recovery
of health. Every one of the associations at Saint John's which in 1556
had half or more of its membership of 1527 — those of Saints Syre,
Fiacre, Edmund, and Maur — were dedicated to saints invoked
against disease. Of all the confraternity saints of the parish, moreover, their relics were the nearest to Troyes, and therefore easily
accessible to pilgrims who could keep the cult vital. Saints Fiacre
and Syre, in particular, were strong. Fiacre, always popular at Saint
John's, now had the single most important confraternity. Syre, who
first appears in the parish ledger of 1525, actually increased her following over the ensuing three decades. At Saint James's Church, the
saints invoked against disease experienced, in general, a more moderate decline than those of the Virgin and the patron. Saint Fiacre
appeared on a permanent basis in the 1530s, and by 1552 had become a leader at the parish. The one exception is Saint Gond, a
saint of Champagne who did suffer severely. At Mary Magdalene's

---

18. AD, Aube, 19G 12, ff. 64v and 67; 16G 64, f. 210; and 16G 65, f. 117.

19. Sixty persons are listed as bâtonniers at Mary Magdalene's from 1553 to 1558, on
91 occasions. Sixty percent of the individuals were women, who were bâtonniers on
64 percent of the occasions. The most nearly comparable years are 1552–1559 at Saint
Pantaleon's, where 58 persons are listed, on 108 occasions. Seventeen percent of the
individuals were women, on 13 percent of the occasions.

Church in 1557 the only confraternities other than the Immaculate Conception which had more than fifty members were Saint Blaise's and Saint Quirin's, whose relics the church possessed. Saints Fiacre and Syre had always been less popular here, but they did retain all of their clientele.

Is it possible that medical or psychological reasons, rather than the proximity of relics, explain the resistance of certain saints to the decline? Fiacre's fistulas and hemorrhoids, Syre's gravel stones and hernias are all in the same general area of the body, and more or less associated with the process of elimination. These diseases were probably no more prevalent in 1550 than earlier in the century. Although I have found no Champenois evidence that people were more conscious or concerned about them, it is known that fistulas affecting women were the object of "a spurt of writing" at the end of the sixteenth and during the seventeenth centuries.[20]

The late Middle Ages, by the common consent of historians, was a time when people preferred their saints close to home, and when local cults abounded. But perhaps this was more true of the sixteenth century than of the fourteenth and fifteenth, at least in the sense that as people began to pay less homage to the cult of the saints, they concentrated on those in their own back yards. Thus saints like Roche and Sebastian, who had no local ties, became vulnerable, as the plague diminished in the second quarter of the sixteenth century.

One universal saint — Joseph, the Virgin's husband — did receive a measure of new attention. Confraternities in his honor were founded at the churches of Mary Magdalene, Saint Pantaleon, and Saint Nicholas in the 1530s and 1540s. They reflected the increasing attention to the Holy Family as a family.[21] But participation decreased in all three associations. Clearly, people in Champagne were not using the confraternity as a vehicle for this new devotion.

In theory a new confraternity had to be approved by the episcopal authorities, at least after the provincial council of Sens in 1528, which also ordered a review of the statutes of all existing associa-

20. Henry Falk and M. Leon Tancer, "Vesicovaginal Fistula: An Historical Survey," *Obstetrics and Gynecology*, 3 (1954), 339.

21. On Saint Joseph see, most recently, Lynn White, Jr., "The Iconography of *Temperantia* and the Virtuousness of Technology," *Action and Conviction in Early Modern Europe: Essays in Memory of E. H. Harbison* (Princeton, Princeton University Press, 1969), pp. 199–201.

tions. The council was primarily concerned by the tendency of members to squander the resources of their associations at banquets in drink. The diocesan statutes of Bishop Jérôme Bourgeois of Châlons, issued in 1557, include a similar injunction on new confraternities, but there is no evidence of any action taken as a result of either of these reforming decrees.[22]

The shape that a more widespread program of reform might have taken may be inferred from *The Way of Salvation, Necessary and Useful to all Christians.*[23] Bishop Guillaume Petit of Troyes wrote this booklet and had it published at Lyons, probably in 1527, a year before exchanging dioceses with Odard Hennequin at Senlis, so that he could be nearer Paris while Hennequin returned to his Troyen home. Petit was a noted Dominican scholar, a member of the circle of humanists about the king. He had been royal confessor, and had defended the Hebraist Reuchlin from attacks at the Sorbonne.[24] Just before Francis I named him bishop in 1517, Petit had spurred the king to invite Erasmus to join a projected new institution of learning, which would later emerge as the Collège royal. In conveying this invitation, the humanist Guillaume Budé noted that on state occasions Petit was invariably chosen to preach to the court, for nature had given him the gift of religious eloquence.[25] But in *The Way of Salvation* Petit's audience was neither the mighty nor the learned. He directed his gift to "the ignorant, and the simple people," although he did include material for any educated reader into whose hands the discourse might fall.[26] Petit wrote on two levels because he was in part addressing the priests, who could in turn instruct the people or simply read the text aloud to them. But he must also have realized that a guide intended solely for those whom he defined in advance as simple-minded would be hollow.

The cornerstone of *The Way of Salvation* is faith, which consists,

22. Joannes Mansi, "Concilium Senonese," *Sacrarum conciliorum nova et amplissima collectio,* vol. 32 (Paris, 1902), col. 1196; *Statuta synodalia, a reverendo in Christo patre ac domino Hieronymo Burgensi, episcopo comite Cathalaunensi, Franciae q pari edita & promulgata, Anno Domini 1557* (Reims, 1557), p. 30.

23. Guillaume Petit, *Le viat de salut nécessaire et utile à tous chrestiens pour parvenir à la gloyre éternelle. . . . Composé par reverend père en dieu Monseigneur évesque de Troyes* (Lyons, [1527?]).

24. Augustin Renaudet, *Préréforme et humanisme à Paris pendant les premières guerres d'Italie (1494–1517)* (Paris, 1916), pp. 646–653.

25. *Opus epistolarum Des. Erasmi Roterodami,* ed. P. S. Allen (12 vols., Oxford, 1906–1947), vol. II: 1514–1517, pp. 444–445.

26. Petit, *Le viat,* sig. a2.

firstly, of belief in Scripture as filtered through the credo and interpreted by the church, without either superstitious additions or critical inquiry. An explicit understanding of the mysteries of Christ, especially those commemorated in the festivals, is also necessary to faith. Hope is built on the foundation of faith, and should be expressed through prayers, which may be directed to the saints as long as it is clear that they are the intermediaries and God the judge. After illustrating acts of charity, Petit concludes with a discussion of each of the Ten Commandments, urging, under the heading of observing the Sabbath, relative restraint at festivals. Petit's tone is not so much guarded as indefinite, reflecting a tension between certain aspects of religious reform and the defense against heresy. Characteristically, in a personal appearance before his cathedral chapter in 1523, he balanced a royal warning against the spread of Lutheranism in France with a personal complaint on the irreverent behavior of the people at the excessive number of religious festivals.[27] In *The Way of Salvation* he has nothing to say about prayers for the dead or purgatory, and touches on the Eucharist only in passing. His ideal seems to have been a laity more attuned to the belief and conduct required for salvation than to the rhythm of the festival year, yet entirely guided, and when necessary restrained, by the clergy. Even had he tried to introduce this educational program into his diocese, it is doubtful whether he would have had much success. For his was a bloodless and patronizing message, which relinquished the convivial warmth of the old ways without offering the personal excitement of distinctly new directions, and which showed no confidence in the ability of his intended lay audience to think lucidly without going astray.

The threat of religious novelty came to Champagne from the west rather than from the Lutherans in Germany. The diocese of Meaux in Brie was an early and independent center of evangelical reform in France, as a result of the activities of old friends of Petit's. Guillaume Briçonnet, great patron of letters and member of a family high in the royal favor, who became the bishop in 1518, intended to make his see a model for the kingdom. Previously, as abbot of Saint-Germain-des-Prés, he had enlisted the influential humanist Lefèvre to recharge the intellectual atmosphere of the venerable and indolent monastery. At Meaux, Briçonnet set out to restore clerical

27. AD, Aube, G 1282, f. 4 (29 April 1523).

initiative by commissioning a preacher for each part of the diocese, rural as well as urban, and enforcing residence on the beneficed clergy. On theological matters, like Petit but much more vigorously, he emphasized the centrality of the Bible to the Catholic faith, and sought to prune some of the more florid branches from the trunk of the cult of saints. To second his efforts, Briçonnet called on Lefèvre and members of the coterie of intellectuals which had gathered around them both at Paris. The new arrivals included Guillaume Farel, the future *enfant terrible* of the French-speaking Reformation. A master of invective from the pulpit and in the pamphlet, Farel would also prove to be a daring and skilled organizer, the man who, one day at Geneva, would show Calvin his vocation. Briçonnet had New Testaments distributed, gratis, to the literate poor. In the busy town of Meaux this meant, essentially, the unruly artisans of the cloth trade, to whom a little learning quickly became a dangerous thing. The bishop was soon outdistanced both by his aides and by members of his flock. The diocese, in the pungent phrase of the guardians of order, began to smell of heresy. Consider for example the activities of one Jean Le Clerc, who despite his name "was not a man of letters but a wool-carder by trade. He was nevertheless excellently versed in the reading of the Word of God, to the extent that it was then available in French," as the *Histoire ecclésiastique,* the official sixteenth-century Protestant account of the French Reformation, described him. Though a layman, Le Clerc felt called upon to preach against purgatory, to peddle heretical tracts, and — in broad daylight — to tack onto an indulgence poster a piece of paper identifying the pope as Antichrist.[28]

Doctors at the Sorbonne had already made a career out of harassing Lefèvre in Paris. Together with the Franciscans, their chief allies in Meaux as everywhere in the provinces, they now escalated their attacks, and broadened them to damn Briçonnet's entire effort. The bishop, who wanted neither to lose royal favor nor to break with his church, was forced to retreat, and then to abandon the enterprise entirely. Disappointed, Farel left for Basel (via Paris) in

28. *Histoire ecclésiastique,* ed. Baum and Cunitz, III, 526. The smell of heresy was noted by the bishop of Châlons (AD, Marne, G 417, f. 8). R.-J. Lovy, *Les origines de la Réforme française; Meaux, 1518–1546* (Paris, 1959), is detailed if unscholarly. Emile Léonard (*Histoire général du protestantisme,* I, 200–206) trenchantly fits the experience at Meaux into the broader French scene. See also Febvre, "Idée d'une recherche d'histoire comparée: le cas Briçonnet," in *Au coeur religieux,* pp. 145–161.

1523. That same year Le Clerc was arrested, and condemned by Parlement to be whipped, branded, and banished from the town of Meaux. He quit the Brie entirely two years later for Metz, where he openly courted and bravely endured martyrdom. Lefèvre himself slipped away to Strasbourg in 1525. To reach their destination all three, and a good many others, had to cross Champagne. Lefèvre was no doubt cautious enough to travel silently, and Farel, too anxious for the greener pastures of Switzerland to evangelize along the way. It is less likely that anonymous, impetuous artisans like Le Clerc held their tongues as they traveled. Early in 1526 Bishop Gilles de Luxembourg of Châlons informed his chapter that he intended to have a preacher in the cathedral for Lent, "because of several errors, superstitions, and other things smelling of heresy and of the Lutheran sect which are now pullulating in certain places," as close to the diocese as possible. In the longer run, to return to the *Histoire ecclésiastique,* "the small flock of Meaux (composed for the most part of craftsmen, wool-carders, and clothiers), not only served as an example of admirable constancy to all the [Reformed] churches of France, but also gave birth to several, even some of the greatest, for the Lord." Parlement had fourteen heretics of the town burned in 1546. Five years later Michel Poncelet, a wool-carder and weaver who had taken refuge in Geneva, was returning to Meaux to settle his affairs. When he stopped in Troyes, the local Protestants induced him to remain, in order to lead the first organized worship there.[29]

Just beyond Meaux was Paris, the Paris that would ultimately become for the French Protestants "the bloodiest and most murderous city in all the world," the Paris of the Sorbonne and of a parlement that treated heresy as it treated any manifestation of independent or divergent policy toward the crown, but also the intellectual and cultural center in which new ideas could be nurtured and then disseminated to the provinces, including nearby Champagne. Robert Estienne, a crown printer, classicist, archenemy of the Sorbonne,

---

29. Richard Cameron, "The Charges of Lutheranism brought against Jacques Lefèvre d'Etaples (1520–1529)," *Harvard Theological Review,* 63 (1970), 122, notes a long-standing conflict between the Franciscans of Meaux and their bishops, which Briçonnet's actions exacerbated; on Le Clerc, see *Les chroniques de la ville de Metz . . . 900–1552,* ed. J. F. Huguenin (Metz, 1838), pp. 824–828; AD, Marne, G 417, f. 8; *Histoire ecclésiastique,* I, 14; Lovy (*Les origines,* pp. 22–23) lists the victims of Meaux. For Poncelet's arrival at Troyes, see Pithou, "Histoire ecclésiastique," f. 66.

and in 1550 refugee to Geneva, bought paper from the Le Bés of Troyes. It was to them, in all probability, that he feigned to send one of his sons for training in 1547 or 1548, with secret instructions that the boy's real destination was Lausanne. Denis and Robert Le Bé became pillars of the Reformed Church of Troyes. Their family was allied to the Saint-Aubins. In 1559 Anthoine de Saint-Aubin, who had just completed a term as a member of the town council, was received as a resident of Geneva. He was one of the few Troyens of substance to take this road in the 1550s. Jacques Douynet, a physician of Troyes "skilled in his art," had a close friendship with François Landry, curé of Sainte-Croix of Paris, who for a time had preached "rather publicly and freely there" until the cardinal of Tournon forced him to abjure in 1543. When Landry came to Troyes in 1555 to accept a benefice, Douynet introduced him around and had him invited to a dinner party of the faithful (where, however, Landry's caution led him to mince his words and unsettle rather than edify his audience). Such links with the capital were crucial in introducing the bourgeoisie to the Reform.[30]

East of the province were the havens for persecuted Frenchmen. From Meaux or Paris refugees took the roads of Champagne. Peddlers of tracts, ministers, and other messengers of the Word traveled in the opposite direction. To reach Strasbourg, the mother church for France in the 1530s and '40s, one either followed the Marne Valley, or cut straight across the plains as far as Vitry, and then continued on into Lorraine. Later, from Geneva "the route of the ministers" slipped through the Jura Mountains at Collonges and crossed Franche-Comté to reach Langres and then either Vitry or Troyes, on the way to Paris and to Normandy, the province in which the Reform was making most progress. To the north, finally, roads led from Champagne toward the Low Countries, on a route that usually went from Vitry through Châlons and Reims. In 1524 Friar Jean

---

30. On Paris, see *Histoire ecclésiastique*, ed. Baum and Cunitz, I, 112. Elizabeth Armstrong, *Robert Estienne, Royal Printer* (Cambridge, 1954), p. 52, refers to the Estienne-Le Bé commerce. There is no evidence that Estienne's other Troyen supplier, the Pietrequin family, to whom the Le Bés were related (Le Clert, *Le papier*, II, 427) were Protestants. See also J. Quicherat, "Lettres de rémission et de main-levée en faveur des enfants mineurs de Robert Estienne," *Bibliothèque de l'Ecole des chartes*, 1 (1839–1840), 565–573. See Pithou, "Histoire ecclésiastique," ff. 315 and 331, on Denis and Robert Le Bé as Protestant leaders, and ff. 79–80 on Douynet and Landry. The relationships between Le Bés and Saint-Aubins are given in Le Clert, *Le papier*, II, s.v. "Famille Le Bé." AC, Troyes, A 12, f. 88v, names Saint-Aubin as an échevin; the *Livre des habitants de Genève* (I, 149) places him at Geneva.

Chastelain, who as an Augustinian was a member of the order "that had a reputation of preaching more purely than the other mendicants," delivered evangelical sermons in Châlons, Vitry, and Bar-le-Duc before meeting his death in Metz.[31]

One of the influential people attracted by Reformed ideas was the lawyer Pierre Pithou, a friend of Lefèvre's who later reluctantly participated in confraternities. In 1539, three years after Lefèvre's death, Pithou engaged Nicolas Stickler, a young man from Flanders teaching at the municipal college of Troyes, to tutor his twin fifteen-year-old sons, Nicolas and François. Like the boys' father, Stickler had "some beginnings and entry into the understanding of true religion, which as yet one had scarcely, so to speak, heard about in Troyes." At that time, Nicolas Pithou later recalled, pamphlets containing "a frontal attack on some of the most glaring abuses of the Roman church" began to pass secretly from hand to hand. Stickler owned several of them. He gave the boys a New Testament in French, and taught them justification by faith and some of the errors of the papacy.[32] Presumably this was all that he knew himself. In time the twins far surpassed their teacher. Nicolas Pithou helped to organize the secret Protestant assemblies that Michel Poncelet, the wool-carder from Meaux, began to lead in 1551. By the end of the decade Nicolas was directing the affairs of the nascent Reformed Church of Troyes. He left for Geneva in 1560, but soon returned, to exercise leadership during the first religious war. The outbreak of the second war in 1567 forced him to quit Troyes for nearby Brienne, and the Saint Bartholomew's Massacre of 1572 to flee France entirely. Pithou returned after Troyes acknowledged Henry IV in 1594, and it was then that he transcribed the manuscript which has been preserved for us. But the elderly refugee who had come home to die did not have to rely entirely on his memory to recall events that had occurred as much as a half-century previously. In the mid-1560s he had prepared a memoir on Troyes for Théodore de Bèze, Calvin's suc-

31. On Strasbourg's importance for France see Febvre, "Une mise en place: crayon de Jean Calvin," in *Au coeur religieux*, p. 262, and Jean Delumeau, *Naissance et affirmation de la Réforme* (Paris, 1965), p. 142. On the road from Geneva, see Febvre and Martin, *L'apparition du livre*, p. 473. Paul Geisendorf (*Livre des habitants*, II, xii) identifies the Haute-Marne as the "rue des pasteurs." For Jean Chastelain, see Eugène and Emile Haag, *La France protestante* (10 vols., 1846–1859; reprint ed., Geneva, 1966), s.v. "Châtelain," and *Les chroniques de Metz*, pp. 809–810. The quotation on the Augustinians is from the *Histoire ecclésiastique*, I, 825.

32. Pithou, "Histoire ecclésiastique," ff. 34v–35v.

cessor at Geneva, who was beginning to compile materials for the *Histoire ecclésiastique,* which appeared in 1580.[33] Pithou's own "Histoire ecclésiastique de l'église de la ville de Troyes" is an amplification of that memoir for the years when he was an active participant, and a more cursory, second-hand account of events which occurred during his absence.[34]

Although Pithou helped to shape the events he was narrating, he expected posterity to consider his account as true. For he was writing history, not martyrology or panegyric. And he had the necessary skills for the task. By profession he was an attorney, and came from a family distinguished in letters and the law. His father Pierre was an important member of the bar at Troyes, and a half-brother, also named Pierre, earned a national reputation as a legal scholar.[35] Nicolas Pithou himself was fully capable of sifting evidence and thinking critically. Living in a commercial center, he rubbed shoulders with merchants and applied to his studies the hard-headed realism that they displayed in trade. The metaphors he uses make this clear. A local tradition held that Troyes had begun as three castles held by three brothers. "That is what these good people say. You may have the merchandise for the weight it cost me, without my wanting to make any profit from it, nor be held to a guarantee." Credulity was his *bête noire,* as befitted a sixteenth-century reformer. In sketching the early history of Troyes he wondered how the pure Christian faith had degenerated. Probably this happened little by little.

The poor and simple people went along only out of good faith — which, however, has no value on either side of the ledger — not suspecting the pernicious and harmful plague that showed through such ceremonies, superstitions, and inventions, because they were covered with the mask and exterior appearance of devotion, the splendor of which dazzled them. They took great pleasure in these new inventions and found them so beautiful and fitting that they received them

33. Compare, for example, the *Histoire ecclésiastique*'s reference to the minister Corlieu's speech (I, 335) with the quotations in ch. 5 below, text and n. 45. The fit is equally close between the two works throughout. The *Histoire ecclésiastique* (ed. Baum and Cunitz), which is composed in large part of just such memoirs sent to Bèze, was probably put into final form by the minister Simon Goulard. See Rodolphe Reuss's introduction: III, lxiv–lxviii.

34. BN, Collection Dupuy, MS 698.

35. On Pierre Pithou the younger, see Donald Kelley, *Foundations of Modern Historical Scholarship: Language, Law, and History in the French Renaissance* (New York, 1970), ch. 9.

willingly, without any discretion and without scrutinizing what was being put forward, according to the rule of God.[36]

Pithou's language, as one might expect, is not that of a disinterested historian. He treats Catholicism with the coarseness that contemporaries used to air their religious differences. This in itself is not serious. We can disregard his venom as long as it does not affect his judgment. In general, Pithou's hatred did not distort his perception of the events of his lifetime. The care and precision with which he describes them give credence to his account, and the other sources we have do not contradict him. He is less reliable when he deals with the character of individuals, for here he let personal animosity govern his opinions. If we are to believe Pithou, most of the men who were attracted to the Reform but then fell away became lechers and died of disease. What he has to say about his adversaries tells us more about himself than about them.

While Nicolas Pithou was growing in the 1540s to manhood, other prominent townsmen including, as he later learned, people of "name and knowledge" who had venerated the Beautiful Cross around 1530, were becoming conscious of "a good part of papal abuses." Antagonism towards the established religion did not, however, necessarily imply understanding or acceptance of a new one. Pierre Pithou the elder understood justification by faith, but nothing of the Eucharist, and so could accept the idea in one of his books that God allowed those whom he had justified to attend the Mass. This was a reasonable point of view for a member of the older generation who was unfamiliar with the ideas that were just beginning to reach Troyes from Geneva. They were brought, gradually, by men like Macé Moreau, who had once sold religious images and other notions on the streets of Troyes but then moved to Geneva, where he placed his vocation at the service of his new faith. John Calvin's compatriot from the town of Noyon, the famous bookseller Laurent de Normandie whose network of distribution reached across France, hired Moreau to conceal Protestant pamphlets under the needles and nails in his sack. Passing through Troyes on his way to Normandy in 1546, the peddler rashly showed Anthoine Marcou's anticlerical and antipapal pamphlet, *The Book of Merchants,* to a fer-

36. Pithou, "Histoire ecclésiastique," ff. 7 and 11v.

vent Catholic who took the tract straight to his curé. Moreau was arrested by the bailiff's lieutenant for criminal matters, Marc Champy. He "had given reason to several people to be considered a good and faithful Christian some time before," but had since completely returned to Catholicism. Parlement condemned Moreau to be burned at the stake, and he went to his death singing hymns.[37]

The high court was now vigorously pursuing religious offenses. Men and women from Langres and Sainte-Ménehould were burned, and people from elsewhere in Champagne hanged or otherwise punished, for owning evil books, holding secret assemblies, or insulting the Mass, the Virgin, or the saints.[38] Those accused of such crimes were not necessarily Protestants, let alone Calvinists. The contours of heresy were vague, although it is true that the court, as so often in such cases, could recognize them much more easily than could its victims. Persecution was in fact the one salient feature to emerge from the religious haze. To all those inclined towards heterodoxy, persecution offered a common challenge while instilling a common fear. It whetted the appetite for a faith capable of making the dead into martyrs.[39] Over the long run, persecution facilitated John Calvin's effort to guide the French Reform towards a single, taut doctrine that broke cleanly with Roman Catholicism.

Since knowledge and protection were the two great needs of the fledgling French Protestants, the clergy and the law officers were the chief objects of their attention. The Pithous and their friends apparently congregated at the sermons of preachers who seemed to them to be leaning away from Rome. They were usually Dominicans, as Troyes had no Augustinian house. All but one of those whose story Pithou tells, however, returned to orthodoxy and bent over backwards in hostility to the Reform. "For to tell the truth, the poor children of God had no worse adversaries, who were more cruel and inhuman to them, than these renegades, who treated them worse than the true papists did." But then perhaps Pithou was simply more

37. Ibid., ff. 32v, 42–44v, and 77v–78. On Moreau, see also BC, Troyes, MS 1291, f. 126.

38. Nathaniel Weiss, ed., *La chambre ardente* (Paris, 1889), publishes cases from Langres, Sainte-Ménehould, Troyes, Reims, Chaumont, Bar-sur-Seine, Bar-sur-Aube, Pont-sur-Seine, Châlons, Château-Thierry, and Sézanne.

39. Donald Kelley, "Martyrs, Myths, and the Massacre: The Background of St. Bartholomew," *American Historical Review*, 77 (1972), 1323–1342, demonstrates the preoccupation of French Calvinism with martyrdom.

sensitive to such men than to those who had never aroused his hopes. One case was especially disappointing to him. Around 1544 his father saw that a Franciscan named Morel, a doctor of the Sorbonne, had a spirited mind. Pierre Pithou cultivated the friar, who began to preach in a different manner, revealing the worst abuses and above all speaking rather well on justification by faith. "This made him remarkable to the people, who had never heard the like." His sermons opened the ears of some of them. Morel continued to preach in the same vein for several years but then, according to Pithou, conceived the ambition of rising in his order. "The seeds that he had sown were lost in some and buried for a time in others."[40] The fact that he had been left entirely unmolested until his reconversion suggests how mild his sermons must have been.

The Pithous also quietly but closely observed potential lay converts, men like the lieutenant Champy whose sympathy would have made life much easier for them. But they must have hesitated before directly approaching anyone. Pierre Pithou's cultivation of the Franciscan Morel is the only attempt to influence a man's beliefs that his son mentions. No one seems to have tried to sway either Champy or his successor Jacquinot, who "had been touched with sentiments of the true religion."[41] The evidence for such a statement may have been nothing more than a chance remark, or a bored look in church. In the early days even a cleric could question aspects of Catholic belief without any intention of betraying his cloth. A layman could show signs of displeasure with the clergy "in familiar conversation," or curtail his participation in ceremonial activities, without meaning to question either dogma or the authority of the church. Pieces of Reformed and Catholic religion could be juxtaposed in one man's mind like an ill-fitting jigsaw puzzle.

The distance at mid-century between the decisiveness of a John Calvin and the fluidity of most Frenchmen who were not old-style Catholics is well illustrated by the man who became bishop of Troyes. Pithou and his circle were elated when they learned that Antonio Caracciolo, abbot of Saint Victor's in Paris, had just exchanged his benefice with Odard Hennequin's successor, Bishop

---

40. Pithou, "Histoire ecclésiastique," ff. 37v–38, 41v, 166v. By 1549 Morel was guardian of the monastery: BN, Fonds français, nouvelles acquisitions, 2825, f. 77.
41. Pithou, "Histoire ecclésiastique," ff. 82v–83.

Louis of Lorraine, for Caracciolo "had the reputation of knowing the truth."[42] The new bishop was then about thirty-six, a member of a Neapolitan family which had taken service with the king of France during the Italian wars. He had entered the court at eighteen but, "pushed by somewhat vague though generous aspirations," as his biographer nicely puts it, turned to religion, and took to the mountains of Provence for a while as a hermit.[43] On his return to Paris the young man became a Carthusian novice. His family, however, quickly moved him on to the plush Augustinian abbey of Saint Victor's. When the incumbent died in 1544, Caracciolo became the new abbot, by the favor of Marguerite de Navarre, sister of the king and patron of evangelical humanism. That same year he published a short exhortation intended for monks "on the manner of living well and religiously." The *Mirror of True Religion* is worth our scrutiny, not merely because it reflects more about its author than he might have liked us to know, but also because it illustrates the difficulty that many thoughtful men had in making unambiguous decisions on religion.[44]

He wrote the booklet, Caracciolo acknowledges, despite his negligence in maintaining the virtues that God had "very copiously" given him. The abbot, then, placed a high value on his talents, but lacked confidence in his ability to use them to advantage. This confession over, he turns to the subject at hand, and strikes an evangelical note. Taking his text from Saint Paul (Col. 1:10), Caracciolo counsels his readers that "the beginning of salvation is the knowledge of the will of God." He follows the Reformers in maintaining that man is justified by God's grace alone. Works are "the witness and corroboration of the free will that he has restored in us." Later on, he veers toward predestination, admonishing us that whether or not "by the grace of God, by his creation of the world, our names are inscribed in the book of life," we are subject to his will and must continually pray him. Several times, Caracciolo belittles the Mass. "The sacrifice most acceptable to God is the fruits of our lips, which renders him honor and praise." "The estate of a true monk consists, not in external ceremonies, even though they are an adornment of

42. Ibid., f. 46v.

43. For Caracciolo, see Roserot de Melin, *Antonio Caracciolo,* or more briefly the same author's précis in the *Dictionnaire d'histoire et de géographie ecclésiastiques,* s.v. "Caracciolo, Antonio," from which the quotation is taken.

44. Antonio Caracciolo, *Le mirouer de vraye religion* (Paris, 1544).

virtue and almost a gold in which the emerald of justice is set, but rather in purity of the heart." There is no mention of the Virgin or the saints in the *Mirror,* and but a single reference to the church, one that could hardly have satisfied traditional Catholics: Christ died "to appease with his blood all things celestial and terrestrial, and . . . to make of all spirits [*esprits*] a triumphal church." [45]

Though he knew his Bible well, and wove paraphases of Scripture into his prose with a certain facile grace, Caracciolo's evangelicalism seems to have been something of a veneer, an excuse for metaphor more often than a source of spiritual inspiration. We are not assured of protection from worldly evil, he warned his fellow monks, simply because "we are shut in the cloister, surrounded by the wall of the evangel, girded by the moat of the prophets, and defended by the rampart of the Psalms." What really moved him was a diluted and popularized notion of Carthusian religiosity, to which he had been introduced as a novice of the order. The topics in the *Mirror* include humility, prayer, sobriety, taciturnity or works of edification, occupation in good works, and obedience. Good monks pray continually and fervently, but silently. They "abhor hypocrisy, and are more comfortable letting their tears flow before God than before men. They demand no trumpet for the solemnity of their fasts." And they resist the artillery of the devil, who assails them with pride, the desire to command, or an appetite for praise, with the ever-useful "wall and ramparts of the evangel." [46]

No true Carthusian, of course, would have mentioned his God-given virtues, as Caracciolo did in the preface. More seriously, what is lacking of Carthusianism in him is a quest for unity with the divine. His attention, rather, is fixed on the physical person of Christ, though perhaps this does not distinguish him from other followers of Saint Bruno at the end of the Middle Ages. In prayer, "a thousand times a day, you must bend the knee of thought, and with the arms of the spirit embrace the cross; kiss the feet of the crucifix with the books of devotion, and like a loyal and tame animal, lick the wounds of our Lord with the tongue of compassion." The cross is in fact "the nerve and substance of all of holy Scripture." When men feel the lure of carnal inclinations — a problem Caracciolo raises more than once — they should "thrust them into

45. Ibid., ff. 2, 6, 11v, 13v, 29.
46. Ibid., ff. 4, 6v, 9.

the cross of Jesus Christ (in which sin has been crucified, and death killed and destroyed), and carry throughout our body and members" his wounds. Morbid sentimentality pervades Caracciolo's treatise. It is also likely that he was afraid to face the world, or himself. For why else would he counsel that "when we hear the cry of the cruel lion, that is the stirrings of the flesh, we must hide within the crevices of the stone, within the wounds of our savior Jesús Christ."[47]

What characterized Caracciolo best, perhaps, is the tacit assumption in the *Mirror* that the Christian cultivates his spirit wholly independently, without interest in fellowship or need for a church. This made it possible for him to regard existing clerical institutions as an indifferent matter — and take full advantage of his benefice. Despite all those words about humility and sobriety, Caracciolo lived in the style to which abbots of Saint Victor's were accustomed, and governed the abbey in a lordly and arbitrary fashion, removing from office those canons who had opposed his candidacy, and making new appointments without consulting anyone. The canons appealed to Rome, and in 1547 Paul III divided the abbey revenues in two, and placed all real authority in the hands of a prior. Isolated — and no doubt humiliated — Caracciolo looked for a more comfortable benefice. After Francis I was unsuccessful in trying to obtain the Provençal bishopric of Saint-Jean-de-Maurienne for him, Caracciolo made the exchange with Louis of Lorraine, despite papal reluctance, and arrived in Troyes in December of 1551, where Nicolas Pithou and the others were eagerly awaiting him.[48]

Caracciolo made a good first impression on them by preaching at the cathedral on the Sunday following Christmas. A great crowd attended, for few Troyens had ever seen "a bishop step up into the pulpit." He "did not let a point of the Christian religion pass when the occasion arose without expounding it purely enough. Nevertheless he scarcely touched the real filth" — in other words the Mass. Judging from Pithou's comments in another context, he probably avoided criticism of purgatory and the saints as well. By implication, then, he was most forthright on justification. After Christmas week, Caracciolo preached infrequently but well. "His language was smooth and engaging, his diction fitting and pure, his tongue discreet, and he used great cleverness and vehemence in persuading

47. Ibid., ff. 3, 8, 15, 16v.
48. Roserot de Melin, *Antonio Caracciolo*, pt. 1, chs. 3–4.

people and appealing to them, with singular grace in explaining himself and making himself understood." Three Dominican preachers took their cue from the bishop and "raised their heads a little, but did not go far without retreating."[49] Franciscans, given the jealousy and competitiveness that divided the mendicants, must have quickly called them to order. Caracciolo himself was soon in difficulty, suspect to his chapter and under attack from the Franciscans, who complained to the archbishop of Sens.[50] The curé of Saint John's urged him to clear his name by preaching orthodox doctrine at the parish church on a Lenten Sunday evening. Caracciolo consented to deliver the sermon, but could not decide what to say. Pithou, present at his table before the service, found him terribly agitated. The bishop did ask that those with Reformed opinions attend his service. They came "full of hope and joy," to hear him retract his previous opinion, at least according to their strict criteria. "Most left their places" — an act of some courage — "and several broke off relations with the apostate bishop entirely."[51]

Caracciolo's later career shows the same restless attempt to meld ecclesiastical status and evangelical ideas, and the same reluctance to take a fixed position in the developing religious confrontation. He went to Rome in 1555 to salute Paul IV the new pope, and stayed on for two years, attaching himself to the literary group patronized by Cardinal Jean de Bellay. He returned in 1557 — by way of Geneva, where Calvin granted him an interview in order to dress him down. The bishop, not a man to welcome criticism, argued back, but when Calvin brusquely stood up to leave, Caracciolo reversed himself and promised to "stop saying the Mass, renounce Roman superstition, and take to heart the advancement of the reign of Jesus Christ in his bishopric." Or at least that is what Pithou was told. Caracciolo then promised a group of Troyens resident in Geneva that he would join them at Calvin's sermon the next day, but changed his mind by morning and set out for home. At Troyes he

49. Ibid., pp. 226–228; Pithou, "Histoire ecclésiastique," ff. 46v, 48–49, for the quotations. A Dominican at Saint John's Church during Advent in 1552 was a much more daring preacher than the bishop, since he criticized the invocation of the saints and purgatory openly, and "gave a terrible blow to the Mass, which the bishop never dared to do" (ibid., f. 68v).

50. Morel, now guardian of the Franciscans, preached against the bishop's doctrine (ibid., f. 64v). A Dominican of Provins who preached in an evangelical vein was reproved by the Franciscans (Haton, *Mémoires*, I, 19–23).

51. Pithou, "Histoire ecclésiastique," ff. 70–71v.

resumed saying Mass and tried to convince the Protestants he knew that they could attend without prejudice to their souls.[52]

Like Nicolas Pithou's father, Caracciolo must have considered the Mass a tolerable evil, with which he could live. The bishop was not a man of systematic thought, any more than of fixed purpose, and he reflected a widespread tendency not to be drawn to extremes. There were some, nevertheless, who committed themselves fully to the new opinions. What did the Reform offer to, and demand of, the potential convert? This is a difficult question to answer, given the intermittent and incomplete information then available to him, and to us about him. Most of the faithful, to use Pithou's stock phrase, had only some beginnings and entry into the understanding of God's truth. But beginnings were enough to negate the Catholic system. Mutual aid among Christians went the way of the private Mass, the confraternity, and the staged funeral. The will of Marie de Montsavion, the wife of a notary and solicitor of Troyes, stipulated an evening burial, "without light or funeral pomp," without any appeal, therefore, for the participation of the community *en masse*.[53] The convert had to renounce the feeling of membership in a community and an estate that depended upon sharing in religious ritual for the benefit of all. This did not make him socially isolated, since he joined a growing movement of individuals who defined themselves normatively and participated in the revival of the true religion, which would culminate in the reestablishment of its church. But in general terms the cultivation of ties among men was less important to him as a religious goal than a renewal of the bond between the individual and his God. And so he had no need for churchmen whose functions had as much to do with life in this world as with preparation for the next. "I, Claude Voisin, damoiselle," begins the Reformed style for the will, which first appears in the surviving notarial archives of Châlons in 1564,

render my soul to God, *my* celestial father [*emphasis added*], of whom I am unworthy to be called daughter, because of the many offenses I have committed against his majesty, supplicating him in the honor of Jesus Christ his well-beloved son, our Lord, who has given satisfaction by his obedience for all the sins of those who believe in him, that he receive me in his paradise, the place that he has prepared for all those who love him.

52. Ibid., ff. 90–91v; Roserot de Melin, *Antonio Caracciolo*, pt. 3, ch. 2.
53. Pithou, "Histoire ecclésiastique," f. 76.

Nicolas Pithou, who needed no formula, makes the case for preoccupation with the self even more starkly. "All my hope," he professed in his will, drawn in 1594, "has been and will be in the death and passion of my Lord, in his precious blood, which has been shed for my salvation."[54]

Anxious to approach his God directly, the convert brushed aside any thought of quasi-divine intercession. He turned on the Virgin and the saints as false pretenders to influence which they did not exercise. For the hotheads among the Reformers, an attack on the Marian cult was the first outward expression of their new faith. Before dawn on Immaculate Conception Day in 1554 several statues were mutilated, including a Pietà on the portal of the Hôtel-Dieu-le Comte, which was decapitated.[55] Sober persons shared the convictions that lay behind such aggressive acts, convictions expressed in the final, crucial phrase of the formula for the will quoted above, which the Damoiselle Voisin's notary, rushed or careless, had omitted in her particular case. Later he would add: "(for all those who love Him) and place their entire confidence in him alone." [56]

Self-reliance, then, characterized the convert; self-esteem did too. Looking inward, he had a heightened perception of his own sinfulness, a stain that he could never wash away. And yet this did not lead him to despair, for he believed that God would accept him as he was, justified by personal faith rather than by social acts. If he had been exposed to the concept of predestination, the need for inner resources to provide confidence that he was among the elect would have been that much greater.

The call to conversion met with differing responses from men and women of the various estates, as Henri Hauser suggested and Emmanuel Le Roy Ladurie recently confirmed.[57] Of all the estates, the peasants of plains like Champagne were least responsive to the new

54. AD, Marne, 4E 6362 (1564); Pithou's testament is published in Société de l'histoire du protestantisme français: *Bulletin*, 15 (1866), 108–110.

55. AC, Troyes, A 11, f. 232v.

56. Cf. Jehanne Le Jeune, wife of the merchant-[joiner?] Pierre Loride of Châlons, AD, Marne, 4E 6363 (1567), and the merchant Gerard Arnoulot of Reims, presently in Châlons, 4E 6364 (1572). The phrase appears frequently in the *étude* of the notary Depinteville.

57. See Henri Hauser, *La naissance du protestantisme* (1940; reprint ed., Paris, 1962), pp. 64–82, and Emmanuel Le Roy Ladurie, "Prises de conscience et luttes sociaux," *Les paysans de Languedoc* (2 vols., Paris, 1966), I, pt. 3, pp. 329–414, which is a "book within a book," a searching examination that significantly advances our knowledge of the social history of religion in sixteenth-century France.

religious climate. Dependent on decent weather for security, if not for survival, they lived, as always, under a cloud of uncertainty. The tightly knit groups into which they were organized required a certain cohesion and the periodic ritual renunciation of personal hostilities, to function with any efficiency. In all probability their concept of sin, to borrow a phrase that has been applied to villagers in highland Colombia today, was built "on man's inharmonious relations with his fellow-men."[58] Illiteracy, to be sure, insulated most European rural communities from the message of those sixteenth-century Reformers who relied so heavily on an appeal to the written word, though peasants in certain places, as in Germany, were well attuned to the anticlerical note and the millenarian dream. But then illiteracy is but one ingredient in the peasant condition, which in a far more generalized way acted in Champagne as a barrier to the Reform. And the outlook of the peasant was not shed by those of his children who peopled the town and worked, when they could, as day laborers and domestics, subject to the hunger and disease that checked their numbers and cleared the way for new arrivals. Unacclimated, they formed "an agrarian world, sunk into the city like a foreign body."[59]

True urbanites could make a freer choice. In fact a root problem of medieval Catholicism was that it never quite succeeded in grafting onto city life a religion that had developed in response to rural needs.[60] Urbanization (the drive toward growth, specialization, and complexity), rather than the mere existence of the town, bred religious dissension.[61] No wonder the heady, expansive twelfth century, as well as the sixteenth, was a time for heresy. And a necessary, though not sufficient, condition for the success of the Czech Reformers at the turn of the fifteenth century, in contrast to the slightly earlier failure of their spiritual cousins the English Lollards, was the vigorous growth of the city of Prague until the end of the fourteenth century.[62]

Among those wise in the ways of the city were the artisans in six-

58. Gerardo and Alicia Reichel-Dolmatoff, *The People of Aritama: The Cultural Personality of a Colombian Mestizo Village* (Chicago, 1961), p. 340.

59. Le Roy Ladurie, *Les paysans*, p. 344.

60. Delumeau, *Naissance de la Réforme*, p. 60.

61. Philippe Wolff, "Villes et campagnes dans l'hérésie cathare," in *Hérésies et sociétés dans l'Europe pré-industrielle, 11e–18e siècles*, ed. Jacques Le Goff (Paris, 1968), p. 203.

62. For the demography of Prague see Ferdinand Seibt, "Die Zeit der Luxemburger und der hussitischen Revolution," *Handbuch der Geschichte der böhmischen Länder*,

teenth-century Champagne. Guild membership gave them a corporate identity, a definite if humble position at the base of the pyramid of urban estates, which set them off from the unskilled and unorganized workers in the social underworld below. The guild also provided enough security to support religious individualism. Many of the artisans could sign their names to notarial contracts, and some were much more accomplished. A joiner of Reims (in this case a Catholic) began his family register of names and significant dates by apologizing to his heirs that it was "rather badly written because of the lack of practice I have had with the pen — which I scarcely have to explain — since they can't be unaware that I was a poor joiner."[63] But still the man could write. Artisans had experience, too, in regulating the affairs of their trade, and a token share in urban politics. Skilled craftsmen and active participants in town life, who were able to draw on a reservoir of literacy from among their equals, had no need to feel inferior to most of those clergymen with whom they came into contact.

But the sixteenth century was unkind to most of them. Municipal governments became more oligarchical as people of quality, reassured by the stronger hand of the crown and greater domestic tranquility, took steps to avoid rubbing shoulders with tradesmen. The town councils of both Reims and Troyes gained royal consent to reserve to themselves the crucial decisions that had previously been deliberated by general assemblies of the inhabitants.[64] Although the guildsmen may not have enjoyed a potent voice at these meetings, at least they felt that their numbers carried some weight and helped the assembly toward a consensus that took their interests into account. Now they would have to watch from the outside. Within the guilds, too, social cleavages were widening. All over France the masters were making it more difficult for those journeymen who were not their heirs, and whose numbers were swelled by the demographic boom, to rise into their ranks.[65]

Established master craftsmen or hard-pressed journeymen, artisans

---

ed. Karl Bosl (Stuttgart, 1967–   ), I, 431; Jaroslav Mezník, "Der ökonomische Charakter Prags im 14. Jahrhundert," *Historica*, 17 (1969), 44–47, 80–82; and Josef Macek, "Jean Hus et son époque," *Historica*, 13 (1966), 61–62.

63. Henri Jadart, "Un troisième livre de famille rémois de 1567 à 1753," *Travaux de l'Académie nationale de Reims*, 121 (1906–1907), I, 265.

64. Roger Doucet, *Les institutions de la France au XVIe siècle* (2 vols., Paris, 1948), I, 372.

65. Hauser's *Ouvriers du temps passé* remains a convincing survey of the artisan condition.

were the kind of men who think more highly of themselves than others think of them. As such, many were ripe for the Reform. Some first learned about it through their connections, near or distant, with members of the liberal professions. The physician Boisonnot of Troyes converted his brother the tanner, who in turn, sometime during the mid-1550s, won over a friend, the scabbard-maker Blaise Chantefoin. But Chantefoin, literate and forceful, was hardly the last, inert link in a chain. He lent a New Testament to his uncle, a Dominican who was "considered one of the most devout in the order," and argued him out of his belief in the Mass. (The friar, though, may already have had "some glimmerings of the truth," since he once told Chantefoin's wife that she would be better off at home than at the Dominicans on All Souls' Day.) Chantefoin also made a vow with Boisonnot the tanner that when the one lay dying the other would try to protect him from pollution by papal abominations. And so in 1558 Chantefoin stationed himself at his friend's deathbed, hoping to ward off the priests sent round by the tanner's wife and his brother the physician, who feared a scandal. The family finally succeeded in persuading Boisonnot to receive extreme unction, but Chantefoin had him spit out the Host, "and then asked him whether he wanted to put his full confidence in Jesus Christ. 'Yes,' replied the sick man. 'I spoke to him; he pardoned all my offenses, and said that I'll be with him by midnight.' " The widow staged a memorable Catholic funeral and had the body buried in Saint John's Church. When Friar Morel, Pierre Pithou's erstwhile protégé, came to preach there, he inveighed against the "Lutherans," and complained that one of them, who had had only a hosier and a scabbard-maker for confessors, lay right beneath them. The body should be burned, he urged, along with the confessors.[66] But then Morel was nothing but a harness-maker's son himself. He was no more distinguished by birth nor, perhaps, by the ability to communicate his faith than Chantefoin and others like him whom artisans in the audience must have known. Morel's cloth did not in itself make him an authority to many of them.

Martin Fournier, an elderly shoemaker, provides a related example of the significant but far from exclusive importance of contact with professional men. One of his sons became a bookseller and "had the fear of God," and a daughter took service in the household

66. Pithou, "Histoire ecclésiastique," ff. 95–97, 109v–113v.

of a Protestant *enquêteur* (investigator) at the bailiwick court. The
influence of his children was less important in Fournier's conversion,
however, than that of another artisan, Michel Poncelet, who led the
first organized worship in Troyes. For Poncelet, Pithou informs us,
brought Fournier to the knowledge of the true religion.[67]

Michel Poncelet is the crucial figure in mid-century Troyes. He
was nicknamed the Picard, which suggests that he was a native of
Calvin's home province. His craft or his religion had taken him to
Meaux. From there he went to Geneva, probably as a result of the
persecutions of 1546. In 1550 Poncelet was returning to Meaux, to
put his affairs in order, presumably so as to move to Geneva for
good. On his way he stopped with some Protestant artisans in a village on the outskirts of Troyes. Pithou learned of his presence and
went out to meet him. Poncelet must therefore already have had
some reputation. But on Pithou's arrival both he and Poncelet's
hosts backed away from one another, "because at the time those
who had some entry into the knowledge of religion kept themselves
so tight and covered that there were few who mingled with one another for fear of being discovered." Poncelet, nevertheless, managed
to bring them together. They convinced him, no doubt after hearing him expound his faith, to teach the Reform in the city, "in order
to increase the faithful flock of Troyes, which was then very small
and scattered, and better to preserve in the fear of the Lord those
already touched with it." For the first time secret assemblies were
held to read the Bible, both in private homes and in the countryside. Initially, such meetings were few and far between. But Poncelet did so well that they were held more frequently, and he helped
many people to see the light.[68]

Judging from his "History," Pithou treated "Michel," the only
person to whom he refers by first name alone, with a respect tempered by condescension. Poncelet was "of low estate," and "knew
only French." But he made a forceful impression on all who met
him, including even the haughty bishop. In 1553 Caracciolo arranged for a bookseller of Geneva to come to Troyes. More likely
the bookseller sent a peddler. The man, whoever he was, declined
to risk going to the bishop's residence, which was in the cité, where

67. Ibid., ff. 68, 81v–84v. Guillaume Fournet was no doubt the same person as Guyot
Fournier, who became an inhabitant of Geneva on 18 Oct. 1557 (*Livre des habitants*,
I, 105).

68. Pithou, "Histoire ecclésiastique," ff. 66–68.

churches and clerics were concentrated. He sent his catalogue with
Pithou, accompanied by Michel, who wanted to meet Caracciolo.
The wool-carder lectured the bishop, as Calvin would later. Caracciolo was "surprised that this man, vile and abject in appearance,
spoke with such boldness and dexterity of spirit, and that he was so
well-read in the Bible." He acknowledged his error in the sermon
of abjuration at Saint John's and expressed a desire to repair it.[69]

The celebrated sixteenth-century potter Bernard Palissy, a Protestant from western France, tells a story that evokes the milieu of
Michel Poncelet. In the city of Saintes, according to Palissy, there
was "a certain artisan, wonderfully poor and indigent, whose desire
for the advancement of the evangel was so great that he voiced it
one day to another artisan as poor and ignorant as himself, because
the two of them taken together hardly knew anything at all." The
first nevertheless convinced the second to prepare "some kind of
exhortation," which he delivered one Sunday to nine or ten people,
who decided to continue to meet. Six of them agreed to alternate
weekly as leader, reading from texts prepared in advance, because
of their lack of experience. By this time, however, they had the advice of a local priest turned Genevan pastor, who had returned to
fertilize the soil of his province with his books and words. "Here,"
concludes Palissy, "was the beginning of the Reformed Church of
Saintes." [70] We may wonder how the second artisan, a man who hardly
knew anything at all, could deliver an exhortation. Palissy obviously used the term "ignorant" in a way different from ours today, for by it he meant, among other things, the inability to quote
and expound Scripture without notes. The enthusiasm and conviction of these men must have compensated for the roughness of their
tongue and the lack of their formal training in letters or in theology.

The only Troyen Protestants mentioned by Pithou who worshipped in a different group from Michel Poncelet's were of equally
modest social condition. Early in 1556 a number of them, who did
not attend the Christian assemblies "for a particular good reason,"
were surprised at a separate meeting, held to pray God and read the
Bible. Those arrested included seven artisans (five clothiers, a cob-

69. Ibid., ff. 66, 71v.

70. Les oeuvres de Bernard Palissy, ed. Anatole France (Paris, 1880), p. 136. For another variation on the beginnings of Reformed worship, this time led by a book-
peddler, see Guillaume and Jean Daval, Histoire de la Réformation à Dieppe, ed.
Emile Lesens (2 vols., Rouen, 1878–1879), I, 7–8.

bler, and a joiner) and two vendors (an oil seller and a hawker of spice bread at the church doors). The last was accused of being the minister. But when Parlement, which heard the case on appeal, learned that the man was barely literate, it released all the prisoners. The court should have investigated the clothiers more closely. Nicolas Pithou, when he wrote of the events of 1562, cited one of them, Jean Lambert, as among the most Reformed of the church of Troyes. The joiner in the group was Claudin Collot — "big Claudin" to his friends. He lived on Middle Street, in Saint John's parish, "which was peopled and full of joiners and other artisans, all good men, strong, robust and of good spirit, and of the [Reformed] religion." By 1560 at the very latest the street itself had earned the same sobriquet that Parisians applied to the faubourg Saint-Germain: "little Geneva."[71]

Given such nests of heretics, contemporaries could not fail to notice the determination of which artisan converts were capable. Claude Haton, with reference to the whole of France in 1558, sneered that "there was no one but the fools of low estate who dared to say, act, and speak in public of the said heresy and so-called religion, such as cobblers, shoemakers, joiners, carders, and drapers, and other mechanics who had themselves burned, and very few others of greater estate." Those who wanted to profess their faith preferred to flee rather than to burn. Jean Lambert and Hugue Collot, who was in all likelihood related to Claudin, were in Geneva by 1559. In general, the registers of new inhabitants of Geneva for the fifties show an overwhelming majority of artisans: twenty-nine out of the thirty-nine from Troyes whose occupations can be identified, seven of the nine from Vitry-en-Perthois, all three from Vertus, fifteen of the nineteen from Reims, and about seven-tenths of the refugees from the kingdom as a whole.[72]

They were able to go because they had less to leave behind, could in many cases carry their tools on their backs, and had acquired as

71. Pithou, "Histoire ecclésiastique," ff. 97v–99, 118, 160, 241v–242. For le faubourg Saint-Germain, see Louis Regnier de La Planche, *Histoire de l'estat de France, tant de la république que de la religion, sous le règne de François II,* ed. E. Mennechet (Paris, 1836), p. 33.

72. Haton, *Mémoires,* I, 81. For Collot and Lambert, see the *Livre des habitants,* I, 150 and 201. The figures for Champagne are derived from the *Livre des habitants,* which supplied Robert Mandrou ("Les Français hors de France aux XVIe et XVIIe siècles," *Annales: E. S. C.,* 14 (1959), 665) with the totals of French emigration to Geneva.

journeymen the habit of travel. To this should be added their vol-
atility. The artisans may have been capable of independent
thought, but not necessarily inclined to reflection. For they were of
the impulsive sort, unsuited to simmer new ideas in their minds for
years as they hesitated before definite choices. The merchant, the
lawyer, the bourgeois, by contrast, were more likely to have had the
habit of waiting ingrained on them by their quest for social promo-
tion, which involved the slow and patient rise of a family, following
a long-term plan. They were accustomed, too, to look above them
for political direction, and religious change was a political question
in the sixteenth century. John Calvin faithfully reflected his social
origins in placing his hopes for the Reform on the conversion of the
magnates of France. The artisans, on the other hand, had just been
excluded from participation in politics. They knew better than to
wait for the truth to dawn on those on high.

Notables tended to be more cautious. On the death of Pierre
Pithou in 1554, Nicolas and his brother, "more afraid of men than
of God," acquiesced in their stepmother's insistence on full Catholic rites. Four years later Nicolas became the town attorney. With
this position to defend, he continued to attend Mass. What choice,
then, did Pithou have but to defer to the leadership of Michel
Poncelet, a man who would not compromise his principles? And
noblemen were even quieter than bourgeois during the 1550s. Later,
once men of the stature of the prince of Condé had declared for the
Reform, a sizable minority of Champagne's rural seigneurs would
reveal their religious preferences and/or their appetite to participate in and profit from civil commotion, but until they received a
cue from above they kept their thoughts to themselves. Only one
scrap of information has come to my attention about the nobility
during these years. Odard Piédefer, whose family held the sei-
gneurie of Saint-Mards in the Othe Forest southwest of Troyes, left
Poitiers in 1551, where he was a student, for Geneva.[73]

The Genevan registers indicate the breadth of penetration of the
Reform. Refugees came from all of the province's areas of vitality,
which had contact with the wider world: the river valleys, the forest

---

73. See Hauser, *Ouvriers du temps passé,* pp. 252–253, on the mobility of the artisans; Etienne Trocmé, "Une révolution mal conduite," *Revue d'histoire et de philosophie religieuses,* 39 (1959), 160–168, analyzes Calvin's policy; Pithou, "Histoire ecclésiastique," ff. 78v–79; see AC, Troyes, A 12, f. 210v, for Pithou as attorney; *Livre des
habitants* lists Piédefer (I, 14).

borders, and the wine country. They came from along the Seine, from Bar and Troyes, and the villages of Payns, Méry, and L'Isle. Bar-sur-Aube and a half-dozen villages down to the confluence of Aube and Seine sent men. In the Marne Valley Protestants left Langres and the Bassigny, Chaumont, Joinville, Saint-Dizier, Perthes, Vitry-en-Perthois, and Châlons. The valley of the Vesle is represented by Reims, that of the Aisne by Gomont, Attigny, and nearby Le Chesne and Voncq. Sainte-Ménehould and Epense, which edge the Ardenne Forest, and Vauchonvilliers and Magny-Fouchard, near the forest of the Orient between Seine and Aube, had their refugees. The list of the places in Champagne from which men went to Geneva may be completed by placing a rough hourglass on a map of the vineyards, with the neck at Epernay. The upper half will trace the villages of Ambonnay, Mareuil, Aÿ, Dizy-Magenta, Verneuil, Ville-en-Tardenois, Tramery, and Nanteuil-la-Fosse, which enclose the Mountain of Reims and its western appendages. The lower half traces Vertus, Coligny, and Loisy-en-Brie, which mark the limits of the Mountain of Vertus.

The far greater number of Reformers who remained in their homes had to endure the watchful eyes of Catholic militants. At Provins Claude Haton and his friends searched for religious deviation. Their mental list of suspects in the late 1550s comprised a handful of people who went to church less frequently than they supped at one another's houses, presumably to pray. Of them only Guillaume de Chesnaye, abbot of Saint James's Monastery as well as a justice at Parlement, acted in a way that gave some small foundation to gossip. The expression on his face was so strange, during his rare appearances in church, that he showed with what "heart and devotion" he attended. To introduce the monks to heresy, Chesnaye brought in a schoolmaster. The man taught so cunningly that he was not exposed until a year and a half later, when an attorney dining at the abbey trapped him into a dispute. What finally gave away Chesnaye's own heresy was his attempt to strip the lead from the church tower, so that he could equip his new lodgings with rain gutters. The absence of firmer evidence encouraged fancy, and made speculation more interesting. Nicolas Pithou characterized his fellow Troyens as people who were by nature "greedy to hear and discover what is kept closed and hidden, even though it does not concern them at all, and prompt to put their nose to the window as soon as they hear their neighbor's door creak." Their usual conjectures about marriage alliances and conjugal behavior, property acquisitions and purchases of royal offices, were overlaid with a new and deadlier game. It was played with that combination of high spirits and intense concentration that makes the chase so gratifying to the hunter. Pithou tells of the Lenten preacher who pointed his finger at his audience as he shouted, "Lutheran, wipe your face, you've eaten lard," to see whether any man would flinch. Emotions were so taut that even good Catholics had to learn to weigh their words. Troyens packed the cathedral on May 7, 1559 to venerate Saint Mathie on her day. A poor shearer, waiting his turn to kiss the reliquary and make his offering, quietly observed to "a certain old bigot, the wife of the solicitor Christophle Douynet . . . that there was a greater crowd at the reliquary than there would have been to kiss a pretty girl." She screamed, "Get the Lutheran who is mocking blessed Saint Mathie," and the crowd killed him on the spot."[74]

By mid-century the church in Champagne had begun to mobilize the kind of people that were most likely to be hostile to the Reform. In 1547 Cardinal Givry of Langres obtained a papal bull granting indulgences to a new Holy Sacrament confraternity that had just been formed at the Dominican church, indulgences which were already enjoyed by the members of a similar Dominican confraternity at Rome. The purpose of the association at Langres, as stated by the general of the order three years later, was to manifest devotion to the Sacrament in answer to the "manifold heresies, sects, and blasphemies" of impious men. Another confraternity was founded in 1550 across the province, in the hospital of Nemours, once again with the express purpose of combatting heresy. Earlier, in the 1530s, the Holy Sacrament Confraternity at Saint Urban's collegial church of Troyes had been revived, though the reasons for the revival are not given.[75] By 1558, finally, a newly founded Holy Sacrament confraternity at Saint John's Church of Troyes, which was distinct

74. Haton, *Mémoires*, I, 53–56. In the event, Chesnaye did prove a Protestant (ibid., II, 569–570) ; Pithou, "Histoire ecclésiastique," ff. 149, 104v ("Lutherian, torche tes babines tu as mangé le lart"), and 123v–124r. For an analogous homicide, see Philippe Wolff, *Histoire de Toulouse*, 2nd rev. ed. (Toulouse, 1961), p. 224.

75. BC, Langres, MS 67, ff. 1–5; Marcel, *Le cardinal de Givry*, I, 163–164. Archives hospitalières de Nemours, H 2 (a document that I was not able to consult) ; the records of St. Urban's confraternity begin with AD, Aube, 10G 757 (1535), and 10G 757.4, cahier 8 (1546–47), f. 11, mentions that the confraternity was "reerigee nagueres."

from the moribund Corpus Christi association that formed a part of the parish's confraternity network, had begun to keep its books. Its officers were priests rather than laymen. These associations were a distant echo of the initiative of Italian clergymen who wanted to enhance devotion to the Eucharist.[76] In Champagne the special Holy Sacrament confraternities must have taken many committed Catholics out of their parishes on Corpus Christi Day. Nine hundred sixty-two people subscribed to the confraternity of Langres at its inception, 151 belonged to the one at Saint James's in 1558.[77] Since the rolls from Saint John's name only new and deceased but not continuing members, I cannot firmly identify any of the participants as parishioners of other Troyen churches. I would nevertheless suggest that here, as well as at Saint Urban's, Langres, and at Saint Quirin's collegial church of Provins, the members were in large part drawn from people who were accustomed to confraternity life, and who welcomed the opportunity to join an association on the grand scale (table 8). They could gain confidence from their numbers, while they manifested the fervor that sustained the true church. A new center of attraction, then, brought Catholic activists together and crystallized their desire to quash the Reform.

Crown policy encouraged them. During the 1550s Henry II progressively intensified the drive "to extirpate and abolish the false doctrines and errors," as the preamble to the Edict of Compiègne affirmed in 1557. It directed the royal judges to take cognizance of all cases of heresy, and show no mercy to the culprits, but to punish each and every one with death. The edict, a papal brief authorizing a French cardinal to designate as inquisitors bishops or doctors in theology, and the investigations at Paris following the discovery of a secret assembly of Reformers, terrified the Protestants of Troyes. They stopped meeting, and asked the wool-carder Michel Poncelet to leave temporarily. He soon returned, to find the faithful "so cold" that he went away for good. The Reform at Troyes underwent a period of latency. For a year the city had neither a spiritual leader nor regular prayers.[78] Then within a short time two ministers stopped at Troyes. Jean Macart, a pastor of Geneva who was returning there after a

76. A. G. Dickens, *The Counter Reformation* (New York, 1969), p. 54; International Eucharistic Congress, 9th (1894), *Congrès eucharistique de Reims* (Reims, 1895), p. 192.

77. BC, Langres, MS 67, ff. 5–15; AD, Aube, 15G 405 (1558–1624), f. 1.

78. François Isambert, *Recueil général des anciennes lois françaises . . .* (29 vols. Paris, 1821–1823), XIII, 494–497; Pithou, "Histoire ecclésiastique," ff. 101–102.

year's stay in Paris, where he had become too well known for his own
safety and that of his flock, passed through in November 1558. Soon
afterwards Jean de La Rivière, known as Le Maçon, made the same
trip in the opposite direction. He had been the first pastor of Paris,
and was on his way back there from Geneva. Both were important
figures in what we might call, from the point of view of the king of
France, the international Calvinist conspiracy, a growing network
to which Troyes was becoming attached.

At the invitation of some of the faithful, each of the ministers
preached. Macart urged the Troyens to establish the ministry of the
Word of God. Rivière drew a larger audience than had been anticipated, and taxed it with "nonchalance and stupidity," admonishing
his listeners to attach little value to their own lives, in a matter concerning the glory of God and salvation. If they were willing, he
would try to send them a minister from Paris. A majority of those
present accepted the offer, and on January 2, 1559 Gerard de Corlieu arrived at Troyes.[79]

Although sixteenth-century bourgeois were unaccustomed to being bullied, a certain number of them at least had obviously bent
before the lash of Rivière's tongue. A sense of guilt may have inclined them to do so. Nicolas Pithou points out later that he himself
had gone "with the others to kiss the baboon, that is to pay homage
to Sunday's beast," even though he knew the pure word of God.[80]

The new minister came from one of the notable, as distinguished
from noble, families of Angoulême. He had gone to Paris to study
for the ministry, and was only twenty-two years old when the call
came from Troyes. But youth and inexperience may have been assets
in dealing with people who were beginning to feel that they were
growing old in the ways of compromise. Corlieu set out at once to
found a full-fledged church, rather than the loose-knit gatherings
that Michel Poncelet had once led. *Surveillants* were named to
maintain discipline, and at Pentecost Corlieu celebrated the Lord's
Supper, the first time that this was done according to Reformed
practice in Troyes. Twenty people communed. About three hundred, in Pithou's judgment, then made up the church, though he
gives no indication of what their degree of commitment or participa-

79. Ibid., ff. 115v–116v. For Macart in Paris, see Kingdon, *Geneva and the Coming
of the Wars of Religion*, pp. 61–64.

80. Pithou, "Histoire ecclésiastique," f. 131v: "baiser le babouin, c'est a dire fayre
l'hommage a la beste des dimanches."

tion may have been. Perhaps Corlieu reached that number in his various prayer meetings, which were kept small to avoid detection. Pithou has him leading four or five a day. Certainly the three hundred were not yet all true converts. Many if not most were probably like Guillaume de Marisy, a poor goldsmith who had "some entry . . . but as weak and feeble as possible." He did know enough to sing psalms while sitting in front of his house with his neighbors, which so angered a passer-by that he stabbed Marisy to death. The surveillants themselves, as a group, were not steadfast. At the end of April 1559, Henry II and Philip II of Spain made peace, in part so that each could hunt the heretics among his subjects, French and Netherlandish respectively. Soon afterwards Henry's officers in Troyes began to search private homes. Most "of the surveillants and principals of the church" decided that for the time being Corlieu should be sent, against his will, to a chateau six leagues away — probably the Piédefer estate at Saint-Mards, forty kilometers from Troyes. When his custody dragged on, the plain people (*simple populaire*) among the Protestants of Troyes criticized the principals, a suggestive if admittedly imprecise distinction between the artisans' willingness to take risks and the discretion of the bourgeoisie.[81]

Henry II's accidental death in June at a tournament held to celebrate the peace brought first a new danger but then new opportunities to French Protestantism, which had grown into an organized movement in the teeth of his persecution. The Reform still commanded the allegiance of only a small minority, who wavered in their determination. It also pricked the curiosity of an indefinite number of others, who wanted to know not merely whether the new religion were true, but also whether it would be safe. As royal authority faltered, the answer to the second question came to depend more and more upon regional and local politics.

81. Ibid., ff. 116v, 123, 124v, 131.

5 / Confrontation

Mapmakers color Champagne Catholic in historical atlases, as a stronghold of the house of Guise during the religious wars. They contrast northeastern France to southern and western portions of the kingdom in which the Protestants were relatively or temporarily successful. Now the Midi was far enough from the levers of command in Paris and the northern might of the Guises to stiffen the resolve of potential Reformers, especially when they were nobles seeking political gains at the expense of a distant, weakened crown. To say that Champagne was significantly more Catholic is not to treat it as monochromatic. If we take a tour of the province we shall find areas of mild or dynamic Protestant activity as well as those in which Catholicism remained more or less intact. Where heresy posed no real threat, there was scant need for repression. In a few localities, conversely, the Reformers were numerous and fortunate enough to survive as a community and to practice their religion openly whenever the vicissitudes of spasmodic war and patchwork peace permitted. Yet elsewhere the Protestant thrust, salient and abrasive, provoked an uncontrollable reaction.

One of the quiet Champenois cities was Reims, citadel of the Guises and symbol of the ties that bound the Most Christian king to his church. Charles de Guise, the cardinal of Lorraine, was not only its archbishop, but abbot of the lordly Saint Remy's Monastery as well. Even though his wider responsibilities precluded sustained residence, the cardinal kept the city well in hand. Jehan Pussot, a local chronicler reminiscing as an octogenarian in 1625, recalled an outbreak of iconoclasm during his adolescence, an imaginary meeting he thought to have witnessed between the cardinal and Calvin's lieutenant Théodore de Bèze, and the diverting history of a heretical college principal whom people called Silver-Nose because the man had undergone a facial operation. There was not much else to remember. At the height of the first civil war the cardinal's propagandist Canon Gentien Hervet could placidly write, in an otherwise polemical tract, that those few Rémois of doubtful religion were under the magistrates' surveillance. A modern historian has in fact found the names of fifty-odd residents whom the municipal authorities expelled, imprisoned, or watched closely during four of the critical years in the 1560s and '70s.[1] No doubt some were under suspicion merely because their politics were anti-guisard. A list of suspects was in any event one of the more temperate forms of punishment in the sixteenth-century repertory.

Ambition rather than cruelty was the original sin of the Guises, a large and close-knit family from beyond the French borders, in Lorraine. Personal courage and soldierly camaraderie made Duke Francis, the eldest son and family head, a popular commander, while meticulous planning and swift execution in attack made him a brilliantly successful one. The cardinal of Lorraine, with his agile mind and aristocratic grace, was an effective spokesman for the duke's sword, especially since the brothers were, in the words of an ill-wisher, "two heads in one hood."[2] Duke Francis sometimes overreached himself, as in attempting to conquer Naples, for France and perhaps for himself. But his errors in the wars of the 1550s against the emperor Charles V and then Charles's son Philip were overshadowed by the military incompetence of his grand competitor for the favor of King Henry II, Anne de Montmorency the Constable of France.[3]

Failure in Italy restricted but did not annul the European ambitions of the Guises. The brothers had been able to marry their eldest sister Marie to James V of Scotland, when the French princess who was James's first wife had died. Marie de Guise survived her husband, and acted as regent for their daughter Mary Queen of Scots. The Guises added another ornament to their family tree by marrying the young Mary to Henry II's adolescent son Francis. This relationship made it easier for them to exercise power after Henry's unexpected death. They elbowed aside the chief prince of the blood, the indecisive Antoine de Bourbon, titular king of Navarre, who was then toying with Reformed ideas. Styling themselves uncles of the king, the duke

1. Pussot, "Journalier ou mémoires," pt. 2, pp. 242–248; Gentien Hervet, *Discours sur ce que les pilleurs, voleurs et bruslers d'églises disent qu'ils n'en veulent qu'aux prestres, au peuple de Rheims et des environs* (Reims, 1562), sig. Aiiii; Henry, *La Réforme*, pp. 429–431.

2. Regnier de La Planche (a publicist for the constable as well as a Protestant), *Histoire de l'estat de France*, p. 178.

3. H. Lemonnier, *La lutte contre la maison d'Autriche, La France sous Henri II (1519–1559)*, in E. Lavisse, ed., *Histoire de France*, V, pt. 2 (Paris, 1911), pp. 154–156, 163–168.

and the cardinal ruled in Francis's name.[4] They cemented their reputation as Catholic champions by implementing Henry's policy of concerted, national repression. A chorus of support from friars in the pulpit helped to organize a vast and pugnacious following of townspeople around the Guisard clients in town halls, courtrooms, and churches. But it was just as fanciful for the Guises to suppose that they could monopolize power in France as it was to have imagined that France could absorb Scotland. One of the persistent problems of the family was that they never set any specific limits to their ambition, so that they could be accused of anything and everything — including the ultimate crime of plotting to assume the throne as pretended descendants of Charlemagne.[5] The Montmorencys and Bourbons had their clients, too, and Guisard prominence blurred the line between political and religious dissent. Navarre's younger brother Prince Louis of Condé took on the defense of the Reform. He stood silently behind the Conspiracy of Amboise of March 1560, in which a group of noblemen tried but failed to seize the Guises and the person of the young king. Resentment against the Guises' harsh reaction to the conspiracy and to their domination at court enabled Henry's widow Catherine de Medici to share power with them. She searched for a religious formula that could dissolve political animosities, or at least maintain them in equilibrium. In June the crown issued the Edict of Romorantin, which removed jurisdiction over cases of simple, as opposed to seditious, heresy from the secular authorities and awarded them to the less harsh or at least less efficient episcopal courts. Meanwhile, the increasing opposition to the Guises of Montmorency's nephew, the experienced and able soldier Gaspard de Coligny, further strengthened the Protestant side.[6]

Some clients of the great Protestant lords had everything but reli-

4. Rosalind Mitchison makes perceptive comments about the Guises, as she discusses Marie of Lorraine and Mary Stuart, in *A History of Scotland* (London, Methuen, 1970), pp. 98, 116, and 128. An example of the avuncular style is given in the collection, *Mémoires de François de Lorraine, duc d'Aumale et de Guise*, vol. VI of Nouvelle collection des mémoires pour servir à l'histoire de France, ed. J.F. Michaud (Paris, 1839) , p. 454. See also Regnier de La Planche, *Histoire de l'estat de France*, p. 5.

5. See the reliable royal judge and Protestant historian Pierre de La Place, *Commentaires de l'estat de la religion et république soubs les rois Henry et François seconds et Charles neufiesme*, ed. J.A.C. Buchon, Panthéon littéraire, XXII (Paris, 1836) , p. 28.

6. J. Shimizu (*Conflict of Loyalties: Politics and Religion in the Career of Gaspard de Coligny . . .* [Geneva, 1970], p. 35, n. 11; pp. 46–47 and 69) treats the question of higher responsibility for the conspiracy, and emphasizes Coligny's independence of Condé before the war of 1562–63. The text of the Edict of Romorantin is in Isambert, *Recueil*, XIV, i, no. 27, pp. 31–33.

gion on their minds. Jean de Mergey was born in a village near Brienne. As a younger son of a bastard daughter, albeit a daughter of the house of Dinteville, he had to strive hard at making a military career for himself. Fortunately he was as adept at drinking as at fighting, and a sure man in a tight spot, whether in trying to escape from a prison or in carrying a message across enemy lands. The enemy for Mergey became the Catholic side in the religious wars, since he took service with the Protestant count of La Rochefoucauld. Mergey's resourcefulness enabled him to survive the wars in general and the Saint Bartholomew's Day Massacre in particular. He wrote his memoirs in 1613, at the age of seventy-seven, and died in bed. They present a man who spent his life in the Reformed cause without ever giving the religious issues a thought.[7]

Family property in northern Burgundy made Coligny a neighbor of Champagne, but not a direct participant in its affairs. The man who would lead the provincial nobility when war began was the "young, aggressive, willful, and yet well-followed" Antoine de Croy, prince of Château-Porcien, northeast of Reims. The Raguier family, which openly declared for the Reform after the June edict, joined him. Their lands stretched along and below the southern portion of the Falaise de l'Ile de France, from Esternay to Villeneuve l'Archevêque, near Sens. A Raguier had been bishop of Troyes at the turn of the sixteenth century. More recently, Louis I Raguier served as a justice at Parlement. His sons the lord of Esternay and the vidame of Châlons brought with them to the Reform their allies and clients, whom Claude Haton of Provins enumerates and excoriates. The bailiwick of Sens selected the vidame as a delegate for the Estates General which the crown summoned to Orléans for the end of 1560. There he defended the loyalty of the Protestant nobility. Not far from Villeneuve-l'Archevêque, Odard Piédefer of Saint-Mards in the Othe Forest also came from a family prominent in the Parisian judiciary.[8] Generally speaking, with the exception of the prince of Porcien himself, Protestant nobles seem to have had their estates in the high, forested,

7. *Mémoires du sieur Jean de Mergey, gentilhomme champenois*, in M. Petitot, *Collection complète des mémoires relatifs à l'histoire de France*, ser. 1, vol. 34 (Paris, 1823), pp. 3–81.

8. Michel de Castelnau, who is introduced in the text below, comments on Croy: *Mémoires*, ed. J. Le Laboureur (3 vols., Brussels, 1731), I, 87; see also Haton, *Mémoires*, I, 127–128. On the Raguier and Piédefer families, see Fourquin, *Les campagnes*, pp. 407 and 414; La Place (*Commentaires*, pp. 109–110) refers to the vidame's speech; Roserot, *Dictionnaire historique de la Champagne méridionale*, s.v. "Saint-Mards-en-Othe."

or wet lands that ringed the plains of Champagne, and were relatively protected from the outside world. It is also true that land in this sort of region was less expensive than in the great open-field area. A high proportion of less prestigious individuals, simple bourgeois as opposed to royal officers and nobles proper, would purchase the lands shortly to be sold by the church to help the royal treasury.[9] Both pronounced social mobility and religious diversity may have characterized the woodlands of Champagne. Later in the 1560s in any event, along the muddy crescent from Troyes to Vitry, at Saint-Pouange, Vallentigny, and Saint-Léger-sous-Margerie, new nobles took advantage of the edicts of pacification that punctuated the religious wars to establish Protestant worship on their estates.[10] At Trémilly, between Wassy and Bar-sur-Aube, Condé's supporter Etienne Menisson could boast that he was a knight of the royal order of Saint Michael. But when Menisson temporized with the Guises in 1574, Reformers in Champagne claimed to remember that his father was a "draper-in-hosiery, a merchant frequenting the fairs. Only three days ago, so to speak, he kept open shop in the said estate in the city of Troyes."[11]

Before the Estates General had convened at Orléans in December 1560, Francis II died. Catherine outmaneuvered the king of Navarre, and endeavored to rule in the name of her second son, ten-year-old Charles IX. The division among the great in 1561, and the sinuous policy of the crown, enabled Protestants all over France to breathe easier. Even a reconciliation of the two archenemies, Guise and Montmorency, in the cause of Catholicism, did not check the Reformers' relief. In Champagne as elsewhere, hidden congregations sought the light and the publicity of day. By the end of the year, although the number of Protestant clergy was inadequate to the demand, ministers had been sent to rural Champagne. Their presence suggests the concern of the Reformed churches of Paris and Switzerland to secure a province that lay between them. The ministers of Neuchâtel dispatched Jean de Beaulieu to Céant-en-Othe, despite the competing

9. Emmanuel Le Roy Ladurie, "Démographie et paysans," in *Histoire économique et sociale de la France,* ed. Fernand Braudel and Ernest Labrousse, I (Paris, forthcoming).

10. "Eglises réformées de la Champagne avec leurs pasteurs et anciens, en 1571," ed. N[athaniel] W[eiss], Société de l'histoire du protestantisme français: *Bulletin,* 39 (1890), 128–134; Boutiot, *Histoire de la ville de Troyes,* III, 589, 597; IV, 22; AC, Troyes, BB 14, first liasse, no. 47; Pithou, "Histoire ecclésiastique," ff. 256v and 384v; Leonard Jones, *Simon Goulart, 1543–1624* (Geneva, 1917), pp. 361–363.

11. Pithou, "Histoire ecclésiastique," f. 411v.

claims of Tournon in the Agenais, a part of the Bourbon domain, "where more than three hundred parishes have put down the Mass and do not yet have ministers." A league from Saint-Mards, Céant was a possession of the duke of Nevers, nephew to the king of Navarre. Beaulieu wrote to Neuchâtel in November 1561 that the little church grew daily, overflowing the barn that it was using. "From several surrounding places the poor people of all sorts, especially the craftsmen, flock toward us, hungry for the pasture of life. . . . Even though we are in a minority, we are the masters in that we have the judicial estate for us and all the biggest heads. We have confidence in God that we will soon have the rest." Beaulieu ranged as far as Sens, where he began preparing the way for Mathurin de La Brosse, who arrived soon afterwards to set up a church.[12]

The conversion of the biggest heads in a little town was however a decidedly mixed blessing, for it helped to identify the Protestants with all the ways in which urban-dwelling landlords, merchants, and tax-collectors profited from rural problems. To the peasantry of Champagne, the Reform may in fact have personified city life and its evils. The church of Sens enjoyed only a few months of formal existence before a troop of villagers, who were in town for an annual pilgrimage on April 7, 1562, aided the residents to murder the local Protestants. The following Sunday the peasants of the region around Céant used their day of rest to sack the barn that served as the Reformed church.[13]

The minister of Châlons, Pierre Fournelet, was more realistic than Jean Beaulieu of Céant about the countryside. He informed Neuchâtel of the difficulties of Jérémie Valet, one of the city's most promising young pastors, who had been sent to Loisy-en-Brie, at the foot of the Mountain of Vertus and near Saint Gond's Marsh. Loisy,

12. Beaulieu to Farel and to the ministers of Neuchâtel, in *Ioannis Calvini opera quae supersunt omnia*, ed. G. Baum, E. Cunitz, and E. Reuss (Brunswick, 1863–1900), XIX, 9–11 (3 Oct. 1561), and 104–106 (7 Nov. 1561); Beaulieu to Calvin, ibid., pp. 103–104 (6 Nov. 1561).

13. *Histoire ecclésiastique*, ed. Baum and Cunitz, II, 484–496. Haton (*Mémoires*, I, 189–195) incorrectly remembered the massacre at Sens as having taken place in 1561 (O.S.), before that of Wassy. For the result of analogous social grievances when sparked by religious conflict, see the account of the siege of Exeter during the Western Rising of 1549, in Hooker, "The Description of the Cities of Exeter," pt. 2, pp. 67–94, esp. p. 68. Paul Bois, *Paysans de l'oeust* (Le Mans, M. Vilaire, 1960), pp. 601–617, argues that the isolation of peasants in hamlets of the *bocage*, during the French Revolution, contributed to their hostility against the bourgeoisie. This isolation was also characteristic of the Othe Forest, which encompassed Céant.

Fournelet reported, was a village "surrounded, hated, assailed, and persecuted by the whole countryside, and truly by a whole world of the wicked; however, the seigneur who has opposed this weak place to the powerful surrounding cities [of Epernay and Châlons] has made this little token grow and flower so that its good odor awakens and gives courage to other neighboring places."[14] Protestant nobles, as Fournelet suggests, had little power in Champagne to make the towns hospitable to the Reform. It is true that a minister came to Sézanne, close by the Raguiers at Esternay.[15] But the country nobility were of limited value to the Reformers at Provins, or so at least Claude Haton tells us.

Born in 1534, country-bred, at home in a small town and yet at ease in Paris, Haton knew his compatriots at the time of troubles as well as any Frenchman could. He disclosed his own background, though presumably not his character, by including in his remarks for 1554 a comment on how plentiful the clergy were in France. Their numbers nevertheless continued to grow: since the times resembled those during which the country was at peace, "village *laboureurs* [prosperous peasants] with three or four sons were delighted to send one to the schools to make him a priest, even though most of them were vicious and evil-living." He settled in Provins, but mentions no specific clerical employment until an allusion to a rural vicarage in 1566. Earlier he had become a militia captain, which gave him the opportunity to engage distinguished travelers in conversation. Haton had also been attached in some fashion to Henry II's household, and even after the king's death frequently went to Paris.[16] He was not merely an inquisitive young priest who lacked pressing responsibilities, made good company, and mixed well in different milieus, but an attentive listener who candidly recorded the opinions of others, and a perceptive, harsh critic of all estates, beginning with his own.

Haton complained of an absentee clergy that neglected "to preach and announce the true word of God to their subjects and parishioners. Their nonchalance enabled the Lutheran heretics to slander the church of Christ, and to debauch its Christians." Conditions at Rome were, if possible, worse. The picture of an open, irreligious

14. *Ioannis Calvini opera*, XIX, 23 (6 Oct. 1561) .

15. Samuel Mours, "Liste des églises réformées, avec date de leur fondation," Société de l'histoire du protestantisme français: *Bulletin*, 103 (1957) , 129.

16. Haton, *Mémoires*, I, 15, and pp. xxii–xxiv, xxviii–xxxi.

city had been fixed in his mind by conversation with men who had
been there with the duke of Guise. Haton even referred to the head
of the church slightingly as "the pope of Rome." But although his
parlance may have acquired a Protestant tinge, his faith remained
intact. He was not misled by those who had returned from Rome by
way of Geneva, "who know so well how to malign pope and clergy
that in censuring them they censure as well the ministry of the holy
church, which in itself is always holy, since its sanctity depends" not
on man but on God.[17]

Even though he initially mislabeled the French Reformers as
Lutherans, Haton was well informed on their activities. Before re-
counting the discovery of the Protestant prayer meeting at Paris in
1557, he noted that the practice at such assemblies was to read the
Bible, enumerate the Ten Commandments, and sing the psalms to
a harmonious, delectable melody, which served to "announce the
praises of the Lord." But he ran a ring of mockery around this
favorable description by prefacing and following it with the common rumor that notable Protestant women drew men to prayer
meetings by offering . . . themselves.[18] The prayer meetings became,
then, just another form of witches' sabbath. This made excellent
sense in the 1550s, when no one knew who the Protestants or the
witches were, but everyone knew that they were there.[19] Haton,
nevertheless, had sufficient information at his command to arrive at
a more sophisticated conclusion. He was credulous by design rather
than by ignorance or stupidity. A man who could argue in 1560 and
1561 that the Reformers tried to provoke Catholics to sedition so
that their friends in the judiciary could arrest the rioters, found it
easy to justify the mob killings of 1562, like the massacre at Sens, as
self-defense.[20]

By 1561 the list of supporters of heresy that Haton kept for Provins included influential men who, one might think, could have
made the town safe for the Reform. The prior of Saint Ayoul's

17. Ibid., I, 89–90, 42–43, 62, 155, 42.
18. Ibid., I, 49–50. Cf. ibid., p. 126.
19. La Place (Commentaires, p. 4) writes that the rumor of the Protestants as forni-
cators was launched after the discovery of the Parisian prayer meeting. Castelnau, in
1559 (Mémoires, p. 7), attributes the rumor to the cardinal of Lorraine. See also
Regnier de La Planche, Histoire de l'estat de France, pp. 35–36. Palissy (Oeuvres,
p. 139) reports that some people in Saintes accused the Protestants of fornicating at
their meetings, while others charged them with kissing the devil's behind.
20. Haton, Mémoires, I, 122, 150, 189–195, 204–206.

Church and the royal prosecutor figured on it. "They had only been shaken Catholics" when they set out for Orléans to represent the first and third estates, "not yet knowing which religion to hold," but returned as "heretics and Huguenots." The two stopped short, however, of signing a request for a preacher at Provins — a petition that Haton may have confused or conflated with one that the lord of Esternay presented to the king for France as a whole. An even more important local figure, Jehan Alleaume the bailiff, whom Haton types as a secret and undeclared Huguenot, did not sign either. During the royal progress three years later, he would harangue king and court at Troyes for the judiciary of his bailiwick, wearing the square bonnet and long robe of the law courts. On concluding his harangue, he retired to change into a velvet bonnet, Spaniard's cape, and sword, in order to represent the nobility. "It was remarked in praise of the said bailiff that he had very skilfully acted two roles on the same day and in the same play, and had acquitted himself very honorably." Alleaume was one of the class of Frenchmen who had shouldered their way into the nobility as bearers of royal authority, only to find that the magnates now claiming that authority were demanding their allegiance. Haton implies that he was partial to Condé, and asserts that he was afraid of Guise, who threatened him once at court. This is plausible as background for a bailiff who administered as best he could the edicts against religious recrimination, and kept his conscience to himself.[21]

Perhaps Haton exaggerates the degree to which men like Alleaume leaned toward the Reform and, conversely, underestimates or understates the number of declared Protestants. He names a mere handful, officials of middling rank, legal and medical practitioners, and artisans. The potential clientele among the artisans of Provins for the Reform was surely restricted, for the extinction of the line of the counts of Champagne and the ruin of their fairs had affected the cloth workshops more severely than the numerous religious foundations. A few clerical dignitaries of dubious religion might influence elections to the Estates, but they could not induce the canons, monks, and parish clergy, who were thick in the town, to change

21. Ibid., pp. 122–125 (a list of presumed local heretics, secret and declared), 134, 139–142, and 178; ibid., II, 710 (Alleaume's partiality toward Condé, which Haton now treats indulgently, because Alleaume has died a Catholic). J.-H. Mariéjol (La Réforme et la Ligue, l'édit de Nantes (1559–1598), in E. Lavisse, ed., Histoire de France, VI, pt. 1, p. 44) mentions Esternay's petition.

their beliefs. Minor inconsistencies and unsecured judgments of individuals do not really undermine Haton's tacit assumption that
religious tension at Provins was in a state of equilibrium. The
presence of some Protestant nobles in the countryside, and the be-
nevolent neutrality of some local notables, aided the Reform. Shaken
Catholics kept shy of outright heresy, however, and the Reformers
neither maintained a preacher nor met as a community, even after
the edict of January 1562 which permitted Protestant services outside the walls. Because they were few in number, they feared both
the vengeance of the Guise and the possibility that the mendicants
might provoke a riot against them. So they worshiped only at the
seigneurial churches.[22]

The duke and the friars served each other's purposes. The sermons of the mendicants had of course long been a potentially explosive feature of urban life. Itinerant preachers, Huizinga wrote,
were able to "shake people by their eloquence." He depicted "the
violence of impression caused by the spoken word on an ignorant
mind lacking mental food." By the sixteenth century in Champagne,
townsmen were replete with at least verbal food, for sermons had
become more frequent. Thanks to a recent foundation by Bishop
Odard Hennequin of Troyes, for example, a Franciscan preached
weekly at Mary Magdalene's, in addition to the sermons at his own
church. The friars attracted not merely the ignorant but also the
literate, who judged them as connoisseurs. Knowledgeable Catholics
at Provins awaited with interest and debated with vigor the relative
merits of the noted preachers whom Franciscans and Dominicans, in
alternate years, invited for Advent and Lent. The two orders were
competing for attendance, alms, and prestige. Their visitors provided variety within a set tradition, but without much threat of religious novelty, since their orthodoxy had already been established
on the oratorical circuit.[23]

In 1561, at Provins as at Paris, preachers tried to distinguish them-

22. Haton, *Mémoires*, I, 122–126. For worship at seigneurial churches, see ibid., p.
189. Isambert (*Recueil*, XIV, pt. 1, no. 44, pp. 124–129) gives the text of the edict.
New evidence for the economic vitality of Provins during the high Middle Ages is
provided by M.T. Morlet, "La vie économique d'une cité au Moyen Age: Provins
d'après les noms de ses habitants," *Proceedings of the Eighth International Congress
of Onomastic Sciences*, ed. D.P. Blok (The Hague, 1966), pp. 304–309.
23. *Waning of the Middle Ages*, p. 4; AD, Aube, 16 G 67, ff. 63 and 84. A heterodox
Lenten preacher of 1554 at Provins was exceptional, for he was a local youth making
his first appearance in the pulpit (Haton, *Mémoires*, I, 11–14).

selves by attacking the Huguenots and insulting the crown, which now sought to temporize with heresy. The history of Ahab and Jezebel, who stood for the king of Navarre and the queen mother, became the model allegory for the year.[24] This evocation of ancient Israel suited the pulpit well. A friar too modest to posture as the new Elijah could at least picture himself among the hundred prophets of Obadiah. In either case he displayed his contempt for the royal warnings against recrimination, and boasted of his readiness to take the judicial consequences. The imagery of martyrdom, at the high tide of the Reform in France, was cultivated most assiduously in Catholic pulpits. The theme of the oppression of true religion by false government gave firm Catholics the sense that they were being jostled into a corner, from which they would have to break out. They could look toward Guise, whose name the preachers were invoking, for leadership.

In eastern Champagne, the Guises were themselves country lords. Antoinette de Bourbon, the matriarch of the family, lived at Joinville on the Marne, where the duke stayed when he wanted to emphasize that he was not at court. Joinville, like Charles de Gaulle's nearby village of Colombey-les-deux-églises, was far enough from Paris to serve as a retreat, though not too distant to keep out of touch or be out of reach. The road that led to Joinville, however, went on to Geneva. Two-score kilometers downstream, the plain of the Perthois was the knot at which a series of individual routes from Alsace, Lorraine, Burgundy, and Switzerland met, before continuing on to Paris and the Low Countries. Jean Chastelain, the Augustinian friar who preached the evangel in Châlons, Vitry, and Bar-le-Duc in 1524, may have been the first but was certainly not the only missionary to pass this way. The Perthois had enough Protestants in 1559 to attract the attention of the duke and the cardinal when they assumed control of government. The bailiff of Saint-Dizier, which lies between Joinville and Vitry, was their man in southern Champagne. His subordinates, through searches, arrests of suspects, and compulsory evening prayers, frightened well-to-do Protestants into taking an uncertain refuge in Troyes.[25] The events of the next year ended the campaign of repression. By 1561, the Reformers of the region were growing in confidence as well as in numbers. The min-

24. Ibid., p. 211. Cf. A.G. Dickens, *Thomas Cromwell* . . . (N.Y., 1959), p. 90.
25. Pithou, "Histoire ecclésiastique," ff. 141–142.

ister Pierre Fournelet, who had been chased from Châlons by a riot soon after his arrival, spent the summer evangelizing in the Perthois. He informed Neuchâtel that as a result of his efforts fifteen villages wanted a pastor.[26]

At Vitry, capital of the Perthois, the Protestants were led by Alain de Vassan the royal prosecutor, a member of an old mercantile family that was entering the nobility of the long, judicial, robe. He wrote at the end of August to ask the help of a prominent French nobleman resident in Switzerland, Antoine de Saussure, in obtaining a new minister. The Parisian church had recently sent Vitry a man, but he preached only on Sundays and Wednesdays, and spent the rest of the week preparing his sermons. Now my brethren, Vassan wrote,

want them daily, because they desire so much to be replete with this holy food (of which we had been deprived so long), that they ask nothing else. Also it is necessary that he go from house to house, making little exhortations, corrections, and remonstrances, which he cannot do. Moreover you know that in this place there are many learned men, who must be spoken to gravely and boldly when it will please God to give us full liberty to serve him publicly in a temple, where we fear our [present] minister would not be well received.

Calvin could not spare a man, so Saussure forwarded Vassan's letter to Farel at Neuchâtel. Vitry, he explained in a covering note, is the seat of a presidial court, which explains the concentration of men of learning. And Farel did send a minister, Pierre Clement, though whether he met Vassan's standards I cannot say.[27]

The fortress-like city of Vitry-le-François was named after the Renaissance king who had ordered its construction, to replace Vitry-en–Perthois which Charles V's army had burned in 1544.[28] Those people who preferred to rebuild the ruins of the old town were not well disposed toward the privileges of their new and favored competitor, nor were the residents of Châlons. On his accession Henry II, who was no friend to his father's memory, listened to the com-

26. *Ioannis Calvini opera*, XIX, 25 (6 Oct. 1561).
27. Vassan to Saussure, 31 Aug. 1561, in H. Dannreuther, "L'église de Vitry-le-François en août 1561, et les de Vassan," Société de l'histoire du protestantisme français: *Bulletin*, 40 (1891), 478–479; Saussure to Farel: *Ioannis Calvini opera*, XVIII, 713–715 (13 Sept. 1561); Gagnebin, "Le Protestantisme en Champagne au XVIe siècle," Société de l'histoire du protestantisme français: *Bulletin*, 12 (1863), 358, n. 1.
28. René Crozet, "Une ville neuve du XVIe siècle: Vitry-le-François," *La vie urbaine*, 5 (1923), 291–309.

plaints, and revoked the new Vitry's privileges. Its settlers nevertheless persevered, and in the years that followed made Vitry-le-François
into an important administrative center. The town was the seat of
one of the new presidial courts that Henry II established, as well as
of the bailiwick, transferred from Vitry-en-Perthois.

We may examine Vitry in the light of Provins, although no full
comparison between an exclusively Catholic source in the person of
Haton, and purely Reformed evidence, is possible. For what we
know about Vitry is not merely Vassan's letter, but the fact that the
Protestants found a home here that lasted, with interruptions, until
Louis XIV accomplished what the Guises had intended: the suppression of the Reform.[29] Neither Provins nor Vitry was a workshop
known for its artisans. The clerical flavor of Provins was nevertheless absent from Vitry, where the church was new and not over-
staffed. Law courts and legal personnel, by contrast, played a more
important part in town life here than at Provins, whose small bailiwick had been but recently carved out of the jurisdiction of Meaux.
The relative weight of rank-and-file clergy to the judiciary was, then,
an important difference. Now even though people like Haton were
inclined to suspect a Protestant head below every square bonnet,
and a Protestant heart beneath every long robe, only a significant
minority of the French judiciary, rather than the bench as a whole,
favored the Reform. This proportion was nevertheless one of the
new religion's important assets. Alleaume at Provins, whatever his
personal beliefs, balanced the staunchly Catholic president of the
presidial court Durand de Villegagnon.[30] We can infer the religious
complexion of some at least of the members of the legal profession
at Vitry from Vassan's call for a minister even more domineering
than his brethren in the faith, as well as from Saussure's covering remark on the court.

South of Vitry, in Humid Champagne, Wassy was the focal point
of Reformed activity. The town fronts the Blaise at the point where
the stream begins to cut a path through the king's forests that will
take it to the Marne. The farms in the valley and minerals in the

29. Georges Hérelle, *Documents inédits sur le protestantisme à Vitry-le-François* . . .
depuis la fin des guerres de religion jusqu'à la révolution française (3 vols., Paris,
1903–1908) .

30. Haton, *Mémoires*, I, 271–272. The president was a brother of the chevalier de
Villegagnon who led an expedition to Brazil. See *Dictionnaire de biographie française*,
s.v. "Durand de Villegagnon, Nicolas."

forest made Wassy prosperous. They account for the presence of enough notable, Reformed bourgeois to request the loan of a minister from Troyes. Jean Gravelle traveled the seventy-five kilometers in October 1561, and spent a week establishing, with some difficulty, "the best possible order."[31] The difficulty is easy to explain. Wassy was less than a fourth as far from Joinville as from Troyes, scarcely a half–day's ride away. It had been assigned by the crown to the dower that sustained Mary Stuart as the widow of Francis II. Guisard officers collected the royal revenues for her. The town was within the family's sphere of influence and along the line of their territorial advance. To flaunt the Reform here was to dance in front of the lion's lair.

In December, nevertheless, Gravelle was called back to perform baptisms at Wassy, where Bishop Jérôme Bourgeois of Châlons met him. Bourgeois had come on the request of the Guises to drive Gravelle away. The bishop confronted the minister during one of his sermons, but Gravelle took the opportunity to draw Bourgeois into debate, demanding to know why he did not preach. The bishop retorted that he preached through his vicars. When Gravelle went on to other subjects, Bourgeois instructed the royal provost at Wassy to furnish him with a written report of the incident, and stormed out. But threats did not daunt the Reformers of Wassy. Were they so convinced of the irresistible advance of true religion, which they could witness at Vitry and infer for Troyes, that they expected both the Roman religion and Guisard power to wither away? Gravelle celebrated the Eucharist on Christmas Day, before leaving for Troyes. Soon afterwards Wassy had its own minister, Leonard Morel.[32] In mid-winter the duke of Guise, returning to Paris from a conference in Lorraine with the duke of Württemberg, paused at Joinville. . . .

In Bishop Jérôme Bourgeois's own town of Châlons, the Reform was less dynamic than at Vitry or Wassy, though not so quiescent as at Reims. Pierre Fournelet the minister had initially been driven from the town. He returned from the Perthois as the summer of 1561 ended, at the same time, perhaps, that Calvin's lieutenant Théodore de Bèze was making his way to the Colloquy of Poissy.

31. Pithou, "Histoire ecclésiastique," f. 182. See also "Discours entier de la persécution et cruauté exercée en la ville de Vassy, par le duc de Guise, le 1 de mars 1562," *Mémoires de François de Lorraine*, p. 477.

32. Ibid., pp. 478–480; Noel Valois, "Vassy," Société de l'histoire de France: *Annuaire-Bulletin*, 50 (1913), 196–200; Pithou, "Histoire ecclésiastique," ff. 185–187.

Catherine had convoked this assembly of Reformed pastors and Catholic prelates in the hope of reaching a religious consensus. The knowledge that ministers were preaching openly at court greatly facilitated the work of their colleagues in the provinces. By harvest time Fournelet sent a report of guarded optimism to Neuchâtel.[33] At first he had experienced difficulty in "leading some of our people entirely to accept the yoke of Christ, after having rejected that of Antichrist." But he must have solved the problem to his satisfaction, for the local Protestants were as "benign, gracious, sweet, debonair, and tractable" as he had ever met, "and the most learned are the most humble." He could only wish equally docile congregations for the pastors of Neuchâtel. No wonder that the city fathers of Châlons spent so much time trying to induce the king to transfer the presidial court from Vitry; they thought that it would toughen the town's character. The Châlonnais Reformers had their own midwife and were baptizing their infants in the faith, as well as beginning to bury their dead and planning to celebrate the Lord's Supper. Fournelet's audience was growing steadily, from a dozen, to thirty, to a hundred . . . "to a recent secret service at night at which we were more than a thousand. I held forth for a good two hours and more, but no one budged." The barns of Châlons, from which grain was shipped down the Marne to Paris, may have been big, but not that big. The pastor's thoughts, as he wrote to his old associates, went back to the night that he held his largest audience spellbound. He saw them all again, the Reformed leaders up front, the novices, the curious, and the spies. Perhaps there really were a thousand — but then his moving pen returned him to the difficulties of his ministry. He and his followers still had to exercise caution, in order to avoid a further riot. Their fears, in October, continued to run high. By the end of the month Leonard Morel had joined Fournelet, but he would soon move on to Wassy.[34]

Six months later, in the spring of 1562, the duke of Guise passed through Châlons, and later informed Parlement that of the seven or eight thousand people in town, the religion of only nine- or ten-score had been "ruined." They however held "a knife at the throat

33. *Ioannis Calvini opera,* XIX, 23–27 (6 Oct. 1561).
34. Pithou, "Histoire ecclésiastique," f. 183v, states that Morel of Châlons preached at Troyes on 1 Nov.

of the others, by the connivance of some royal officers."[35] This was another way of saying that the new edict which tolerated Reformed worship outside city walls was being respected, and plain-speaking friars reproved. The duke's figures must have come from the episcopal palace. The total population of Châlons had passed the mark of nine thousand as early as 1517, but the figures for the Reformers do seem acceptable. Some may style them impressionistic, a term that denotes the attempt to capture a swiftly changing landscape by the juxtaposition of rapid brush-strokes of pure color. Taken together, Guise's vivid report to Parlement and Fournelet's hotly imaginative calculations picture Châlons as a city whose bishop felt the loss of two hundred souls and whose minister dreamt of a thousand. A study that deals in appearances rather than truths cannot risk further precision. Too many people declined to declare themselves. From the viewpoint of the committed, they were the kind "that swam between two waters, that were neither yet entirely heretical, nor perfectly Catholic." [36] The reader may perhaps recognize the tone of our man in Provins. Haton was surely quoting a preacher's variant of "How long halt ye between two opinions?" Elijah's question to the people of Israel as he confronted the prophets of Baal. The truths of 1561 were theological rather than typological. Claude Haton knew better than Pierre Fournelet how hard it was that year to yoke the hesitant and the stubborn to either religion.

Châlons-sur-Marne was a military staging-ground for the northeastern front, a center for the distribution of food and other commodities, and a town of some small handicrafts. There were too few of the proud lawyers of Vitry, too few of the boisterous artisans of Troyes, to make the Reform a real threat to the stability and security of the established church. By the beginning of 1562 the episcopal officials who took their cue from Reims, and the royal officers who followed the zigs and zags of crown policy, were working at cross purposes, without however coming into direct conflict with one another. The Protestants after early difficulties had planted their church. In future they would be endured, at least as individuals, and to a degree even accepted by Catholics in town. If France had

35. "Discours faits dans le parlement de Paris par le duc de Guyse et le connestable de Montmorency, sur l'enregistrement de la déclaration du 11 avril 1562, sur le tumulte de Vassy, et sur ce qui arrivé depuis." *Mémoires de François de Lorraine*, p. 490.

36. Haton, *Mémoires*, I, 152.

been Châlons writ large, perhaps civil war would not have begun. But the kingdom also included towns like Troyes, which enjoyed too much character. As well as its artisans, the "capital of Champagne" had screeching friars, a new Guisard bailiff, an iconoclastic bishop, an untried and undeclared provincial governor, and a lay leader of the Reform whose courage had risen to the level of his faith by the time war broke out.

Towards the end of Henry II's reign, Nicolas Pithou tells us, virtually all the affairs of the local Reformers rested on his shoulders. We may therefore ascribe a good measure of their caution to him. First, in 1557, Michel Poncelet was asked to leave. Then the church leaders enforced a rural sanctuary on Gerard de Corlieu, the regular minister who succeeded Poncelet at the beginning of 1559. While Corlieu was in hiding, Pithou fell critically ill. He tormented himself with the fear of damnation that must also have been on his mind when he was well. Corlieu, who either had returned by this time to Troyes or else slipped in to see him, convinced Pithou that his soul was not necessarily lost. The sick man recovered, and decided that he would go to Geneva in order not to pollute himself any more. His convalescence must have been slow, for he did not leave until high spring of 1560, as we know because others began to clamor for his position as town lawyer.[37] In the interval, Corlieu tightened church discipline. He had deacons elected, and increased the number of the surveillants. Their duties included watching out for scandals, distributing alms, and counseling the church. Those earlier surveillants who continued to pollute themselves with "papal superstitions and abuses" were dismissed. We can infer something of what the church expected of members from its instructions to an apothecary to stop furnishing the candles for offerings at Saint Pantaleon's. Suddenly, however, Corlieu was arrested. The lieutenant for criminal affairs entered his lodgings while hunting a thief, and discovered a minister. Corlieu was sentenced to be drawn on a hurdle to the gallows, where he would be hanged and his body burned. He appealed, and was sent under guard to Parlement. But the underground network of the Reformers was efficient, and their movement through wooded areas unimpeded. Outside the capital, in the valley

---

37. Pithou, "Histoire ecclésiastique," ff. 131v–133. He attended the town-council meeting of 16 April 1560, but by 11 June his absence was noted (AC, Troyes, A 12, f. 283v; A 13, ff. 14–16).

of Gros Bois, eight masked men stopped the carriage conveying the minister and set him free, to resume his vocation in Paris.[38]

The Troyen leaders remained prudent. Their new minister, named Paumier, who had been born in Béarn and had previously served at Caen, arrived in March 1560, right after the Conspiracy of Amboise. He was told to stay put in his rooms. Paumier finally managed to hold an "exhortation" in a house in the fields belonging to a Protestant merchant. But the bailiff, Anne de Vaudrey, seigneur of Saint-Phal, surprised the meeting and arrested everyone present. The religious amnesty that followed the conspiracy enabled most of them to be released. Paumier himself was transferred to the episcopal prison, from which a band of men freed him in November.[39]

While he waited in prison, Troyes prepared for the Estates General. Town and crown officials, clerical dignitaries, and guild leaders met in mid-October to nominate representatives to an assembly of the three estates of the entire bailiwick, which would name the actual delegates. The joiners, the surgeons, who were skilled craftsmen rather than physicians, and the guild of gunsmiths, swordsmiths, cutlers, and scabbard-makers all voted for Jacques Menisson the Protestant anobli. Menisson's leanings, if not his convictions, were well known. Their other choices included Bishop Caracciolo and President Jean de Mesgriny of the presidial court, certainly one of the judges whom the friars were condemning for laxity against the heretics. The locksmiths supported these same men, save for Menisson. The other guilds, however, supported Guisard Catholics like the merchant Pierre Belin.[40] Even among the artisans, the Protestants were far from dominant.

On Middle Street at least they were in a comfortable majority. Every day the residents passed a house with a Pietà in a niche on its outside wall. The statue faced an alley off the street. It was clothed in silk, honored by a lamp that burned before it on Sundays, and

38. Pithou, "Histoire ecclésiastique," ff. 143–149, 170, 174v.

39. Ibid., ff. 159–163, 167v–168.

40. Documents inédits tirés des archives de Troyes et relatifs aux Etats-généraux. Ed. T. Boutiot. Collection de documents inédits relatifs à la ville de Troyes et à la Champagne méridionale publiés par la Société académique de l'Aube, I (Troyes, 1878), 28–42. The delegates named, all good Catholics, were, for the clergy, Dean Yves Le Tartier of Saint Stephen's and Archdeacon Anthoine Perricard of the cathedral; for the nobility, the bailiff and Fery de Nicey; for the third estate, Belin and Mayor Denis Clérey. In August 1562 Mesgriny was incorrectly accused of attending Reformed prayer meetings (Pithou, "Histoire ecclésiastique," f. 235).

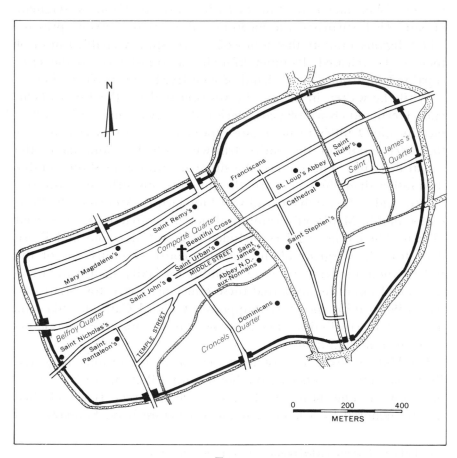

Troyes

venerated in the neighborhood — which suggests how close Catholic and Protestant groups stood to one another on the urban checkerboard. One summer Sunday night in 1561, some Protestants hung a stinking cat from the Virgin's head, and covered her body with mud and manure. The affront warranted a general procession, which broke up in confusion after leaving the Pietà for the cathedral, because of the marchers' fear that they might be attacked by the Middle Street artisans, who for their part were trembling behind closed doors.[41]

Nicolas Pithou called the vandals crack-brained ("estourdis"), a common epithet of Protestant apologists for those who would not observe Reformed discipline.[42] But calculated insult was becoming central rather than incidental to the movement. Claude Haton sedulously collected reports of abusive words and acts, from calling the Host "John White" (*Jehan le Blanc*) to greasing one's boots with holy oil. A dispassionate if not disinterested observer, the traveler, courtier, diplomat, and soldier Michel de Castelnau also noted the sting of French Calvinism. Castelnau judged religions by how well they justified the social order. He wrote, with reference to 1560, that since the learned and clever ministers had been driven out or executed, most of the remainder were "poor fellows, ignorant and uncouth." They "ordinarily began their sermons," two years later after the Edict of January officially recognized the Reform, "against the abuses of the church, which no prudent Catholic would want to defend. But from there they generally entered into invectives." These comments must of course be sifted. While the ministers were speaking most freely, in the year that began with the summer of 1561, Castelnau was in Scotland with Mary Stuart. When he wrote his memoirs years later he was under the spell of Elizabeth of England and therefore partial to proper, docile sermons. The ministers were neither uncouth nor of low estate. Of those whose condition Robert Kingdon could identify, some were nobles, most bourgeois, and only a few artisans.[43] Castelnau was echoing royal propaganda, which in 1560 characterized most of them "as mechanics and of no

41. Ibid., ff. 168–169. Pithou, however, incorrectly remembered the incident as having taken place in 1560. Cf. AD, Aube, G 1284, f. 462v (20 Aug. 1561).

42. Pithou, "Histoire ecclésiastique," f. 168v. Cf. *Histoire ecclésiastique,* ed. Baum and Cunitz, II, 440.

43. Haton, *Mémoires,* I, 150; Castelnau, *Mémoires,* pp. 70, 75; *Dictionnaire de biographie française,* s.v. "Castelnau-Mauvissière, Michel de"; Kingdon, *Geneva and the Coming of the Wars of Religion,* pp. 5–8.

literature," an anachronistic reference, by now, to men like Michel
Poncelet.[44] What nevertheless may be believed is that many of the
ministers were not the suave, accommodating types that Castelnau
would have preferred as religious adversaries. Instead of calm, cere-
bral sermons they delivered cut-and-thrust attacks on Roman Catholicism. A letter that the minister Corlieu wrote in 1560 from Paris
to his former Troyen congregation suggests the tone of his sermons,
while it evokes their as yet hesitant attitude, which would change
within the year. He begins by lashing them into repentance. As their
pastor he had been too soft and pliant, when God commanded him
full rigor and severity. He had nevertheless told the Troyens to
"avoid flattering yourselves, and lulling yourselves in your vices, in
accordance with the tendency of your perverse natures." Remember
that the Lord condemns principally those who are neither hot nor
cold, but lukewarm. Having been this harsh toward his own, he was
consistent in showing the other religion no quarter. "Look, then,
that is if you have eyes, and see this great idol swaying and falling,
see our enemy who sighs, close to his death — and you don't want to
put your hand to it. And he will fall then without you, you whom
the Lord has reserved for these times, to destroy and win victory
over those who rose against his Christ. You don't want to give back
to the devil, to the son of perdition, the evil he has done you?"[45]

Corlieu's tone was eager as well as acid. One side of the Reform
was an explosive gaiety, which is perhaps best captured in the joyous
psalm-singing. The French Calvinists were capable of laughter, principally at their opponents. They regarded those who continued to
practice the old religion as ridiculous, because they prayed to hu-
mans, believed in the halfway house of purgatory, and worshipped
a flour-God.[46] Raucously or sardonically, and as often as not scato-
logically, the Reformers intended to laugh Roman Catholicism to
its death.

Catholics were not pleased to be the object of other people's scorn.
But they also had deeper, less circumstantial reasons for coldness to
the Reform. The final profession of faith of the Protestant solicitor

---

44. Isambert, *Recueil*, XIV, pt. 1, no. 22, p. 22 (Edict of Amboise) .
45. Pithou, "Histoire ecclésiastique," ff. 152–159.
46. For the Protestant contention that Catholics worshipped "un morceau de paste,"
see ibid., f. 312v; or analogously, "ce vain dieu de paste," *Le chansonnier huguenot du
XVIe siècle,* ed. Henri-Léonard Bordier (Paris, 1870) , pp. 97–99, quoting a song dated
1532.

Pierre Clement may suggest why so many people responded to the new religion with mortal hatred, and most remained deaf to its appeal. Clement was hanged at Troyes in 1562. His last words were " 'Lord, you know that I die not for a murder or other crime, but for having sustained your quarrel.' To which some Catholics responded, in blasphemy, '(Damn), does God have quarrels?' "[47] Reformers like Clement saw the quarrel as a struggle for purity of doctrine, and for a church that would preach and defend that doctrine, while it administered the sacraments that made a Christian life possible. But the spectators around the scaffold who answered Clement back considered the very idea of a divine quarrel repugnant. God's purpose was to promote unity among his people, and to enable them to aid one another in the quest for the good things of this world and a place in the next, not to split them into two by raising up a faction that claimed a monopoly of religious truth.

The word "religion," in sixteenth-century Catholic parlance, was a synonym for devotion. It meant the honor and respect paid to God, the Virgin, and the saints, or else the estate of the regular clergy, who were devout by profession. Too much as well as too little devotion could expose a lay person to public comment. To the Protestants, however, religion meant belief rather than practice. It was a qualitative term: either one had it or one didn't. They referred to themselves as being "of the religion," and left everyone else to the devil. Such a position must have seemed, to people comfortable with the older ways, not an alternative to their present beliefs but a negation of any creed at all.[48] The official royal term for Calvinism was "the so-called Reformed religion"; a notary from Dauphiné in the southeast shortened the formula to "the so-called religion." [49] Its adherents formed a faction that generated confusion

47. Pithou, "Histoire ecclésiastique," f. 250; see also *Histoire ecclésiastique*, ed. Baum and Cunitz, II, 471. Pithou crossed out "mort Dieu" in his manuscript, probably in the interests of divine honor rather than of historical precision. The French *querelle* and the English quarrel then meant, at one and the same time, a complaint in search of redress, a cause, and a dispute. Another reference to the Protestants' *querelle de Dieu* occurs in Bruslart, "Journal," I, 69. It is true that the duke of Guise also considered himself a fighter for the *querelle de Dieu*. See Regnier de La Planche, *Histoire de l'estat de France*, p. 116, and *Mémoires de François de Lorraine*, p. 517. Guise was however refuting the charge that he was pursuing his private, political quarrel. See Castelnau, *Mémoires*, p. 125.

48. Pierre Imbart de la Tour, *Les origines de la Réforme* (4 vols., Paris, 1904–1935), III, 424, points out that Catholics looked on the Reformers as nihilists.

49. See *Mémoires de Eustache Piémond, notaire royal-delphinal en la ville de St.-Antoine en Dauphiné (1572–1608)*, ed. J. Brun-Durand (Valence, 1885), p. 50,

and promoted conflict. They, rather than the Catholics, were led by the father of discord, the devil. Here was a further reason to conflate witchcraft and heresy.

Royal display, if not royal policy, reinvigorated the meaning of devotion. On Corpus Christi Day of 1561 Charles IX participated in a "particularly solemn" procession at the Abbey of Saint-Germain-des-Prés, where he was lodging. Not merely the queen mother but Antoine de Bourbon and Coligny's brother the cardinal of Châtillon joined him. The gentlemen of the royal guard, torches in hand, conducted them. In addition, as Canon Pierre Bruslart of Notre-Dame tells us, "several of the princes and great lords were distributed among the parishes of the city, and attended the processions to show a good example to the people of Paris." On the octave, the royal procession was "yet more excellent and devout." The cardinal of Lorraine carried the Host, and sang high mass at the abbey.[50] He may also have been responsible for distributing the lords around town. Catholic festivals were becoming self-conscious, a defense and illustration of both institutional resilience and enduring truth. The cardinal was one of the early directors of Counter-Reformation theatre.

Corpus Christi became the crucial moment of the year for the public expression of religious preference, since the Protestants regarded it as the most abominable holiday of all. In 1560 Corlieu convinced the man with whom he lodged to leave Troyes for the day, despite the dangers. The marchers talked of pillage as they passed the one house that had no hangings to honor the procession, but did not carry out the threat. A year later, while the king and his entourage were marching from Saint-Germain, someone on a street in Lyons tried to seize the Host from a priest. Catholics countered by attacking all whom they suspected of heresy.[51] A festival that was intended to symbolize the search for social cohesion now manifested

---

which relates to the later 1570s. But since he was born in 1550, Piémond was old enough in 1561 to have begun to learn his insults.

50. Bruslart, "Journal," p. 39, and Jean Lafosse, *Journal d'un curé ligueur de Paris sous les trois derniers Valois*, . . . , ed. E. de Barthélemy (Paris, [1886]), p. 43.

51. Pithou, "Histoire ecclésiastique," ff. 124v–125r, calls Corpus Christi "the greatest idolatry," and tells the story of Corlieu's landlord; see also Antoine Péricaud, *Notes et documents pour servir à l'histoire de Lyon . . . 1560–1574* (Lyons, 1842), pp. 3–4, and Natalie Davis, "Missed Connections: *Religion and Regime*," *Journal of Interdisciplinary History*, 1 (1971), 386.

the disarray within the community. Devout Catholics could not help but experience an affront.

But suppose that we take one short step along the path of doubt and ask ourselves, as someone whose loyalty was wavering might have, whether God could really have a quarrel with the Roman Catholic church. If so, how would he act? Why, in the way that he always had acted — by creating a saint, at least one saint, to purify the church. The saint would prove his mission the way that saints do, by performing miracles. Reformers who portrayed all mankind as steeped in sin could not possibly be saints, and in any event they had no miracles to their credit. Bèze spoke to the problem at the Colloquy of Poissy. He denied that miracles were necessary to confirm ministers who were not of the established church, and went on to argue that the change in behavior of the converts and the fact that men who had burned Reformers during the past year had adopted the religion in this one were miracles enough. What sophistry! The sick, the lame, the people possessed by the devil provided a heaven-sent opportunity for Calvin or Bèze to show who was behind their mission. The bourgeois of Paris who kept a diary from 1515 to 1536 was not the only man of his time to live in a world in which it was easier for a miracle to occur than, say, for the countryside to be cleared of brigands.

At Troyes, for example, the Beautiful Cross twice recovered the curative powers that it had enjoyed in 1500. Around 1530 the Cross was again suddenly frequented by a mob of people, who gathered before it and remained day and night, imploring renewed health. Even Nicolas Pithou was troubled as he remembered what he had heard about the results. For among those who claimed to have benefited from the miracles was a deaf and dumb man who did odd jobs for a monastery near Troyes. The abbot had brought him to town so that he might be cured. After the customary nine days of waiting the man suddenly rose and seized the Cross, crying out something that sounded like "Jesus" to those near him. Then he gradually learned to speak. Some time previously a group of people who believed that the fellow was shamming had shot off a gun at his ear, but he did not budge. Several prominent Catholics nevertheless suspected the abbot of staging the miracle. Pithou rules out this possibility, arguing that the abbot had no motive since he did not receive any of the offerings made by the worshippers. Perhaps, Pithou speculates, the man was not physically handicapped, but rather possessed by an evil spirit from which Satan released him at the Beautiful Cross. The histories of the ancients recount similar happenings in pagan temples, for God permits Satan to seduce idolatrous men. Whatever its cause, Pithou concludes, the incident enhanced the prestige of the Cross. When miracles began to occur once more in 1561 Pithou had no difficulty in suggesting an explanation. He detected a scheme by priests who were eager to counter Protestant gains. They hired a whitewasher to come by night and bleach the pillars that held up the Cross. Catholic Troyens who duly believed in a miraculous transformation flocked around to pray for an end to their ills. The good word spread at least as far as Provins, where Claude Haton could see that God had convincingly refuted the Protestants.[52]

Not everyone needed miracles to sustain or change his convictions. The devotion of many Catholics to the saints, after all, was decreasing. But many a man sheds old habits and allegiances slowly, without regrets or hard feelings, firmly convinced that he is what he always was. That man does not take kindly to someone who flaunts the change, throwing out the old ways like a pair of worn-out shoes. Catholics who did not expect church reformers to be saints could easily have shrunk back when pastors and other proponents of the Reform acted as if they intended to turn the traditional standards of sainthood, which Saint Francis had set early in the thirteenth century, upside down. First among the standards was humility. Perhaps the cardinal sin of the Reformers was a self-assurance that led as often as not to arrogance. Pithou eulogized François Bourgoin, who served as pastor to the Reformed churches of Chaumont and then Troyes, as a "most excellent minister, well versed in holy writ, as eloquent as possible, of a very good judgment, and well suited to the consistory: harsh to the obstinate and the stiff necked, but sweet and humane to the humble and the meek in heart—in short the kind of person needed for this church, in which there were sometimes more Champagne heads [stubborn people] than one would have

52. *Histoire ecclésiastique*, I, 644; *Journal d'un bourgeois de Paris sous le règne de François Premier,* ed. V.-L. Bourrilly (Paris, 1910), pp. 60, 147, 232, 294, and 346; Pithou, "Histoire ecclésiastique," ff. 30–32v, 172v–177; AC, Troyes, A 13, f. 88 (16 June 1561); Haton, *Mémoires,* I, 196–197.

wanted. He knew most often how to bend some of them, and to align them with reason, according to the Word of God." [53]

The saints taught mainly by example — by doing — rather than by precept; the Reformers began with a new doctrine, which alone led to a new way of life. Sobriety was expected as the pattern for that life, although of course Protestants did not always live up to it. Even the best behaved were not necessarily ascetics, or even prudes. Nicolas Pithou tells a lewd story or two in the course of his "History" with as much gusto as the next man. But his standards of propriety were high, and his threshold of tolerance when faced with the foibles of others exceedingly low. If a sobriquet is any indication of deportment, then men like the mason Guillaume sans Rire must have been a standing affront to the expressionists among the Catholics, who regarded religion as an occasion for the display of emotions.[54] In some cases, the older religious forms that appealed to such Catholics no longer enjoyed institutional support. But they could be revived by people who still remembered them. When the peasants marched to the cities of Champagne in 1556, they galvanized townspeople into activities that included representations of scenes from the Passion. One impromptu performance took place in Troyes, and another elsewhere in the province.[55] Pithou regarded the plays as an ungodly farce, but the actors and other spectators considered them a means of reaching the Lord so that he might send them desperately needed rain. The contrast in attitudes and behavior was sharp.

Thus far we have considered the type of person whose blood the Reform, as it was preached and practiced in Champagne, made boil. No one can say how numerous they may have been. Fewer, perhaps, than those who were not preoccupied, or even very much concerned, with religion, and who for that reason were cold to any challenge to the survival of Catholicism. In 1563, after the first war had ended, the Troyen town council sought to block the re-formation of

53. Pithou, "Histoire ecclésiastique," f. 324. See also Emile and Eugène Haag, *La France protestante,* s.v. "Bourgoin, François."

54. Pithou, *"Histoire ecclésiastique,"* the stories (ff. 26, 42v–45v), and the sobriquet (f. 251). It was not applied to him by Protestants alone, nor did it become current only with the coming of the Reform, for in 1536 Saint Pantaleon's Church paid "Guillaume sans rire, mason" for his labor (AD, Aube, 19G 9, f. 75).

55. Pithou, "Histoire ecclésiastique," ff. 88–90v.

the local Protestant church. It sent two notaries from door to door,
to ask householders whether they would support a request that the
royal council refuse permission for prayer meetings. Lyebault Lye,
a cobbler, after condemning the Huguenots and their services, volunteered that "there are enough other churches" already. The notaries also polled the widow Borincard, a domestic, and recorded
that "as for the prayer meetings, she leaves them up to God, the
king, and the world, because she can't understand them at all."
Some sophisticated Frenchmen expressed equal bewilderment. During the reign of Francis II, the Guisard Gilles Bourdin, prosecutor-
general at Parlement, was heard to offer unsolicited and unwelcome
advice to the authors of certain anonymous but obviously Protestant memoranda on religion and politics. "These fools," he said,
"had marvelously good arguments, which however are badly applied, and it was a pity that they didn't employ their talents elsewhere than in these contentious reveries of religion." Michel de
Castelnau, who expressed his opinions as historical maxims, affirmed
that since dispute necessarily engenders doubt, it is a signal fault
"to doubt Religion, of which we must be entirely assured. All heresies are but the result of excessively curious disputes on the Christian religion." Castelnau objected to the Reform because it raised
political issues, Bourdin because it obscured them. Both could ask,
together with our Troyens, how an institution like the Roman
Catholic church, which had lasted so long, could suddenly be proven
so wrong. This was the major question that Bèze had to face at
Poissy, one much more important than the matter of miracles.[56]

Castelnau was right to insist on the political implications of religious novelty, since to challenge the church was to oppose the
crown. Until a Bourbon became ruler of France, none of the Most
Christian kings of the period ever considered abandoning a partnership that may have turned somewhat querulous and occasionally
even stormy in the past few hundred years, but all things considered
had paid handsome dividends, especially to the junior partner. For
four decades before the great majority of Frenchmen learned of the
Reform firsthand they had been taught by the state that the new

56. AC, Troyes, BB 14, first *liasse* (troubles civils et religieux, 1540–1565), no. 24,
ff. 17v, 53v. Regnier de La Planche (*Histoire de l'estat de France*, pp. 34–35) relates
Bourdin's remark. See also *Dictionnaire de biographie française*, s.v. "Bourdin, Gilles";
Castelnau, *Mémoirs*, p. 73; *Histoire ecclésiastique*, ed. Baum and Cunitz, I, 619–639,
for Poissy.

doctrines were subversive, as well as by the church that they were evil. Most adults around 1560 had been born into a growing climate of suspicion, hatred, and perhaps even fear of Protestantism. Even after the crown conceded a measure of grudging toleration to the Reform, it took considerable effort to shake these habits of thought.

In Europe as a whole, a reformation against the will of the established political authority was successful only when the government itself was alien to the people, so that an intense political issue, hatred of the foreigner, became interwoven with the religious question, as in Hussite Bohemia and the Netherlands of Philip II. In German Central Europe religion became food for xenophobia, since a good deal of anti-Catholic feeling centered on Italian domination of the church. In Champagne, which was as French as the Ile-de-France, no deep currents of antagonism flowed through the rivers toward Paris. The only political threat *per se* came from those stock figures in French history, malcontent nobles and their network of clients, which extended down to the rag-and-tatter squires who re-emerged during the wars as Protestant zealots, partisans of the prince of Condé, or Catholic zealots, adherents of the duke of Guise.

During 1561, nevertheless, the dynamism of French Protestantism was more apparent than the limitations to its appeal. The cardinal of Lorraine, well aware of the Reform's progress, supported the idea of a colloquy among theologians of different persuasions. Whether he genuinely wanted to negotiate, or rather sought to isolate the Calvinists by publicizing their differences with Lutheranism, remains an open question.[57] There was in any event no confluence of ideas at Poissy, in August and September, despite the attempt of a few participants to further the queen mother's plans for a settlement. Caracciolo was one of her supporters. Characteristically, he called attention to himself by remarking to his fellow prelates that the authority of priests equalled their own.[58]

The bishop of Troyes, for whom wishful thinking was no novelty,

57. After a searching examination Donald Nugent (*Ecumenism in the Age of the Reformation: The Colloquy of Poissy* [Cambridge, Mass., 1974], ch. 8) awards Lorraine a "grey innocence" for his sincerity.

58. *Diario dell'assemblea de' vescovi à Poissy*, ed. Joseph Roserot de Melin. "Etude sur les relations du Saint-Siège et l'église de France dans la seconde moitié du XVIe siècle: I. Rome et Poissy (1560–1561)," *Ecole française de Rome, Mélanges d'archéologie et d'histoire*, 39 (1921–1922), p. 108.

decided that the time had come when he could reconcile his conscience and his estate. He asked Catherine in September whether he
could put the bishropic in royal hands, "as for the spiritual," and
keep the temporal for himself. She replied that he was always welcome to resign. He turned next to the Reformed Church of Troyes,
and with due apologies for his previous faults, asked to be received
as a minister . . . and confirmed as bishop.[59]

Almost all the lay leaders of the church were delighted by Caracciolo's request, which must have struck them as the crowning success
to a brilliant year. In January 1561, a month after Francis II's death,
they had received a new minister from Paris, as a successor to Paumier. Jean Gravelle, called Du Pin, a native of Dreux in Normandy,
soon resumed the prayer meetings, which were held "more boldly
than before." In time the Protestants dared to assemble openly.
They gathered in the churchyard of Saint Pantaleon's one evening
in May to hear Gravelle preach, and again on the following Sunday
night in Temple Street. A thoroughfare of the upper town, this was
the residence of the wealthiest among them, men like the merchant
Robert Le Bé and the former alderman who had recently returned
from Geneva, Anthoine de Saint-Aubin. Warned that Saint-Phal the
bailiff hoped to attack them, they barricaded the entrances to the
street and organized a protective guard. Unable to destroy the whole
assembly, Saint-Phal lay in wait in the cloister of Saint Stephen's
Church for the "rather good number" of worshippers who marched
back after services to their homes in the cité. His ambush was foiled,
however, when Daniel Coulon, the rock-throwing rotisseur and ha-
bitué of confraternities, forced them to change route.[60] Pithou's urban
geography, if not necessarily his cloak-and-dagger story, inspires full
confidence. The Protestants were strongest in the workshops and
residential areas of the upper town, as exemplified by Middle Street
in Saint John's parish and Temple Street in Saint Pantaleon's,
where eight years earlier Pierre Pithou the elder had gone to confraternity. They were less well established in the cité, although far
from absent even there.

59. Roserot de Melin, *Antonio Caracciolo*, pp. 287–292; Noel Valois, "Les essais de
conciliation religieuse au début du règne de Charles IX," *Revue d'histoire de l'église
de France*, 31 (1945), 258–259; Pithou, "Histoire ecclésiastique." f. 179, for the approaches to Catherine and the consistory.
60. Ibid., ff. 171–172v, 179.

Gravelle was sufficiently encouraged to ask Bèze for a co-worker.[61] The Genevan ministers forwarded his request to Neuchâtel, which lent Troyes Jacques Sorel, a native of Sézanne, for six months. When he arrived during the course of the summer, Sorel was immediately sent out to evangelize in the neighboring countryside. His presence also encouraged the Troyens to complete the organization of their church by adding a council of twelve elders, which met when necessary to make all the important decisions, and a consistory composed of the twelve surveillants and the ministers. In Genevan practice the authority that Troyes entrusted to the council was exercised by the state, and it was the elders and ministers who made up the consistory. But in Troyes the state was no friend, and the notables intended to keep church affairs, which were matters of life and property as well, tightly in their own hands. So no ministers sat on the council.

By mid-October, while Caracciolo's candidacy for the ministry was pending, attendance at services numbered from four to five hundred people, at least by Sorel's count. The meetings took place "in a very ample and spacious" rented barn, as Pithou, who by this time had returned from Geneva, tells us. We are, Sorel informed Neuchâtel, more than a thousand in all. "The priests, who are in great number, and the papists, scarcely know where they are." In a companion letter to Calvin he acknowledged that in addition to the open meetings on Sundays and holiday mornings and evenings, secret services were held on other days after dark, "because there are still plenty of fearful people, as are some of the rich, who don't dare go there openly, being too weak." Sorel asked Neuchâtel to allow him to remain permanently at Troyes, even though he and Gravelle had been joined by Pierre Le Roy, a former Carmelite friar whom Geneva had sent to Dijon. Le Roy had been forced to move on after a disturbance during a baptism. With three ministers, Sorel noted, it was possible for one to be in the countryside at all times.[62] If Caracciolo were accepted they would be four, but the ministers were not delighted by the prospect of the bishop as a colleague. Le

61. *Ioannis Calvini opera*, XIX, 425–426 (29 May 1561). The editors place Gravelle's letter, which is undated as to the year, in 1562, but the text refers to his recent arrival and requests a second minister. Troyes already had Sorel in 1562.

62. Sorel to Calvin and to Neuchâtel, ibid., 49–53 (13 Oct. 1561); Pithou, "Histoire ecclésiastique," ff. 177v, 183v.

Roy held forth against Caracciolo in his sermons, only to be told on one occasion that "he wanted to be wiser than the whole consistory," and to keep to his text without digressing.

Nicolas Pithou said out loud what Sorel was thinking, at a meeting of the consistory and other notable people of the church. Pithou based his case on Caracciolo's immoral life, inconstancy, and continued singing of the Mass. Above all he stressed the bishop's betrayal at the sermon at Saint John's in 1551, which he would never forget. This last argument could not have swayed most of the others at the meeting, since at the time they still were Catholics. The solicitor Pierre Clement replied that stringent standards were all very well at Geneva, but that things were done differently in France. "Would it please God," sighed Pithou, "that everything went as well in all the churches in France as they are going in several places, and in Geneva." But the man who had tasted exile proved to be more rigid than the ministers in Switzerland. Peter Martyr of Zurich, who stopped by Troyes on his return from Poissy, pointed out that Saint Peter too had abjured. When Calvin was asked for advice he addressed himself to the general issues. A bishop who converted and had the necessary qualities could be received as a minister, provided that he renounced the priesthood and stopped saying Mass. If he insisted he could keep his temporalities, since the times were so confused, but a man to whom the revenue and authority meant so much would do better to act as a protector rather than a minister of the church.[63] With this qualified approval, Caracciolo began his new career on November 16, by preaching for the first time in a decade, at his own residence. He announced a second sermon for the 23rd at Saint John's, but the mayor and clergy convinced the young duke of Nevers, who had just made his formal entry into the town as governor, to cancel it. Next day, nevertheless, the bishop attended a service in the Protestants' barn.[64]

63. Ibid., ff. 178v–183v; Roserot de Melin, *Antonio Caracciolo*, pt. 3, ch. 4; Peter Martyr to Bèze: *Ioannis Calvini opera*, XIX, 100–102 (6 Nov. 1561); Jean Calvin, "Pour les évesques et curéz de la papaulté," ibid., X, 184–187. For a guarded comment of Sorel on the bishop, in a letter to Calvin: ibid., pp. 182–183 (16 Dec.). Nicolas Camusat, *Promptuarium sacrarum antiquitatum Tricassinae dioecesis* (Troyes, 1610), ff. 250–251, transmits a rather indulgent if necessarily critical account of the bishop's actions in 1561, by Dean of the Cathedral Guillaume de Taix.

64. Pithou, "Histoire ecclésiastique," ff. 184v–185; Louis, cardinal-archbishop of Sens, another of the Guisard brothers (30 Nov. 1561), and the lieutenant-general of the bailiwick Coiffart (26 Nov.), to the cathedral chapter: AD, Aube, G 2553.

The church leaders, meanwhile, had taken steps to create a second generation of ministers, of local origin, and thus avoid depending on Paris, Geneva, and former Catholic clergy. They used the Saint Martin's Day holiday, November 11, to hold theological exercises which would help train men for the cloth. The physician Jacques Douynet and the attorney Claude Girardin, both old-timers in the cause, participated, no doubt to initiate the program and set an example for others rather than to become ministers themselves.[65]

By the time that the crown, three weeks into 1562, issued its edict tolerating Reformed worship outside city walls, churches had been established (if we move counterclockwise from the southwest) in the town of Chaumont, as well as at Wassy and Vitry; in the market village of Heiltz-le-Maurupt and the village of Bettancourt, both in the Perthois; in Epense and Le-Vieil-Dampierre, slightly to the north of Bettancourt, bordering the Argonne Forest; and in Voncq, on the upper Aisne River, north of the forest. There were churches, too, in Châlons, Loisy, Sézanne, Céant and neighboring Villemoiron, a Piédefer property, Troyes, and Bar-sur-Seine, whose bailiff and lieutenant were of the faith.[66] Reims was conspicuous by its absence.

While the Reformers in Champagne grew bolder, and the timid and the indifferent waited on events, fervent Catholics had to be more patient, as Claude Haton complained, than sheep at the butcher's. Leaving aside the bathos, his picture of people who found it increasingly difficult to contain their passion rings true. The people knew, even if the queen mother and her advisers did not, that their churches, their statues, and their saints would have to be avenged. And the voice of the people, as Haton liked to say later in life, is sometimes the voice of God.[67]

A self-righteous minority, tasting what it took to be the first fruits of victory, had created an angry, threatened multitude, which called itself, with some plausibility, the majority, and in any event had first claim on those who would have preferred to sit out the struggle. The two sides eyed each other during the winter of 1561–62. On the last day of February, the duke of Guise set out from Joinville for Paris. Next day he entered Wassy, to find the Protestants violating the recent edict of toleration by holding a service in a barn within

65. Pithou, "Histoire ecclésiastique," ff, 183v–184.
66. Mours, "Liste des églises réformées," pp. 52–54, 59, 129–130. On the lieutenant of Bar, see Bruslart, "Journal," p. 89.
67. Haton, *Mémoires*, I, 183, and ibid., II, 993, for one example of the homely wisdom.

the town. Thus provoked, his men charged the barn, and initiated religious war.

Protestants condemned the killings as a massacre, and politic Catholics deplored them as a misfortune. These reactions only redoubled the exhilaration of Catholic militants, who greeted Guise when he arrived at Paris as if he were a king.[68] Condé soon found it necessary to withdraw from the capital. He failed in retreat to take custody of Charles IX and Catherine at Fontainebleau. Without them he was constrained to announce as his war aims the liberation rather than the protection of the royal family, together with the defense of the royal edicts. The king of France and his capital remained in Catholic hands, but Protestants gained control of Rouen and Lyons, as well as important cities in the south. Their power was most concentrated along a rough ellipse that enclosed the middle Loire, from Orléans where Condé took his stand, around to Bourges, Poitiers, and Angers. Troyes may have been outside this orbit, but it was scarcely closer to Paris than to Orléans. Neither Guise nor Condé could offer meaningful aid to their partisans in the city. Much depended upon Nevers the provincial governor, much upon the local Reformers themselves.

On receiving the news from Nevers, the morning after the massacre, they secretly mustered men and munitions, in the event that the duke of Guise were coming their way. Together with the Reformed seigneurs in the area, they maintained the alert, after Nevers wrote to them to be prepared if necessary to march for Condé. Outwardly, nevertheless, Troyes remained relatively calm. Toward the end of March Catholic and Reformed notables met to agree on coexistence, which did not prevent each of the parties from trying to elect its own candidates to replace the four aldermen (échevins) whose terms would expire on Easter Monday. The issue was crucial, since three of the four continuing aldermen were Protestant. The Reformers caucused under Nicolas Pithou's leadership at Calvary Mountain in Saint Nicholas's Church. When questioned later, they claimed to have met in the form of the college of nobles and bourgeois, the most influential of the voting corporations. At town hall, however, a week's postponement was decided on, presumably by Denis Clérey the Catholic mayor and the town council as a whole. It was composed, not only of the aldermen, but of twenty-four coun-

68. Bruslart, "Journal," p. 75. See also Castelnau, *Mémoires,* p. 83.

cilors proper, who were selected by coöptation and served for life. Delay gave the Catholics time to appeal to Guise. The duke sent the sieur d'Esclaverolles, a member of his household, to Troyes, but could spare him only twelve horsemen as an escort. He introduced himself as royal lieutenant, with oral instructions but no written commission from the king and queen mother to prohibit the election of Protestants. Pithou challenged d'Esclaverolles's authority, while observing that the people for whom he himself spoke were not, as they had just been called, of the new religion, but "of the old one, as it was at the time of the apostles." This information did not stop the Catholics, who had had the time to organize themselves and prevent an electoral coup, from winning all four seats.[69]

A few days later Troyens learned of the second massacre, at Sens. In response the Reformers quickly but quietly summoned the neighboring seigneurs of their party. D'Esclaverolles left his lodgings in the Belfroy Quarter of the upper town for the protection of the cité, barricading himself in Saint Stephen's cloister. Those canons who refused to shave their beards and crowns on major holidays, even though in their choir stalls they did not look to the lay worshippers like proper priests, now had a legitimate excuse. They could plead that if their estate were easily recognizable, they might be mocked or abused on the street. Mayor Clérey, meanwhile, a man of peace who had struggled to keep the city calm during his two-year term, announced that he was quitting his office. He protested that Nicolas Pithou, who came to council to protest alleged military preparations, had insulted him once too often. By mid-April the Protestants had seized the gates. They were in full control when the duke of Nevers made his way toward Troyes on their request — and ordered them to disband if they wanted him to enter the city. At the council of the Reformed Church, Pithou and a few others urged noncompliance, for they feared that Nevers was following Navarre, his senior uncle, into the royal camp. The majority of a council composed of merchants, lawyers, and medical men was not, however, about to defy one of the great lords of France, especially since he still seemed to have Condé's confidence. The Protestants gave up their advan-

69. Pithou, "Histoire ecclésiastique," ff. 193–195, 197–200; AC, Troyes, A 13, ff. 145–150 (see 145v for the complaint on the pre-election meeting, and Pithou's defense of the Reform). Of the continuing *échevins*, Pierre Mauroy, Antoine de Marisy, Guillaume Desrieulx, and Claude Le Mercier, the last three were absent for religious reasons in August 1562, and were replaced by Catholics (ibid., ff. 64 and 229).

tage. Clérey was back in office by April 30, and in May the citizenry
were disarmed. June was the month for mayoral elections in Troyes.
When Clérey refused to stand for reëlection, the Protestants decided
to support Claude Pinette, a good-natured, tractable merchant who
had a Reformed brother-in-law. Since he was also "reasonably well
liked by the people," Pinette won with ease, to everybody's satisfaction.[70]

By the end of spring the Troyen Reformers had found themselves
unable to dominate the town council, and unwilling to challenge
the provincial governor, despite promises of support from nobles in
the countryside. But at worst Nevers seemed neutral or indifferent,
and Pinette was promising. The hope of local power was gone, but
not the expectation of tranquility. At the beginning of summer the
plague, which had been gathering strength since May, threatened to
become an epidemic. Nevers quit town for the greater safety of Saint
Lyé, an episcopal retreat, where he joined Caracciolo. Open warfare
had made the bishop's ambiguous position untenable. He resigned
his benefice to Claude de Bauffremont with the understanding that
he would receive a healthy pension, and was now waiting to see how
the queen mother would react to the transaction.[71]

Nevers left Des Bordes, a noble in his entourage, as the king's lieutenant in Troyes. In July Des Bordes went to court seeking authority
to proceed against the Protestants, and came back with one decree
compelling churchwardens and lawyers to take oaths as Catholics,
and another ordering the arrest of the officers and ministers of the
new sect and of anyone who tried to hide them. During his absence
the municipality raised a company of three hundred soldiers. Des
Bordes was ready now. On Sunday, August 2, he put his cannon on
the walls and closed all but two of the gates. The Protestants who
went out that day to the field in which they were now holding services did not come back — if they had the means and a place of
refuge. Others had already left because of the plague. Troyens in
town were stopped by soldiers wearing oversized rosaries, and in-

---

70. Pithou, "Histoire ecclésiastique," ff. 203–217; AD, Aube, 6G 25, f. 173v (23 April
1562) . See also ibid., ff. 194v, 196v, 241v, 251v, 292, and 293v, and for similar concern
at the cathedral chapter in 1563, G 1285, ff. 161 and 180. AC, Troyes, A 13, ff. 161 and
166 for Clérey. Pinette's brother-in-law Pierre Perricard was one of the Protestant
delegates to a municipal assembly in 1571 (AC, Troyes, BB 14, second *liasse*, no. 35) .
71. Pithou, "Histoire ecclésiastique," ff. 223, 187v; Roserot de Melin, *Antonio Caracciolo*, pp. 331–333.

vited to kiss the cross that hung from them or take a beating instead. Monday Des Bordes led an attack on Middle Street. When that apparent bastion was taken without resistance, Catholics knew that the whole town lay at their feet. As they ran through the streets they shouted, parodying the titles of mystery plays, that the Protestants had played the *Passion,* but that *they* would now play the *Vengeance.*

Reformers who had recently ridiculed Catholicism were now being forced to recognize that, in the eyes of a hated adversary, impotence is the most ridiculous state of all. During this same summer of 1562, peasants slit the throat of a village weaver near Le Mans who used to conduct prayer meetings, and then stuffed pages from their victim's Bible into the mouth of his corpse. Looters in Troyes found a barrel containing Bibles and books of psalms in the cellar of an absent Temple Street merchant. A crowd danced around a bonfire of the books, singing, "We're burning the truth." Their meaning was more ironic than sacrilegious, for as the duke of Guise was reported to have exclaimed at Wassy, when a New Testament was shown to him, "What! By the blood of God, Holy Scripture? It's been 1500 years since Jesus Christ suffered death and passion, and these books have been in print for only a year." [72] Did a Protestant propagandist invent or embellish these words? Catholics like the duke, in any event, were intent on proving that truth did not reside in the Book, as the Reformers read it. Laughter and scorn were among their major weapons.

The task of reunification at Troyes began on Wednesday, August 5, when the children of Reformed artisans were dragged off to church for a Catholic baptism. Since the ministers had escaped, a crowd hauled their pulpit from the field to the spot in the grain market where executions took place. They tied a Bible and a smoked, *sour* herring, as an effigy of Jacques *Sorel,* to the pulpit, and gaily burned it down. Sunday the ninth was a day of rejoicing and general processions. Everyone in town was ordered to attend Mass, and the clergy began to remarry couples originally wed in the Reformed Church. For the rest of the summer the soldiers virtually had the run of the town, molesting and sometimes murdering the Protestants on whom they could lay their hands, and pillaging the houses of some who

---

72. *Histoire ecclésiastique,* ed. Baum and Cunitz, II, 627; Pithou, "Histoire ecclésiastique," ff. 222v–229, and AC, Troyes, A 13, ff. 196v–223v; *Mémoires de François de Lorraine,* p. 483.

had fled. Mayor Pinette did nothing to stop them, and later egged on the populace to murder individual refugees as they returned. He was not the only pacific man turned ugly that year. Christophle Angenoust, town councilor, had been considered "among the most humane, sweet, and gracious of the city." When asked in the fall how to treat Protestant notables who were back in Troyes and professing Catholicism, he replied "high and short." Here was someone who, according to Pithou, had once read Calvin and thought about Reformed ideas. It will not do, then, to write off the persecutors (who in some other parts of France might have been the Protestants) as religious extremists, political opportunists, unbalanced minds, or simply the rabble of each estate. Pinette and Angenoust were honorable men, but the unheard-of arrogance of the Protestants, religious dissidents who had tried to become political masters, caused a shock that unnerved men to the point of forgetting honor. For every Denis Clérey who retired to cultivate his garden, there was a Claude Pinette who developed a thirst for blood. Even in 1563, after the kingdom was at peace, those who continued to profess the Reform in Troyes could not be sure of their lives — the only city in Champagne that was not yet tranquil.[73]

We have only cursory information on the first war elsewhere in the province. Soldiers and peasants sacked Céant in August. At about the same time the royal commander at Saint-Dizier tried unsuccessfully to organize the peasants in Humid Champagne to revisit the Reformers at Wassy. The ministers in the cities either fled back to Switzerland or took refuge with nobles locally, while abjurations reduced the number of their faithful.[74]

National peace was made possible by a fatal wound to Navarre outside Rouen, the capture in battle of Condé by the Catholics and of the constable by the Protestants, and the assassination of Guise outside Orléans. (Nevers was also killed in the war, but his death made little difference.) The terms of peace provided for one place of Reformed worship in each bailiwick, in addition to the privileges of seigneurs and the continuance of those urban churches that were

---

73. Pithou, "Histoire ecclésiastique," ff. 232v–233 and 278v. For Pinette, see ibid., ff. 228, 273, 392v; for Angenoust, ff. 257 and 264. Bèze to Farel, 3 July 1563: "In Campania, solis Trecensibus exceptis, res satis sunt compositae," *Correspondance de Théodore de Bèze,* ed. Hippolyte Aubert et al. (Geneva, 1960–), IV, 166.

74. *Histoire ecclésiastique,* ed. Baum and Cunitz, II, 484; *Mémoires de François de Lorraine,* 487.

still in existence at the end of the war. The Protestants of Vitry
simulated continuity by immediately resuming public worship.[75]
But in Troyes the Catholics acted first. Officers of the guard conducted the two notaries whom the town council dispatched, from
house to house. Pithou implies that they went through the whole
town, but stopped only at the doors of Protestants and suspects. The
single surviving register of their poll, however, covers the residents
of only one of the four quarters of the city, and seems self-con-
tained.[76] The notaries were instructed to take the names of heads
of households,

and to learn from them whether they intended and wanted to live according to
the true and ancient religion, Catholic and Roman, in which they had been
baptized and brought up, and which has been maintained and kept by our sire
the king and his predecessors; and whether the king, queen mother, and privy
council should be asked that no assembly and exercise of the new, so-called
Reformed religion should be allowed in the suburbs.

The law courts gave the tone to Comporté Quarter, which was on
the opposite side of the upper town from Temple Street. Court personnel and legal officials, together with some merchants, lived among
the artisans here. A large majority of the residents, especially those
who worked at court and were accustomed to formulas, simply accepted the statement as it was read out to them. No doubt in most
cases they would have done so even in the absence of the guard. A
substantial number of people, however, who more often than not
were artisans, either gave their own loquacious twist to the formula,
or else substituted another one for it. Their reactions offer some clues
as to how the war had sifted opinion.

Several residents, like Jehan Huterot the shoemaker, gave coura-
geous yet politic answers that clearly identified them as Reformed.
Huterot said that he "wants to live according to the law of God and
of the king. As for the prayer meetings, he leaves them up to the
king, and won't say anything else." [77] *Noble homme* Guyon Merat

75. Pithou, "Histoire ecclésiastique," f. 291v. For the text of the edict, see Isambert,
Recueil, XIV, pt. 1, no. 35, pp. 135–140.

76. Pithou, "Histoire ecclésiastique," f. 278v; AC, Troyes, BB 14, first *liasse*, no. 24.

77. Ibid., f. 18v. Similar responses were made by a hosier Jehan Prevost: f. 3v; the
widow of Simon Dargilieres, a murdered glass-painter: f. 13v and Pithou, "Histoire
ecclésiastique," f. 268; the wife of a bookseller, in her husband's absence: AC, Troyes,
BB 14, first *liasse*, no. 24, f. 21v; a merchant-apothecary: f. 29v; a merchant-goldsmith:
f. 67v; an innkeeper: f. 71v; a widowed linen-maid who could not sign her name:
f. 75v; the merchant Odard Perricard and his wife: f. 82v; and a physician's wife, in
her husband's absence: f. 86v.

and his wife, by contrast, stumbled between the formula that Huterot had adopted and the one that the notaries proposed. "They in-
tend to live according to God and his commandments, Catholicly
and as it will please the king our lord to command, and according
to the Catholic and Roman church, at the pleasure of the king," to
whom they, too, referred the question of Reformed assemblies. The
very redundancy of the statement suggests equivocation. Merat was
in fact an ex-Protestant, whom Nicolas Pithou identifies, more precisely if less honorifically than the notaries, as a merchant draper. In
the fall of the previous year the town council had taxed the Protestants and the suspects for the cost of the late troubles. Merat was
forced to pay 1200 livres, even though he had returned to the Mass.
Some Catholics asked him, according to Pithou, how much that was
for each prayer meeting he had attended, which really angered this
old man. He "abandoned the Religion entirely, and from then on
had such an aversion to it that he never ceased criticizing it." [78] He
may have criticized, and even abandoned, the Reform, but judging
from his response to the notaries he did not repudiate it.

Others were more frank about the nature of their religious experi-
ences. Jehan Noe, a merchant, was "good and drunk of having gone
to the prayer meetings," and Jacques Manguin, a pursemaker, "has
been deceived about this new religion and will never trust it again
in his life." Loyse the wife of the glass-painter Pierre Sondan, who
was not in town, perhaps for religious reasons, "said that the prayer
meetings have cost her much, and she will feel it all her life." Among
the other women who responded in the absence of their husbands,
the wife of Pierre Millet, blacksmith, was not able to answer the
notaries' question, but "if she were the only one to satisfy, the matter would quickly be solved." The wife of Claude Gaulard, a sergeant-at-law for the countryside, of the Châtelet at Paris, affirmed her
own Catholicism but left the assemblies up to the king, adding that
"she didn't care whether there were any of them or not, and she
made a similar declaration for her six children." [79] These indifferent
spouses had been dragged into the religious hurricane, where they

78. Ibid., f. 84v. Pithou, "Histoire ecclésiastique," ff. 261v–262. Merat had been replaced as a town councilor because of his religion (AC, Troyes, A 13, f. 248v: 18 Sept.
1562.)

79. Noe, however, also left the prayer meetings up to the king: AC, Troyes, BB 14,
first *liasse*, no. 24, f. 68v; Manguin: f. 25v; Sondan's wife: f. 37; Millet's wife: f. 22v;
Gaulard's wife, Jehanne Leguissey: f. 64.

would remain. During the second war Millet again fled Troyes. As
he made his way back, his wife went out to Saint-Mards to meet him.
The couple stopped to wait at a village near Troyes — where some
Catholic ruffians from town surprised them and almost raped her.
In 1569 a very young daughter of the Gaulards, at home alone one
evening, began to sing a psalm of David. "Some of the most mutinous neighbors on the street" had her mother arrested. Gaulard himself was arrested three years later, following Saint Bartholomew's
Day, and murdered, like others, in jail.[80] Among the Gaulards' mutinous neighbors in 1563 was the weaver Nicolas Gros. He offered
"to be among the first to prevent prayer meetings, under the authority of the king." The caveat was not the weaver's but the
notaries', who dutifully added it whenever such sentiments were expressed.[81] Some fervent Catholics echoed Gros, others put the matter
in more personal terms. Nicolas Lhuillier, a skinner, "would prefer
to have his throat cut rather than to go to the prayer meetings." If
the wife of the shoemaker Loys Guerrapin "were to learn that her
children became Huguenots she would break the neck of every one
of them." The largest set of vocal responses came from Catholics
who stressed the violence of people other than themselves. "Prayer
meetings would serve only to kill people," said the schoolmistress
Guillemette Aubry. The merchant Pierre Bel affirmed that public
tranquility could be maintained only in the Catholic religion.[82]

After the notaries had completed their survey of the quarter they
went beyond the walls to the suburb of Comporté, but the task of
interviewing seemed both formidable and unnecessary. The residents were usually out working in the vineyards, and they were all
Catholics anyway, as the vicar assured them. No doubt he was virtually right, for relatively few artisans, professionals, or notables were
to be found on the outskirts of town.[83] But even in the heart of the

80. Pithou, "Histoire ecclésiastique," ff. 338v–339v, 364v; BN, Dupuy, MS 333:
"Mémoire des principaux événements survenus à Troyes en 1572 . . . ," f. 73v.

81. Gros: AC, Troyes, BB 14, first *liasse*, no. 24, f. 60. Other, analogous statements
which required the caveat were made by a cooper: f. 12v; a needle-maker: f. 16; a
justice: f. 17; a hatter: f. 18v; a tinsmith: f. 19; a goldbeater: f. 20; a weaver: f. 48v;
and a roofer: f. 54.

82. Lhuillier: ibid., f. 79v; Guerrapin's wife: f. 16; Aubry: f. 15v; Bel: f. 69. A
needle-maker observed that with prayer meetings, "lon se batteroyt tres bien" (f. 44),
a joiner that "ce n'est que troublerye davoir des presches" (ff. 53v–54).

83. Ibid., ff. 89–96; Henri Drouot, *Mayenne et la Bourgogne; étude sur la Ligue
(1587–1596)* (2 vols., Paris, 1937), I, 60, 119–120, 147, is especially good on the social
and religious contrast between city and suburb.

city, an attitude of naked hostility to the Reform was once again
fully respectable. A certain number of former Protestants, as our
survey shows, joined many Catholics in believing that a religion that
clearly could not triumph need not be endured.

The Protestant Church of Troyes had been shaken but not crushed
in the first religious war. A whole world of lost illusions nevertheless
separated 1563 from 1562. Looking backward, Nicolas Pithou remembered Troyes as in the flower of youth, touched by the preaching of the Word of God. Now he deplored the return of the mores
as well as the theology of decadence. Protestants could henceforth
hope to keep only their own community reformed. At the turn of
1564 the church leaders went to Joinville to ask the duke of Aumale,
Guise's brother and Nevers's successor, for a suburb of Troyes as a
place of worship. Instead he granted them Céant, "a wretched little
town" at the very corner of the bailiwick and in the midst of the
forest. It was "on a bad, hilly road, surrounded by good-for-nothings
who were very badly disposed to those of the Religion, and was so
deserted and ruined that it could not lodge a third of the church
members." Céant was better than nothing, at least for the bourgeoisie, since not every artisan could take the time and spend the
money involved in the trip. On May 7, 1564, the Reformers had
their own day of reunification, when church members who had been
to Mass repented, asked pardon of God, and were welcomed back
into the fold. In June, for "the so-called Fête-Dieu, they decided to
act as duty commands, using the liberty of conscience granted them
by God and by the edict" of peace, and refused to decorate the front
of their dwellings. Some of the Protestants went to Céant. Catholic
Troyens hung tapestries from the Reformed houses that faced the
streets along which the processions were to pass.[84] To do otherwise
would have destroyed the meaning of Corpus Christi.

Nothing infuriated Catholic militants more than the attempts of
Protestants to worship in or near the city. In 1567 the merchant and
town-councilor Pierre Belin, among others, accused the tanner
Claude Boisonnot and the currier Jehan Valleton of using their
homes for secret prayer meetings. Belin had led the Guisard faction
in town since the troubles first began. Of necessity he was involved
in the successive efforts that the council made to end assemblies at
Antoine Menisson's village of Saint-Pouange, south of Troyes. Prot-

---

84. Pithou, "Histoire ecclésiastique," ff. 226, 289v–291v, 298, 309–312. See AC, Troyes,
BB 14, first *liasse*, nos. 33 and 34, for corroboration on Corpus Christi in 1564.

estants countered by obtaining permission in 1572 to meet at Isles (L'Isle-Aumont), nearby, which belonged to Marie de Clèves, who was about to marry the young prince of Condé. In July the council sent Belin, who had just finished a term as mayor, and another councilor, to object at court. Some Catholics in Troyes, rather than await the results, took to stoning the Reformers as they returned from Isles.[85]

During Belin's stay in Paris, the queen mother plotted the murder of Coligny, who was about to make war in the Netherlands. When the assassins succeeded only in wounding the admiral, Catherine and the young duke of Guise felt obliged to protect themselves by ordering more killings, which in the hands of the king's brother Henry, later Henry III, and the provost of merchants of Paris became a general massacre.[86] Belin wrote to inform Mayor Pierre Nevelet of the events of Saint Bartholomew's Day. After conferring with Guise he wrote again, advising Nevelet of the king's determination "to make an end, to exterminate the relicts" of the Protestants. The mayor, Belin knew, had received instructions to act accordingly.[87] As Belin wrote, Protestants were already being attacked on the streets of Troyes. The town council, which wanted to wait until calmer instructions were received from Paris, demanded imperiously that "force remain on the side of justice." Instead Bailiff Anne de Vaudrey imprisoned more than thirty adherents of the new religion. Together with Belin, who had returned posthaste from Paris, he arranged to have them murdered in jail.[88]

When Vaudrey asked permission to search Saint Stephen's cloister for Protestants in hiding, the canons responded by offering him a present of wine. At the same meeting they listened to a report on the recent efforts to abolish the assemblies at Isles.[89] The news from Paris had separated the militant Catholics who wanted to suppress

85. AC, Troyes, BB 14, second *liasse,* nos. 13, 14, 40; Pithou, "Histoire ecclésiastique," ff. 366 and 369.

86. H. G. Koenigsberger, "Western Europe and the Power of Spain," *New Cambridge Modern History,* III, ed. R.B. Wernham (Cambridge, 1968), pp. 289–290; Philippe Erlanger, *Le massacre de la Saint-Barthélemy, 24 août 1572* (Paris, 1960).

87. Belin's letter of 27 Aug. makes reference to an earlier letter to Nevelet, which is no longer extant: AC, Troyes, BB 14, second *liasse,* no. 47. See also Pithou, "Histoire ecclésiastique," f. 371v.

88. AC, Troyes, A 17, f. 225v (27 Aug.); "Mémoire des principaux événements survenus à Troyes en 1572, contenant un récit de la Saint-Barthélemy à Troyes," BN, Collection Dupuy, 333, ff. 65–75, on which Pithou acknowledges that he has based his own account ("Histoire ecclésiastique," f. 382v).

89. AD, Aube, 6G 29, ff. 30v–31r (4 Sept. 1572).

the Reform by legal means from the toughs on the street and in high places who wanted to suppress it by any means. Over the years the former group had helped to maintain hatred at a level high enough to suit the purposes of the latter. For a few crucial days Vaudrey and Belin placed the law on the side of force. They believed that an end had to be made of the Protestants, who were acting as if they had not already been defeated.

Further discussion about Isles was unnecessary, for the Reform, if not all its supporters, had been destroyed in Troyes, the one city in Champagne that was fully charged by the passions that made mass murder possible. Elsewhere in the province the Protestants had created less of a furor. After the peace of 1576, which closed the fifth religious war, a conciliatory Henry III permitted the Protestants in Châlons to worship, although their church may not have survived the outbreak of the sixth war in 1577.[90] In 1585 the bishop responded to a Guisard charge that the Reformers had tried to disrupt the Corpus Christi procession by assuring the king that "the small number of the Religion who are in my city of Châlons have always conducted themselves, as they still do, most peacefully, and in all modesty, without any scandal." [91] The Châlonnais seemed to have learned to endure one another. Protestant notaries drew up wills for Catholic clients that began with a pastiche of two contradictory formulas. A man or woman "recommended his soul to God the creator, praying him in favor of his well-beloved son Jesus Christ, our Lord, by the intercession of the Virgin Mary and the saints of paradise to receive him in his holy paradise, a place that he has prepared for all those who love him and have their confidence and love in him alone."[92]

During the wars of the Catholic League from 1585 to 1594, Châlons broke with almost all of the rest of the towns in the province to declare for King Henry III rather than for Henry, duke of Guise.

90. AC, Châlons, GG 148.
91. Pithou, "Histoire ecclésiastique," f. 452.
92. Margueritte Hurtault: AD, Marne, 4E 6374 (11 June 1582). Slight variants of the formula may be found in eight more of our wills, including those of Jehanne Philippe, wife of a master-joiner: 4E 6370 (1 Sept. 1578); the Hon. Jehan Babault, merchant and bourgeois: 4E 9766 (1 Dec. 1582); and the shoemaker Paul Doynyn and his wife: 4E 6380 (6 Oct. 1590). A.G. Dickens notes that "in Venice from 1540 solid citizens commonly made wills expressing in passionate terms their entire dependence on the merits of Christ; this conviction continued for several decades, yet was often combined with the veneration of saints and other Catholic elements" (*The Counter Reformation,* p. 38).

After both duke and king were murdered the city remained loyal to the crown, even though the new, Bourbon king, Henry IV, began his reign as a Protestant. The Reformed Church of Châlons started to meet once more in 1591. The church's baptismal records furnish the Christian names that parents chose for their children. One third of the girls from 1591 to 1600 were named Marie, and a third of the boys Pierre or Jean, because parents followed the standard practice of using the name of the child's godparent of the same sex. Another third of the girls and four-tenths of the boys received names from the Old Testament: Sarah, Rachel, Esther, Suzanne, and Judith; Isaac, Jacob, Benjamin, Samuel, Nathan, David. . . .[93] They would be reared by parents who had lived all their lives in the faith. In 1598, after Henry IV had renounced his religion to secure his throne, he issued yet one more royal grant of freedom of belief and limited worship, in the Edict of Nantes. The Protestants of Châlons were joined by churches in Bar-sur-Seine, Vitry, several villages in the Perthois and the Argonne, Sézanne, Aÿ, Chaltrait near Loisy-en-Brie, and Saint-Mards. They re-formed for what must have seemed the nth time, and prepared to face the trials of the seventeenth century.[94]

As an epilogue to one of the tragedies of history, we might ask, from a Champenois perspective, whether a generation of civil war could have been avoided. In preparing for the Estates-General of 1560, the Troyen town-councilors, Catholic and proto-Protestant, were able to agree on a cahier of grievances that included a religious chapter. The council wanted a more dedicated, more moral, and less numerous clergy. They asked that priests be ordained only at the age of thirty. Each was to hold but one benefice, in which he would reside, and perform the sacraments without cost to his parishioners. A curé should be limited to a single maidservant, who must be above suspicion, and to only one or two clerks. A fixed number of priests was to be set for each parish. Clergymen without a benefice or regular stipend should return to their own dioceses (just as the poor were expected to remain in the place of their birth, rather than

---

93. AD, Marne, Châlons, Protestants, Registre de l'état civil.
94. "Liste des églises et des pasteurs réformées de France en 1660," Société de l'histoire du protestantisme français: *Bulletin*, 15 (1866), 513–514; "Fragment de statistique officielle des églises réformées en France, trois ans avant la Révocation," *Bulletin*, 7 (1858), 22–26; Hérelle, *Documents inédits sur le protestantisme à Vitry*, vol. 1.

wander about, disturbing the peace while they looked for work).
Family heads should attend Sunday and holiday services, and compel
the rest of their household to go too — at least every other Sunday,
as a later article of the cahier stipulated. The number of festivals
should be reduced, public dancing and dissolute songs prohibited,
and shows by traveling actors and acrobats ended, for these idle
players diverted the people from their work.[95] The cahier reflects the
concern of notables for a more disciplined populace as well as a
more subdued religion. It is a restatement of Bishop Guillaume
Petit's *Way of Salvation* in the language of municipal politics.

Had the king of France in 1560 been an adult with the talents of
a Henry IV and the good fortune to escape assassination, he might
have succeeded where the cardinal of Lorraine had faltered and
Catherine the queen mother had failed. A mature king might well
have been able to assemble a sufficiently weighty number of Frenchmen around a Gallican solution that went beyond the Troyen councilors' list to include a married clergy, communion in both kinds,
and the disestablishment of purgatory. This program, like the
Troyen one, would have been too little for Nicolas Pithou and yet
too much for Claude Haton. It would however have suited Antonio
Caracciolo, and have allowed him to remain at his post. With such
a program a strong monarch could conceivably have prevented the
conflation of religious passion and noble faction, and kept France,
while he lived, at peace.

95. *Documents inédits relatifs aux Etats-généraux,* pp. 60–82.

6 / The Ghost of the Past

For the better part of forty years Frenchmen fought one another in the name of religion, but with much more than religion on their minds. The "second sixteenth century," as Pierre Chaunu has styled it, was a time of frequent and intense famine, accelerated inflation, and renewed plague.[1] The duke of Guise had a soldier's answer to the demographic problem. When some Catholics complained to him that members of their own party had suffered in the recapture of Blois, he snorted that "there were too many people in the kingdom, and he would have so many of them killed that foodstuffs would all become cheap."[2] The source of the quotation, the *Histoire ecclésiastique,* makes its attribution a bit suspect, but does establish that both the problem and a possible solution were on men's minds. Fifteen years later, in Issoire in central France, interested parties spread a rumor that the town had been betrayed by its notables to the commander of the army of the Catholic League, which was attempting under Guisard leadership to impose a stringent religious policy on Henry III. It was said that the local commander planned to have the men and children of the ordinary people murdered, and the wives remarried to his soldiers.[3] Even without such remedies, the population of France declined by a tenth or even a fifth, depending on the region, from 1560 to 1590.[4]

The hardships of the period exacerbated the discontents of men at the base of all the estates. A host of soldiers whom the peace of 1559

1. Pierre Chaunu, *La civilisation de l'Europe classique* (Paris, 1970), p. 446. Narratiev evidence of natural disasters in Champagne is provided by Pithou, "Histoire ecclésiastique," ff. 88–90 (famine of 1556) and f. 405v (1573); Haton, *Mémoires,* I, 223–229 (plague of 1561) and 332–333 (plague of 1562); ibid., II, 601 (plague of 1570), 714–731 (famine of 1573), 1056 (plague of 1581), and 1081–1089 (plague of 1582). Records of the municipal bureau of poor relief refer to the plague in 1595, 1596, and 1597: AC, Châlons, GG 218. Jehan Pussot of Reims gives grain and wine prices annually in the course of his "Journalier." For Paris, see Baulant and Meuvret, *Prix des céréales.*

2. *Histoire ecclésiastique,* ed. Baum and Cunitz, II, 678.

3. [Julien Blauf], *Annales d'Issoire,* ed. J.-B. Bouillet (Clermont-Ferrand, 1848), p. 193.

4. Le Roy Ladurie, "Démographie et paysans," *Histoire économique et sociale de la France,* ed. Braudel and Labrousse, I (forthcoming).

with Spain had momentarily deprived of employment brought their habits as well as their skills to civil war. They were no more adept at plundering than were the beggars and the underemployed. Settled artisans wanted to use the troubles to regain a voice in municipal politics. Duke Francis's son the cardinal of Guise, after entering Troyes in 1588 by a coup d'état in defiance of the crown, set out to win the nonpatrician members of the bourgeoisie and the artisans to the Catholic League. Nicolas Pithou heard, plausibly if not authoritatively, that the cardinal soon became disgusted by the tanners and curriers with yellowed fingernails who frequented his table. Yet he had to suffer them if he were to maintain the League's position, and keep in exile from the town those notables and judges who supported the crown. Petty nobles, meanwhile, saw the wars as a way to gain revenge on merchants in particular and towns in general — the sources, they thought, of their troubles. Those who were Protestants murdered clerics and sacked abbeys as well. Claude Haton called the marauding gentlemen of the Brie champenoise "gens pille et tue hommes." Peasants shared the hatreds of the squirearchy, and also had a grievance against the church. Opposition to the Reform did not prevent the inhabitants of a score of the villages in Champagne from refusing to pay their tithes, at some time between 1563 and 1567.[5] Orchestrating these several and sometimes conflicting interests were the great noble families. If they undid royal authority they could enjoy regional autonomy while competing with one another for power at court, as their late-medieval predecessors had done.

Just as the plagues and political strife of late-sixteenth-century France replicated late-medieval economics and politics, the public devotion of the time included a recollection and spastic revival of earlier religious forms. The king of France himself exemplified the febrile religious atmosphere. Henry of Valois had been elected king of Poland while Charles IX was alive. On Charles's death he fled Poland, and returned to France as Henry III. Traveling by way of Venice, he took advantage of his passage through Avignon to join the

---

5. Pithou, "Histoire ecclésiastique," f. 472, and BN, Fonds français, 3396, ff. 8–16: "Mémoire des choses les plus remarquables qui se sont passées en la ville de Troyes au commencement des derniers troubles"; Haton, *Mémoires*, II, 786, 813, 838, 852, 854. The nonpayment of tithes, from 1562 to 1567, is documented in Victor Carrière, "Les épreuves de l'église de France au XVIe siècle," *Introduction aux études d'histoire ecclésiastique locale* (3 vols., Paris, 1934–1940), III, 319–352, and discussed by Le Roy Ladurie, "Démographie."

Confraternity of the White Penitents at the Dominican church. The cardinal of Lorraine, who was now fifty years old, joined the king in its procession. He exposed his head and feet to the December air, and contracted a fatal fever.[6] In 1575 Henry had oratories set up in the churches of Paris, which he visited continually. To earn the pardon of the papal jubilee in August 1576, he went from one Parisian church to another, holding an outsized rosary and mumbling his prayers as he walked. Such fervent devotion had not been common in sixteenth-century French kings. Nor had Henry's other traits. His minions, or royal favorites, were a haughty, bellicose, foppish, and effeminate group of young men. The king staged elaborate and costly festivals with them and the ladies of the court, in which each sex masqueraded as the other. In short, Henry gave Frenchmen the impression of much sin and even greater repentance. During the 1580s he became progressively more pious. He founded a confraternity of penitents in March 1583 under the patronage of the Annunciation, which had become an old-fashioned devotion. His favorites, other courtiers, royal judges, and notable bourgeois were all pressed into service. The confraternity members, including the king, dressed in white like the penitents of Avignon and other southern European cities (and the peasants around Troyes in 1556), for the procession on Annunciation Day. It was said that during a second procession, on Holy Thursday, a number of the penitents, including some minions, flagellated themselves. The confraternity met regularly in the following years. Its more robust members also sometimes accompanied the king on foot in pilgrimage.[7]

Intelligent, sensitive, lacking any self-discipline, Henry III was hardly an ordinary personality. Yet it was not his religious behavior that made him an individualist. An anonymous politique (one who put political unity above religious purity) wrote a satirical tract in 1584 entitled *An Accord in Several Particulars between the Curés and Theological Doctors of Paris, and the Ministers of the So-Called Reformed Religion*. The author charged, among other things, that

6. Pierre de L'Estoile, *Mémoires-journaux*, ed. G. Brunet et al. (12 vols., Paris, 1875–1896), I, 37–40. On the penitential confraternities of Avignon, see *Dictionnaire d'histoire et de géographie ecclésiastiques*, s.v. "Avignon," and, more generally, Maurice Agulhon, *La sociabilité méridionale (Confréries et associations dans la vie collective en Provence orientale à la fin du 18ème siècle)* (2 vols., Aix-en-Provence, 1966), which has much material on the late sixteenth century.

7. L'Estoile, *Mémoires-journaux*, I, 93, 151, 142–143, 109–110, 113, 148–150, 333.

the clergy of both confessions were trying to delude their flocks by initiating them into new and extraordinary devotions. The assertion that the Catholic laity were simply responding to clerical direction is, however, questionable. The people of Provins, Claude Haton noted in 1578, had become "more fervent in devotion." During this year and the previous one, they set out on pilgrimages, in much greater numbers than usual, to Saint Fiacre in Brie, Saint Nicholas in Lorraine, Saint Claude in Franche-Comté, and elsewhere. Some twenty or more even journeyed to Saint James's relics at Compostela. On their return from Spain they revived the Confraternity of the Pilgrims of Saint James, with all the trappings, including a full-dress representation of Jesus and the apostles as part of their procession, and a dinner at the standard-bearer's. Haton confirmed his observations of the religious effervescence of his fellow townsmen with news from elsewhere in France. An earthquake in January 1579 frightened the residents of Tours sufficiently to make them all want "to convert their wicked life into a better one." Next day they assembled in their parishes, and set out on a procession through the countryside. More than three hundred people marched, wearing nothing in mid-winter, Haton wrote, but a simple sheet: the white robe of penitence, which would appear at the royal court four years later. As a mark of repentance and in self-punishment, some weighed themselves down with iron bars, others with heavy pieces of wood. The priests went barefoot, too, and in simple dress. During the earthquake many men and women had vowed pilgrimages. They hastened to accomplish them in the days following the procession.[8]

Haton's narrative, unfortunately, breaks off in 1582. During the next year, in which the king founded his confraternity, religious revivalism reached a climax. "The sky gave no rain in May," reported Jacques Carorguy, *greffier* (clerk of the court) of Bar-sur-Seine, and so "the people rose by themselves," first in Burgundy and then at Les Riceys in Champagne. On June 1 the villagers of Les Riceys marched in a general procession to Bar. The boys were naked to the waist, the girls dressed in white, and the widows in black. They sang hymns to the patron saints of the places through which they passed. The residents of Bar placed tables on the city streets, laden with bread, meat, and wine for them. Another day, the marchers from the village of Loches "came, ceaselessly whipping a poor man whom they said re-

8. Ibid., II, 170–172, quotes the tract in full; Haton, *Mémoires*, II, 926–928, 974.

sembled our Lord, spitting on him with the countenance of tyrants similar to those who oppressed him at the time of the Passion."[9] The summer that followed was extremely hot, and brought an epidemic of the plague.[10] From July to October thousands of people in northern Champagne and elsewhere donned the white habit, to go in procession to the Cathedral of Reims. Canon Hubert Meurier published the three sermons he delivered that year in defense of the processions, with an appendix giving the number of marchers and their places of origin. They came from more than two hundred villages and towns: from the Ardennes, the Tardenois, Châlons and its environs, the Mountain of Reims and the valley of the Marne. Meurier numbered them, with the precision that was beginning to characterize the sixteenth-century mind, at 72,409.[11] Since villagers on procession to the Cathedral of Paris from the Ile-de-France told the diarist Pierre de L'Estoile that the movement had begun when ten or twelve thousand inhabitants marched to Notre-Dame-de-Liesse and the Cathedral of Reims, Meurier's figures were in fact on the order of those that were being bruited about in France. The carpenter Jehan Pussot of Reims wrote in his journal that during the processions hardly anyone was left in the villages to guard the livestock.[12]

Many of the peasants came barefooted. They carried wooden crosses, and sang and chanted prayers in honor of the Virgin and the Mass. Their priests, conducting the monstrance of the parish, accompanied them. As Meurier put it: "You can see that it is not the bishops, nor the curés, nor the preachers who exhort the people to such extraordinary devotions. On the contrary, it is the people who solicit and by a saintly persistence force, so to speak, the bishops, curés, and preachers to lead them where their devotion impels them." The fervor of the peasants had a catalytic effect on the townsmen of Reims. Pussot noted that "some rich Catholics who were cold in devotion were stirred and swayed, as they saw and considered, among other things,

9. *Mémoires de Jacques Carorguy, greffier de Bar-sur-Seine, 1582–1595*, ed. Edmond Bruwaert (Paris, 1880) , pp. 2–4. A colorless minor official, Carorguy provides copious if snickering descriptions of religious effervescence on the march between Champagne and Burgundy, as well as a provincial royalist's view of Paris during the League.

10. AD, Troyes, 6G 33, f. 83, and AC, Troyes, A 21, f. 81v.

11. *Traicté de l'institution et vray usage des processions, tant ordinaires, qu'extraordinaires, qui se font en l'église catholique, contenant un ample discours de ce qui s'est passé pour ce regard en la province de Champaigne depuis le 22 de juillet jusques au 25 d'octobre 1583. . . .* (Reims, 1584) .

12. L'Estoile, *Mémoires-journaux*, II, 134; Pussot, "Journalier," pt. 1, p. 167.

that the good villagers did not fear the season, the time of their grain and wine harvests, and left their villages to accomplish such long and diverse processions without regard for profits or damages." The Rémois themselves, Meurier points out, were moved to march through the city in white. And on one Saturday in August residents of five parishes of Châlons, 960 by the canon's count, arrived at the Cathedral of Reims. Not merely ordinary townsmen, but people of quality — cardinals, great lords, and the like — took part in the processions. Meurier notes, moreover, that young people took pleasure in representing the mysteries of the Passion, which reinforces the suggestion in Carorguy's memoirs of a fleeting revival of the religious theatre.[13]

Villagers and city dwellers were on the march in 1583, hoping for an end to famine and plague, and seeking relief from other, less tangible anxieties as well. Meurier defined the white processions as "nothing else in truth than a public and solemn profession of the sincerity of the faith that we hold, and the purity of the doctrine that we believe. And although the life of most of us is often horribly soiled with sin, to our great confusion, nevertheless our faith and doctrine remain always whole, clean, and pure, to our great consolation." [14] The Reform had been crushed as a movement in nothern France, but the religious wars continued, sustained by the Protestants south of the Loire and by the conflict between Valois king and Guisard duke. Until the wars would end and heresy disappear, the truth of Catholicism had to be proven, rather than taken for granted. That proof required a demonstration that the sins of Catholics as individuals, which were held in large part responsible for the natural disasters, did not taint their creed. Penitential processions accomplished this purpose.

When L'Estoile asked the peasants why they had marched to Paris they did not, however, invoke the defense of the faith. Rather "they had been moved to make these penitences or pilgrimages because of some fires that had appeared in the sky and other signs, like prodigies seen in the sky and on the earth, especially towards the Ardennes." Earlier, the comets of 1577 and 1581 had fascinated astronomers, but unnerved other Christians, who saw in them portents of evils to

13. Meurier, *Traicté des processions*, ff. 26–28, 36, and appendix; Pussot, "Journalier," pt. 1, p. 167.
14. Meurier, *Traicté des processions*, f. 36.

come.[15] Like the earthquake of 1579, they helped to bring to the surface generalized uncertainties and fears, which fed on themselves, leading to the search for yet more signs of disaster, and requiring rituals of propitiation.

But the drive toward unity, which had once been a precondition for a successful appeal to God, was manifestly impossible to achieve now. Lawrence Stone's observation on England holds for Champagne, too: "As the religious fanatics on all sides shouted louder and louder, so more and more sober men began to adopt a latitudinarian attitude of watchful skepticism." Jacques Carorguy scoffed that most of the girls in white from Les Riceys were chambermaids, who sported with the boys in the fields on the way home from Bar in the evening, and shook the heavens so hard that the rains came down. In the longer run, however, Carorguy continued, devotions like the whipping of the boy who played Christ angered God, who sent "the scourges of his ire," in other words, famine, plague, and war. One man's atonement was another's evidence of the multiplication of sin. Henry III's religiosity was mocked by the politiques and condemned by partisans of the Catholic League, who saw a flagrant contradiction, rather than a mutually reinforcing tension, between the king's public piety and his personal sins. In 1583, during a Lenten sermon at Notre-Dame of Paris, a friar denounced the new royal confraternity as an association of "hypocrites and atheists."[16]

The word "atheist," as a strong and often loosely construed epithet, was not new to the later sixteenth century, but does seem to have been used more frequently.[17] Claude Haton felt it necessary to provide a definition. In 1563 a Parisian Protestant seized the Host and stepped on it. The priest who interrogated the "poor miserable" creature saw that he was an *athée ou athéiste, that is to say without any belief in a God, which is the most pernicious error that ever was or ever will be.* Nicolas Pithou described an important adherent of the League in Troyes, whom he preferred not to name, as a person

---

15. L'Estoile, *Mémoires-journaux*, II, 134; Haton mentions the popular reaction to the comets (*Mémoires*, II, 909–914, 1036–1037).

16. Lawrence Stone, "The English Revolution," in *Preconditions of Revolution in Early Modern Europe*, ed. Robert Forster and Jack Greene (Baltimore, 1970), p. 93; *Mémoires de Jacques Carorguy*, pp. 3–4; L'Estoile, *Mémoires-journaux*, II, 111.

17. See Febvre, *Le problème de l'incroyance*, esp. pp. 138–153.

"who believes nothing at all, and is one of those who go around saying, when the subject is the certainty of Holy Scripture, that paper endures anything." Friar Chrestofle Blaiseau, guardian of the Franciscans of Troyes, urged in a sermon of 1587 delivered in support of Henry III that all the divisions prejudicial to God's honor would end, "so that people no longer say, this one is an atheist, that one a heretic, and the rest nothing but half-breeds (*métis*), politiques, and libertines."[18] The concern about atheists suggests that the sense of religious community among Catholics was disintegrating. A man could not be sure what, or even whether, people believed, if their religious sensibilities differed from his own.

The patterns of confraternity membership also suggest an increasing disjointedness in Catholic religious practice. Everywhere in Troyes the confraternities of patron saints were dying. Troyen notables had once congregated at Saint Pantaleon's on the church's festival day, and had taken a candle in the patron's name. The confraternity had fifty-eight participants in 1558, but only seventeen in 1585, and three in 1593 (table 2). The evidence from Saint Quirin's Confraternity, at the parish altar in his collegial church at Provins, is complementary if not so dramatic. Here, the patron's association declined from two hundred or more members in the 1550s and 1560s to sixty-six in 1595 (table 8). Quirin was also a healing saint, which may in part explain the survival of his confraternity at Provins. For now at the end, as earlier in the second quarter of the century, saints who cured diseases fared better than patrons. Quirin's and Blaise's confraternities remained popular at Mary Magdalene's Church of Troyes, though even they were slipping badly in the 1590s (table 3). Fiacre and Syre held their attraction at Saint John's and Saint James's churches, which was that much more remarkable in the light of what was happening to the other parish associations (tables 4 and 5). Sebastian and Roche, who protected against the plague, came into prominence at Saint John's during the epidemic of 1564, and were singularly popular at Saint Nizier's in the cité, at the plague-ridden turn of the seventeenth century (table 8). Even the curé belonged to both in 1604, and to no others.[19]

18. Haton, *Mémoires*, I, 375; Pithou, "Histoire ecclésiastique," f. 437; Chrestofle Blaiseau, *Coppie du sermon prononcé en l'église cathédrale de Troyes, au retour de la procession générale, le dimanche trentiesme iour d'aoust, mil cinq cens quatre vingts et sept* (Troyes, n.d.).

19. AD, Aube, 18G 17, ff. 28 and 33v.

Saint Nizier's is also remarkable for the popularity of the Virgin's Nativity, and of her mother Saint Anne. This parish was in Saint James's Quarter, the poorest part of the city, which housed many newcomers from the countryside.[20] The quarter's roll for the *taille* of 1606 shows that the largest single group of inhabitants were weavers, 136 of the 611 whose occupation is given, or 22 percent.[21] Taken together, the few substantial and the many impoverished weavers were assessed a bit more than 18 livres. This sum was little more than a fifth of the 87 l. 10 s. that the one notable on the taille roll, François Mauroy, and his wife, had to pay. Confraternities at Saint Nizier's did not, however, maintain their membership by drawing from the underside of the social order. Not one of the forty day-laborers, gardeners, or vine-growers in the quarter who paid the taille purchased candles at the parish confraternities from 1604 to 1606. Equally precise statements are hard to make for other crafts, given the ambiguities of certain names and trades. Was it Simon Casin the prosperous butcher, or Simon Casin the poor skinner, who belonged to the confraternities of saints Sebastian and Syre? In any event, during the same years no more than 20 of the 136 weavers participated in Saint Nizier's confraternities. The confraternity members listed on the taille roll generally came from among the more well-to-do practitioners of the various trades. The three most heavily assessed cake-makers, oil sellers, and tavernkeepers, for example, all belonged to confraternities. The twelve most prosperous clothiers also appear on the confraternity lists in 1605, all but one under the Virgin's Nativity, together with seven other members of their craft. In an association of ninety-one members these nineteen clothiers, of the fifty-two on the taille roll, formed a nucleus that helped to attract participants from other occupations. In this modest parish, then, established tradesmen kept some of the confraternities strong.[22]

20. Françoise Bibolet 1974: personal communication on patterns of migration into sixteenth-century Troyes.

21. The *taille* roll is in AC, Troyes, F 28.

22. A guild confraternity of the clothiers met at Mary Magdalene's: AD, Aube, 16G 65 (1557), f. 125. Separate and amalgamated lists of those appearing on the taille roll and the Saint Nizier's confraternity lists (18G 17 and 18G 19), together with the codes I have used for classification, are deposited in and available from the Archives of industrial society at the Hillman Library of the University of Pittsburgh, under the title of this book. For the occupations, I adapted the excellent code of Jean-François Bergier and Luigi Solari, "Histoire et élaboration statistique. L'exemple de la population de Genève au XVe siècle," *Mélanges d'histoire économique et sociale en hommage au professeur Antony Babel* (2 vols., Geneva, 1963), I, 203–209.

Few Marian confraternities elsewhere in Troyes retained any appeal. The Immaculate Conception at Mary Magdalene's and at Saint Remy's did still enjoy a measure of popularity, at least relative to the other confraternities in these churches (tables 3 and 6). People who wanted to pay the Virgin special honor, but could no longer do so comfortably at their own parish since their numbers were so few, gathered at either Mary Magdalene's or Saint Remy's for her Immaculate Conception. They continued the trend toward the aggregation of the devout, which we noted at mid-century.

The Holy Sacrament confraternities, similarly, withered in the parishes, but survived and sometimes prospered in the form of the special associations that had been founded to defend the Mass. The confraternity at Saint John's, in a spectacular advance, increased its membership from 142 in 1575 to 254 in 1580, slipped to 190 in 1584, and plunged back to 123 in 1585 (table 8). The temporary appeal may be related to the period of religious revival around 1580. Saint Quirin's Holy Sacrament Confraternity at Provins, on the other hand, followed the pattern of the church's confraternity of the patron, and declined steadily from the 1570s onward.

As participation declined in the parish confraternities, the residual members may increasingly have been women. The names listed in the churchwardens' accounts, when lists were made, are those of the individuals who purchased a candle. If a man's name appears, then his wife may have honored the devotion and participated in the festival, too. But if a woman is listed, she acted alone. At Saint Fiacre's Confraternity of Saint Remy's Church, 22 of the 23 members in 1571 were male, but only 2 of the 7 in 1591. In Saint Syre's Confraternity 16 of the 18 members were male in 1571, but only 1 of 6 in 1591. Fiacre remained strong, on the other hand, at Saint James's Church. Here, 22 of the 31 members in 1563 were male, and 27 of the 34 in 1594. At Saint Nizier's, analogously, 86 of the 91 people listed under the Confraternity of the Nativity of the Virgin in 1605 were men, and the proportion of women was small for all of the other popular confraternities of this exceptional parish. But if there was in fact a general drift toward female membership in declining confraternities, then we have further evidence that an institution that had once enjoyed general appeal was now attractive, more and more, only to specialized clienteles. So, for example, forty-odd supporters of the Catholic League joined together at Saint John's Church on September 17,

1591, to honor Saint Lambert with a confraternity, since on the saint's day one year ago a company of royalist exiles and Protestant seigneurs had tried but failed to surprise the town of Troyes.[23]

It was easier, at the end of the sixteenth century in Champagne, for old institutions like confraternities to decay than for newer ones to flourish, as the history of poor relief demonstrates. The municipal bureau of Troyes succeeded in providing regular support to the poor on its rolls, and in this way helped to prevent the problem of poverty from overwhelming the town. But the grand design of eliminating beggary remained visionary. In the first place, the hospitals could not be fully integrated into the municipal system of poor relief. The jealousy of the patrons, their defense of tradition, autonomy, and privilege, did not give way entirely until the seventeenth-century monarchy, tired of clerical foot-dragging and intent on social discipline, merged all the city's hospitals into a single institution under secular control, in 1635. Our period continued to live with the practices of the past. In 1590 Lieutenant-General Deber of the bailiwick of Troyes drew up a caustic memorandum on the hospitals, for he hoped, vainly, to unite them and use part of their resources to found a seminary, in accordance with a decree of the Council of Trent. Saint Bernard's, he charged, was a "receptacle" for cutpurses and other rascals, and the Hôtel-Dieu-Saint-Esprit held but fifteen to eighteen women who continued to beg from the streets.[24]

Apart from the hospitals, if the bureau were to provide for its own charges effectively and govern them with the necessary rigor, the town would have to be kept free of outsiders who could not support themselves. This meant constant vigilance at the gates, slowing traffic to a virtual standstill so that every itinerant artisan, seedy peddler, and insufficiently laden peasant could be questioned about his business in Troyes. It also meant turning away people to die on the roads. In normal times the first reason alone was a sufficient deterrent to action. As for the native poor, the bureau's assumption that the guild masters could provide continuous employment for every man who had a skill was utopian. A renewal and redraft of the statutes in 1570, after the

23. AD, Aube, 15G 124, f. 52. Only the total sum paid for candles is given, and I cannot precisely calculate the number of members. Pithou ("Histoire ecclésiastique," f. 493) informs us that Catholics "attributed their deliverance to one Saint Lambert, because the event took place on his day." A general procession of the clergy, as well as of the confraternity at Saint John's, marked the anniversary.

24. AC, Troyes, A 23 (16 Feb. 1590).

early religious wars had interfered with the bureau's work, did not even pay lip service to this principle.[25] Employment was simply not that plentiful, and the master who had to lay journeymen off whenever a famine drove up grain prices and emptied customers' purses was hardly prepared to hire all comers, even when times were good. The objectives of the guild, in any event, were much less to serve the general weal than to protect the special interests of its members and to enable them to pass on their monopoly to their heirs.

Public works were no solution to the problem of unemployment, despite the provision in the statutes that the able-bodied, unskilled poor on the rolls be set to work on them. Their real purpose was as much moral as economic. In the words of the 1570 draft, "the mayor and aldermen will determine whether they have the means to set up public works to occupy and employ the powerful and healthy poor, and in so doing avoid laziness, which is the mother and nurse of all vices." The mayor and aldermen, however, were not willing to pay the price, save under the pressure of real crisis, when the number of men without work reached alarming, rather than merely disturbing proportions.[26]

But the most severe check on the bureau was the resistance of townsmen in their private capacity as donors of alms. The wills, once again, tell their story. A few of the notables did make major bequests. The merchant Jean Nervost and his wife endowed the bureau with 2,400 livres, to feed and clothe the poor on the rolls of Troyes, and to provide funds for travelers stopping at Saint Bernard's Hospital; Jean Mauroy, who had founded a new hospital in the village of Colvardey, left 100 livres for the bureau.[27] But among the sixty Troyen wills extant in the notarial archives from 1580 to 1604, not a single testator offered the bureau a penny. Some of them did acknowledge its existence, though hardly with satisfaction. Pierre Beau, a canon of Saint Stephen's, instructed his executors in 1581 to distribute three livres to the poor, unless the bureau's regents wanted to prohibit "the said manual distribution," in which case he ordered it annulled. Both

25. A printed copy of the revised Troyen statutes is in AC, Châlons, GG 215 (11 Dec. 1570).

26. In 1586, for example, when the cloth masters were constrained to "mectre hors leurs maisons leurs gens et serviteurs" because of general high prices, the price of wool, and the poverty of the people, the town instituted public works for those who had lost their jobs, but not for those who had previously been unemployed (AC, Troyes, A 22: 27 July).

27. Boutiot, *Histoire de la ville de Troyes*, IV, 122–124.

Anthoinette Deberleze, wife of the *huissier* (sergeant-at-arms) at the bailiwick court, and Catherine Porcherat, a merchant-cooper's wife, made the same reservation.[28] The former left a setier of rye to the poor widows, at her executors' discretion. The latter directed them to sell a plot of her land and distribute half of the proceeds to the poor of the parish in which she lived, and half to those of the one in which she would be buried. In each of these cases the testator made his executors into surrogates, who would represent him after death by handing out pittances personally and individually, in the same way, assuredly, that he had practiced charity during his lifetime. They would not allow themselves to be reduced to anonymity.

An even more striking case of hostility to the bureau is provided by a man who shared at least part of its vision. The merchant Nicolas Dare was at one time the receiver for the office to control the plague, a matter of such concern in the 1580s that the office was detached from the bureau and given semi-autonomous status. He set aside the 50-livre income on a sixty-year mortgage, both for the needy poor and to apprentice boys who would otherwise have no trade. But Dare directed the bureau to allow his heirs to administer the legacy, or else to see it annulled. Anne Coquault of Reims, who like Dare left funds for apprenticeship, also enjoined the bureau from interfering.[29]

No wonder that many, perhaps most townsmen of Troyes regarded their weekly contribution to the bureau as a thinly camouflaged tax. In 1558, a decade after having founded the bureau, the town council substituted the curés for the two parish notables who, with the church-wardens, had collected pledges and, when necessary, had levied assessments. But this attempt to emphasize the religious nature of the bureau's task and increase its moral authority was unsuccessful, especially since the laymen complained, as was their wont, that the clergy were not carrying a fair share of the burden.[30] The redraft of 1570, after inveighing against begging, "permitted the said inhabitants, over and above their assessments, to bring alms to any place and person for whom they have the desire and affection, provided that they do not interfere with the regulations."[31] During the famine of

---

28. AD, Aube, 2E 3/110 (1581), 2E 7/7 (1586), 2E 3/111 (1595).

29. *Mémoires de Nicolas Dare*, pp. 133–134. For Coquault, see AD, Marne, 4E 16743 (1575), and above, ch. 2, text and n. 58.

30. AC, Troyes, A 12, f. 180 (17 June 1558); ibid., f. 283v (16 April 1560): complaint by Jean Mauroy and a second town councilor.

31. AC, Châlons, GG 215.

1573, each townsman of means was made personally responsible for one of the poor people on the rolls, whom he was to provide with bread.[32]

Old habits died hard in this period. There was simply too much diversity of intent and style among donors for a bureau to impose its ideology by fiat. Consider, for example, the nuance in attitude of two bishops of Châlons, both charitable men. The town had instituted its bureau during the epidemic of 1564, after a disappointing canvass by the churchwardens for voluntary contributions. In the same year Parlement ordered, but could not implement, the union of all the city's hospitals and the charitable confraternity. Bishop Jérôme Bourgeois set up a charitable trust on his personal estate in 1572, to distribute 1,100 livres annually. Of that sum, 600 livres would endow a seminary and provide for the education "in the liberal or mechanical arts," in town or at a university, of poor children whom the bishop and his successors would name. The Hôtel-Dieu was to receive the remaining 500 livres and use them for the town's poor, on condition that the hospitals be united. The bishop and his heirs, but ultimately the bureau, would administer these funds. There was resistance to union, initially by the town council, which had succumbed to the temptation of using the revenues of the leprosery to keep up the fortifications, but more doggedly by the cathedral chapter, as patron of the Hôtel-Dieu. These delays gave the bishop's heirs the opportunity to renege on their obligations. Parlement eventually compelled one of them, Bishop Cosme Clause, to maintain six students at the local college. Their pension was styled a seminary.[33] In his own right, however, Cosme Clause was a generous man. He left 30 livres to the bureau in 1621. Any more, he said, would have diluted his foundation for the poor, which consisted of a principal sum of 20,000 livres. The income was to be used to apprentice and train for service orphan boys and girls. The bishops of Châlons, together with their grand vicar and a representative of the chapter, would select the beneficiaries from among beggars at the church door. In the draft of 1621 Clause specifically excluded from consideration the members of families on the rolls. A year later he modified the language, but not the intent, to exclude "the children of the so-called hidden [poor], especially since those of their relatives who are rich should provide for them."[34] The

32. AC, Troyes, A 18, f. 47 (23 May 1573).
33. AC, Châlons, GG 213.
34. Ibid., GG 216.

bishop accepted the bureau, and even showed it a certain limited good will; it had, after all, become an established institution by his time. Yet he could not accept its criterion for distinguishing among the poor.

The attitude of the townsmen of Châlons to the bureau seems more positive than at Troyes. Four testators made bequests to it, and of considerable sums at that. One of them, Hierosme Goujon, had obviously made a successful adjustment between the older ideals and the institution, since he entrusted the bureau with monies to feed the homeless poor who were lodged in a barn, so that they would pray for his soul.[35] As an explanation for the relative détente at Châlons we can invoke the long tradition and demonstrated usefulness of the Confraternity *dudit denier*, which worked closely with the bureau in distributing allowances to the poor, and in all likelihood helped make it respectable.[36] Goujon, like so many of the charitable testators, mentioned the confraternity in his will.

In Reims, finally, the cardinal of Lorraine was instrumental in establishing the bureau. In 1557 he received the approval of a general council of notable inhabitants to add what was left of the funds of the chartreries to the sum that he intended to provide for the erection of buildings that would house and instruct one hundred boys and one hundred girls, especially orphans, in the liberal and mechanical arts, and maintain an equal number of indigent old people. Excerpts from the bureau's ledger of 1562-63 do in fact show outlays for apprenticeship, and for the maintenance of almshouses for children. Moreover, beyond a rate levied on the townsmen and miscellaneous collections, fines, and legacies, the major part of the bureau's income came, for once, from the clergy.[37] Among our testators only the Damoiselle Coquault mentioned the bureau; she disliked it enough to show overt hostility.

Troyes, Châlons, Reims — to type precisely their public responses, and the private feelings of their inhabitants, toward the poor would require the kind of evidence that the sixteenth century was chary of

35. Nicolas Dehuez, merchant bourgeois, 5 livres to the confraternity and 1 livre to the bureau: AD, Marne, 4E 8826 (1573) ; Hon. Jehan Babault, 15 livres to the bureau: (above, ch. 5, n. 92) ; Marguerite Hurtault, wife of Claude Dehuez, 10 sols to the bureau: 4E 6374 (11 June 1582) ; and Hierosme Goujon: 6 livres to the confraternity and 18 livres to the bureau: as above, ch. 2, text and n. 60.

36. AC, Châlons, GG 218: requests for aid by the poor in 1595-1597 to the bureau, which ruled on them and forwarded the applications it approved to the confraternity for payment.

37. Varin, *Archives législatives*, pt. 2 (Statuts), I, 905-906; ibid., II, 93-94.

recording, and later periods not always careful to preserve. But the complexity of the response, even at the end of our period, and the tendency of many men and women to continue looking toward the past for moral guidance is at least clear. Whether the position embodied in the Troyen statutes of 1546 became the norm of individual conscience as well as the official policy of the Old Regime is a matter for seventeenth-century historians. In our period a man was free, perhaps even compelled, to make up his mind for himself.

A decline in the spirit of neighborliness has been plausibly associated, by English historians, with the hunt for witches in the last decades of the sixteenth and the first part of the seventeenth centuries. Many people would not give personal charity, yet were troubled in their conscience after denying a poor old woman, and fearful that she might repay them in the devil's coin.[38] I have not studied the judicial archives of Champagne, but shall for the sake of completeness mention the cases of witchcraft cited by contemporaries. On Corpus Christi Day of 1594, either at or near Bar-sur-Seine, a woman was tested for sorcery, as several others had been from the time that the spring frost began to threaten the vines. She was tied hand and foot, and thrown in the water to see whether she would sink like a true Christian. Unfortunately, according to Jacques Carorguy, she floated like a boat — or, better, like a witch, since the water had rejected her. Jehan Pussot noted in 1609 "that at this time there was a great rumor of and hunt for sorcerers and sorceresses, but no punishment was meted out in this city, save for the executions in some of the villages around Reims." [39]

The fear of witchcraft indicates a basic uncertainty as to whether rational forces governed social relationships. One sign that the social universe was "out of joint" was the misbehavior of clergy, who no longer necessarily paid lip service to the obligations of their estate. At Troyes in 1572 Saint Stephen's chapter reprimanded a petty canon named Tristan Beaufilz for, among other faults, failing to carry his breviary or learn his hours. Nor would he wear a flowered hat on the appropriate festivals, a custom which, the canons asserted, had been practiced in their church since time immemorial. The youth replied

38. Macfarlane, *Witchcraft,* p. 174; Thomas, *Religion and the Decline of Magic,* pp. 552–569.

39. *Mémoires de Jacques Carorguy,* p. 189; Pussot, "Journalier," pt. 2, p. 106. See also F. E. Sutcliffe, "A propos d'un procès de sorcellerie," *Studies in Modern French Literature Presented to P. Mansell Jones* (Manchester, University Press, 1961), pp. 296–310.

that "he didn't want to be a hypocrite and act like some," who carry the breviary but don't recite it. Beaufilz was no clerical supernumerary who would vanish from view, for a year later he became, by royal appointment, a member of the chapter.[40] Not surprisingly, complaints about the clergy became ever more vocal and acerbic in the late sixteenth century. The meetings of the Estates General, necessitated by the political situation, enabled the people to make their grievances known. The cahier of Arcis-sur-Aube in 1576 demanded that all those who had left the faith be compelled to return to Catholicism, and went on to blame the existence of heresy on the lack of instruction by a negligent and unlearned clergy, and on the evil conduct of priests "who are the shadows rather than the light of the world." The villagers of Bourdenay, east of Troyes, echoed a general theme in calling for reformation of "the frequent and public vices" of churchmen. Criticism of a dissolute clergy was repeated in the cahiers of 1614, together with a strong demand that curés either reside in their villages or at least provide capable vicars.[41] Such grievances were stated articulately, and suggest the lawyers' hand, but they may also have spoken the minds of the people. Repeatedly in the general chapters that met twice a year at the Cathedral of Troyes, Dean Guillaume de Taix exhorted the canons to reform themselves, and quell the general complaints.[42]

The beginnings of a clerical reform in particular, and a Catholic reformation in general, are also apparent during the period, but they did not reach fruition until well into the seventeenth century. On his return from the Council of Trent the cardinal of Lorraine had Gentien Hervet publish a French translation of the decrees, which however the cardinal could not induce the queen mother to promulgate as law. Hervet also published a catechism. The cardinal himself founded a seminary in 1567, the first of its kind in France.[43] At a pro-

40. AD, Aube, 6G 29, ff. 20v (7 Aug. 1572), 22, 25, 26, 108, 178.

41. *Documents inédits relatifs aux Etats-généraux*, pp. 141 and 144; Yves Durand, *Cahiers de doléances du bailliage de Troyes pour les Etats-généraux de 1614* (Paris, 1966), pp. 77–89, 99, 103–107, 118–124, 138, 168–172, 184–194, 198–204, 205–209, 285–287.

42. AD, Aube, G 1288, f. 38v (5 July 1576), f. 114v (1 July 1577), f. 231 (2 July 1578), ff. 285v–286 (3 Jan. 1579), and regularly until de Taix's death: G 1292, f. 268 (4 Sept. 1599).

43. Gentien Hervet, trans., *Le sainct, sacré, universel et général Concile de Trente* . . . (Paris, 1564), and *Catéchisme et ample instruction de tout ce qui appartient au devoir d'un chrestien* . . . (Paris, 1568); AD, Marne, G 178–180: accounts of the seminary, 1575–1577.

vincial synod in 1583 his nephew and successor the cardinal of Guise issued a number of decrees designed to counter the centrifugal tendencies of earlier religious practice. No confraternities were to be held during Sunday parish masses; no one was to say his hours aloud during the Mass; and no masses were to be said outside church, save in oratories that were specifically dedicated to divine services.[44] But innovations were often condemned as vigorously as continuing abuses. In 1576 the curé of Saint Nizier's parish of Troyes, Canon Molé, had to clear himself of the suspicion of heresy. He had had the parish children recite their catechism in dialogue form. The Jesuits who preached at Reims were accused of heresy because of the novelty of their sermons. No doubt here as at Provins, they did not pay sufficient attention and do appropriate honor to the Virgin and the saints.[45] Toward the end of the century there was a cacophony of opinions among Catholics on proper belief and appropriate religious behavior. All may have agreed that the clergy needed reform, yet no common denominator of understanding indicated the direction in which a reformed clergy should lead the people. Too much emphasis on innovation led to the charge of heresy, too little to that of sloth. During the next hundred years the clergy would benefit from strong direction and saintly inspiration, and bring a Catholic reformation to France. But by that time the divergences among the laity may have been too pronounced and too apparent for any illusions about a quest for unity.

The dissipation of the previous religious mood is one sign that over the course of the sixteenth century the changes to Catholicism in Champagne had been more impressive than the similarities. Revivalism in the later decades may have recalled the earlier, expressionist religion, but only in a brittle, superficial manner. Around 1500 the prevailing themes of religious life had been deeply rooted, as parish confraternities, mystery plays, and a poignant, sentimental art were reaching maturity. Men and women entrusted their hopes for this world and the next to the mediation of the Virgin and the saints, while at the same time they professed the unity that, ideally at least,

44. *Les actes de la province ecclésiastique de Reims,* ed. Thomas Gousset (4 vols., Reims, 1842–1844), III, 443, 447, 449. For a fine discussion of the general movement of which these particular decrees are a part, see John Bossy, "The Counter-Reformation and the People of Catholic Europe," *Past and Present,* no. 47 (1970), 51–70.

45. AD, Aube, G 1288, f. 12v (20 April 1576); Pussot, "Journalier," pt. 2, p. 213; Haton, *Mémoires,* II, 636.

bound them all together as Christians. For they perceived deep con-
flicts among the estates of society, and were concerned about God's
attitude toward themselves. It was difficult for them to delimit the
boundaries between his prerogative and the saints' influence, since
the hierarchies of church and state, which served as a model for the
divine order, had long been in disarray. This religious climate nurtured a teeming rather than a disciplined clergy, and suited an elite
which, in patronage and participation, showed an example to the rest
of the people.

But by the second third of the century changing social and political
conditions vitiated forms that had by now become traditional. A more
sophisticated, international art appealed to the tastes and prejudices
of those who commissioned works of sculpture and stained-glass windows. The mystery plays seemed naive and bizarre to the Parlement
of Paris and to provincial oligarchies. Some people also sensed an affront to God when amateur actors represented divine figures before
huge crowds that sought amusement as well as spiritual benefit. Confraternities declined in popularity as many men and women became
less interested in public, collective religious behavior and less devoted
to the Virgin and the patron saints. A minority of Christians went
further, and rejected the established religion. Even in a prosaic province like Champagne, the Reform was vigorous enough to give its
leaders confidence of rapid and complete triumph, once they had seen
the hand of God in the accidents of royal succession. Their movement
attracted some, left many indifferent, and repelled a third group that
included the advocates of bloody repression. At the same time the
Protestant challenge led many committed Catholics to manifest their
loyalty by reinvigorating the religious style of their fathers. But now
the number of sardonic spectators was considerably larger, and they
had no hesitation about voicing as well as recording their thoughts.

Contemporaries sometimes tried to deny the pervading atmosphere
of religious hostility. Nicolas Pithou alleged to the queen mother in
a petition of 1565 that "we are all, whether Catholics or of the Religion, related, or allied by marriage to one another, and there is so
good a congruity and unity among us all that the purse of one is not
closed to the other. We often see and visit each other in banquets and
in familiar conversation." The threat of disorder came, he maintained,
not from "the good and notable Catholic bourgeois," but rather from
"a pack of some sort of rascals and idlers," who were drunken with

the license that they had learned in the wars, and not prepared to return to their trades.[46] But the days of dinner parties at which religion
and politics could be discussed were over, and only in Pithou's imagination did the demon of discord wear the rags of the lower class. The
divisions among the elite, within Catholicism as well as between the
two religions, precluded the strong governing hand that would have
given direction to ordinary people. As a result, the fragmentation of
belief and behavior, and mutual suspicion and disgust, characterized
the late sixteenth century, and created a widespread longing for an
effective Catholic reformation.

Appendix

Bibliography

Index

Appendix / Membership in the Confraternities of Champagne

1. Saint Nicholas's Church, Troyes.
2. Saint Pantaleon's Church, Troyes.
3. Mary Magdalene's Church, Troyes.
4. Saint John's Church, Troyes.
5. Saint James's Church, Troyes.
6. Saint Remy's Church, Troyes.
7. Saint Nizier's Church, Troyes.
8. Other confraternities.

The churches of Troyes are listed west to east. The choice of dates is governed by the completeness of the evidence as well as by the desire to illustrate general trends.

Figures in parentheses were calculated by me from the total amount of money contributed. An "x" means that I cannot calculate the number of members with precision. An "n.g." means that the confraternity met, but the number of members was not given. An "sb." means, unless otherwise noted, that the confraternity did not meet, but that someone nevertheless agreed to keep the baton, and made an offering for the privilege. In other words the confraternity was dormant.

Totals are provided only when the information for a given year is complete.

Table 1.   Confraternity membership at Saint Nicholas's Church, Troyes[a]

Confraternity	1540	1544	1548	1552	1554	1589	1595
St. Sebastian	—	—	—	—	—	10	10
St. Joseph	16	16	(12)	—	2	2	3
Annunciation	—	—	—	—	—	4	2
Notre-Dame of Loreto	—	(150)	108	—	—	—	—
Holy Sepulcher	—	x	—	—	—	—	—
Our Lord (or the Resurrection)	—	—	—	—	—	—	1
St. Nicholas in the Summer	24	23	11	7	—	1	3
St. Gond	6	10	5	7	4	4	4
Corpus Christi	18	x	12	—	10	4	4
St. Claude	—	x	—	—	—	—	2
St. Margaret	10	9	10	7	12	—	0
St. Anne	—	—	—	—	—	11	4
St. Roche	—	x	—	—	—	13	7
St. Adrian	17	3	4	2	2	—	1
Holy Cross	—	—	—	8	x	—	1
St. Catherine	—	—	—	—	—	3	0
St. Nicholas in the Winter	—	x	—	52	—	8	4
Immaculate Conception	—	x	—	8	—	—	1

Source: AD, Aube, 17G 12–30.

[a] The increasing number of confraternities reflects the successive stages in the construction of the chapels of this church.

Table 2. Confraternity membership at Saint Pantaleon's Church, Troyes

Confraternity	1515	1519	1522	1537	1553	1556	1558	1585	1593
St. Genevieve	44	40	27	30	19	15	18	10	2
St. Maur	29	23	26	13	3	5	5	1	—
St. Sebastian	20	25	27	22	6	6	5	—	sb.
St. Joseph	—	—	—	—	14	18	8	3	—
Annunciation	—	—	—	—	15	6	8	—	—
St. Gond	20	35	28	14	2	sb.	0	—	—
Corpus Christi	57	54	59	40	17	16	14	—	—
St. Claude	40	33	36	19	15	10	12	2	—
St. Margaret	—	—	—	—	12	6	5	—	—
St. Pantaleon	125	140	125	126	76	65	58	17	3
Assumption	36	35	27	23	8	10	9	—	—
St. Roche	48	72	54	27	7	7	3	—	—
St. Adrian	17	26	15	9	1	1	—	—	—
St. Lambert	—	—	—	—	—	—	—	—	4
Immaculate Conception	37	37	19	19	8	4	7	1	sb.
Totals	473	520	443	342	203	169	152	34	9

Source: AD, Aube, 19G 3–23.

Table 3. Confraternity membership at Mary Magdalene's Church, Troyes

Confraternity	1411	1412	1442	1472	1512	1519
St. Maur	n.g.	42	9	51	50	57
St. Sebastian[a]	—	—	4	36	43	68
St. Blaise	—	—	—	—	83	107
St. Joseph	—	—	—	—	—	—
Translation of the Magdalene's Relics	—	—	—	—	80	70
St. Quirin[b]	—	—	—	—	—	—
Corpus Christi[c]	—	3sb.[e]	113	138	93	102
St. Claude	—	—	10	9	34	41
St. Syre	—	—	—	—	—	25
St. Mary Magdalene[d]	—	—	42	—	—	—
St. Anne	12	10	—	—	26	30
Assumption	—	—	—	—	—	111
St. Roche	—	—	—	—	27	88
St. Fiacre	—	—	—	—	37	41
St. Reine	—	—	—	—	—	—
St. Michael	—	—	—	—	14	15
St. Urse	—	—	—	—	3	2
St. Loup	—	—	—	—	17	20
St. Barbara	—	—	—	23	36	41
Immaculate Conception	144	124	59	89	138	138
Totals without Quirin	—	—	—	346	681	956
Totals with Quirin[b]	—	—	—	—	—	—

Source: AD, Aube, 16G 6–92.

[a] Occasionally called Saints Sebastian and Fabian, until 1451.

[b] Until after 1519, Quirin's confrères were listed in a separate ledger, which has not been preserved.

[c] Called the Confraternity of Jesus until 1444.

[d] The clothiers' guild preëmpted the festival with its guild confraternity; the fifteenth-century figure, but probably not the sixteenth, is the clothiers'.

[e] The presence of three standard-bearers suggests, but does not prove, that the confraternity had a substantial membership.

Table 3 (cont.)

Confraternity	1542	1551	1557	1562	1589	1600
St. Maur	39	32	17	20	10	5
St. Sebastian	53	40	25	18	15	12
St. Blaise	115	114	80	51	26	14
St. Joseph	36	38	26	17	10	4
Translation of the Magdalene's Relics	51	23	10	5	—	—
St. Quirin	218	196	150	123	62	29
Corpus Christi	72	38	17	5	—	—
St. Claude	41	21	14	9	7	4
St. Syre	47	40	31	30	23	12
St. Mary Magdalene	26	—	—	—	—	—
St. Anne	35	33	29	24	12	4
Assumption	41	23	11	7	1	—
St. Roche	38	28	19	21	18	15
St. Fiacre	46	48	43	23	23	16
St. Reine	—	—	—	—	—	9
St. Michael	15	12	8	5	3	—
St. Urse	1	5	3	0	—	—
St. Loup	27	17	20	13	9	2
St. Barbara	27	20	13	5	5	4
Immaculate Conception	182	186	147	104	59	32
Totals without Quirin	892	718	513	357	221	133
Totals with Quirin	1110	914	663	480	283	162

Table 4. Confraternity membership at Saint John's Church, Troyes

Confraternity	1442	1509	1513	1527	1544	1556	1561	1564	1595
St. Maur	110	144	127	88	58	45	(40)	(53)	n.g.
St. Sebastian	—	60	48	(67)	34	13	(12)	(20)	n.g.
Jesus (Corpus Christi Day)	110	93	87	(45)	—	—	—	—	—
Corpus Christi	—	—	—	—	39	18	(10)	(8)	—
St. Claude	22	114	105	(63)	40	23	(11)	(18)	3
St. Syre	—	—	—	(41)	62	56	(45)	(72)	37
St. John the Baptist	—	121	119	(122)	103	48	(32)	(28)	2
St. Anne	—	—	—	—	32	33	(18)	(22)	1
Assumption	—	71	55	(41)	29	10	(16)	(6)	—
St. Roche	—	176	153	(157)	89	42	(27)	(55)	10
Decapitation of St. John the Baptist	12	56	53	(27)	11	3	(2)	(4)	0
St. Fiacre	—	136	137	(102)	98	88	(77)	(84)	79
Nativity of the Virgin	—	15	(14)	(1)	—	—	—	—	—
St. Edmund	—	n.g.	75	(78)	105	53	(35)	(45)	—
St. Barbara	—	n.g.	83	(46)	28	14	(10)	(10)	—
Immaculate Conception	—	n.g.	sb.	—	36	10	(9)	(20)	—
Totals	—	—	1056	(878)	764	456	(344)	(445)	—

Source: AD, Aube, 15G 27–131.

Table 5. Confraternity membership at Saint James's Church, Troyes

Confraternity	1432	1434	1464	1494	1503	1520	1525	1530	1538	1554	1563	1583	1594	1600
St. Maur	—	—	9	14	19	16	30	22	21	19	14	12	12	4
St. Sebastian	—	4	28	12	10	19	30	26	14	9	17	7	9	3
Annunciation	—	37	28	23	25	19	22	18	7	6	4	2	—	—
St. Gond	—	—	—	—	—	—	31	20	15	6	17	8	10	3
Corpus Christi	43	60	44	26	22	29	23	18	12	5	4	2	11	—
St. Claude	—	—	—	9	14	25	24	23	19	15	10	7	22	—
St. Syre	—	—	—	—	—	—	—	—	—	—	13	8	1	8
St. James	1	sb.	—	26	40	44	35	25	15	6	3	5	—	—
St. Anne	—	x	—	—	—	—	—	—	—	—	—	—	—	—
St. Roche	—	—	—	—	22	22	34	33	12	13	17	24	34	20
St. Fiacre	—	—	—	15	—	—	—	—	8	32	31	—	—	—
St. Adrian	—	—	—	—	—	—	—	—	—	—	—	—	—	—
St. Andrew	—	—	—	—	6	—	—	—	—	—	—	—	—	—
Immaculate Conception	n.g.	29	26	15	34	37	26	21	15	9	7	—	—	—
Totals	—	—	135	140	192	211	255	206	138	120	137	75	99	38

Source: AD, Aube, 14G 2–55

Table 6.   Confraternity membership at Saint Remy's Church, Troyes

Confraternity	1435	1473	1501	1522	1571	1575	1580	1583	1588	1592
St. Maur	10	1	32	n.g.	9	7	7	2	0	4
St. Sebastian	—	—	24	n.g.	6	2	3	2	1	—
St. Joseph	—	—	—	n.g.	3	2	—	sb.	0	—
St. Marcou	—	—	—	n.g.	30	17	12	13	5	4
St. Avoie	—	—	5	n.g.	1	sb.	—	—	—	—
St. Gond	—	—	—	n.g.	4	3	—	0	—	—
Corpus Christi	20	7	65	66	7	5	4	2	sb.	sb.
St. Claude	—	2	23	n.g.	6	3	1	sb.	1	sb.
St. Syre	—	—	—	21	18	13	6	5	1	2
St. Main	—	—	—	25	4	2	2	sb.	—	—
St. Margaret	—	—	—	7	2	0	—	0	—	—
St. James	—	—	5	2	—	—	—	—	—	—
St. Anne	—	1	8	6	15	8	8	6	0	—
St. Memmie	—	3	1	1	—	—	—	—	—	—
St. Lawrence	—	—	3	2	—	—	—	—	—	—
St. Roche	—	—	19	41	9	8	3	6	2	—
St. Fiacre	—	—	—	33	23	28	20	14	13	9
N.-D. de Liesse	—	—	—	—	21	15	21	16	11	9
St. Remy	4	1	57	56	14	12	11	10	3	sb.
St. Edmund	—	—	—	11	6	4	2	2	3	—
St. Barbara	—	1	25	10	0	0	sb.	—	—	—
Immaculate Conception	45	1	77	103	44	48	56	35	23	14
St. Anthony	—	—	—	—	4	5	3	1	—	—
Totals	79	17	344	—	226	182	159	114	63	42

Source: AD, Aube, 20G 15 (1435), 20G 16 (1473), 20G 19 (1501), 14G 17 (1522), at present mistakenly classed with Saint James's Church, and 20G 13 (1571–1592).

Table 7. Confraternity membership at Saint Nizier's Church, Troyes

Confraternity	1524	1588	1599	1600	1605
St. Maur	n.g.	n.g.	n.g.	4	6
St. Sebastian	n.g.	n.g.	n.g.	120	108
St. Nizier	n.g.	n.g.	n.g.	2	—
St. Gond	n.g.	n.g.	n.g.	15	13
Corpus Christi	93	n.g.	n.g.	x	x
St. Syre	56	40	n.g.	38	41
St. Barbara	x	—	—	—	—
St. Eloi	18	11	n.g.	12	8
St. Anne	—	47	47	n.g.	46
St. Roche	116	88	88	n.g.	75
St. Fiacre	75	15	12	n.g.	20
St. Gilles	—	3	20	n.g.	14
Nativity of the Virgin	—	5	62	n.g.	91
St. Hubert	—	0	sb.	n.g.	5
St. Edmund	26	4	7	n.g.	8
St. Barbara	—	0	0	n.g.	1
St. Nicholas	—	0	0	n.g.	0
Immaculate Conception	—	19	7	n.g.	3
Totals	—	—	434a		439

Source: AD, Aube, 18G 9–19.

a Total for July 1599 to June 1600, since only the second half of the first year and the first half of the second are given.

Table 8.   Membership at other confraternities

Confraternity	1499	1505	1535	1545	1550	1555	1558	1559
The Cross, at St. Remy's Church, Troyes	—	—	—	—	—	337	311	—
The Holy Sacrament, at St. Urban's collegial church, Troyes	—	—	107	147	135	—	—	—
The Annunciation, at St. Urban's Church, Troyes	(145)	—	—	—	50	—	—	—
The Holy Sacrament, at St. John's Church, Troyes	—	—	—	—	—	—	—	151
The Holy Sacrament, at St. Quirin's collegial church, Provins	—	—	—	—	—	213	225	218
St. Quirin's, at his church, Provins	—	—	—	—	—	200	206	197
St. Gibrian's, at St. Remy's Monastery, Reims	—	32	—	—	—	68	—	—

Sources: The Cross: AD, Aube, 20G 135–141; St. Urban's Church: 10G 757–765 and 10G 133–138; St. John's Church: 15G 405; St. Quirin's Church: BC, Provins, MS 221; St. Remy's Monastery: AD, Marne (Reims depot), H 1306 and 1308.

Table 8 (cont.)

Confraternity	1561	1565	1569	1575	1580	1585	1592	1595
The Cross, at St. Remy's Church, Troyes	289	240	251	—	—	—	129	127
The Holy Sacrament, at St. Urban's collegial church, Troyes	—	—	—	129	—	149	—	—
The Annunciation, at St. Urban's Church, Troyes	—	—	—	—	13	—	—	11
The Holy Sacrament, at St. John's Church, Troyes	131	148	172	142	254	123	—	—
The Holy Sacrament, at St. Quirin's collegial church, Provins	224	203	216	176	165	93	55	56
St. Quirin's, at his church, Provins	204	207	208	172	167	109	67	66
St. Gibrian's, at St. Remy's Monastery, Reims	—	25	—	—	—	22	—	—

Bibliography

Abbreviations

AC   Archives communales
AD   Archives départementales
BC   Bibliothèque communale
BN   Bibliothèque nationale

Principal Manuscript Collections

Troyes

AD, Aube   The copious set of parish archives for the city, and the fragmentary remains from the rest of the department, in the subseries of series G, were complemented by the archives of the cathedral and collegial churches, notably the minutes of the canons' deliberations. Series E, on family records, contains wills, inventories, and foundations; 2E, the notarial archives, includes late sixteenth-century wills. Gildas Bernard, *Guide des archives départementales de l'Aube* (Troyes, Impr. la Renaissance, 1967), provides an excellent orientation.

AC   Series A: the town council minutes; M and AA, carton 35, on poor relief; AA, carton 60, on the mystery plays; BB 14, on religious troubles.

BC   MS 2282 is the text of the Passion play performed at Troyes.

Châlons

AD, Marne   The wills in series 4E, principally from Reims and Châlons, are as rich in their class as are the parish documents of Troyes. Series G, conversely, was of limited value, with only a scattering of parish records.

AC   The town council minutes, series BB, necessarily command less attention than the highly-charged affairs of Troyes, but series GG has important if disparate information on Protestants, plagues, hospitals, and poor relief. The Protestant *état civil* has also been preserved.

Reims

AD, Marne   Visitations of the diocese, and the accounts of Saint Gibrian's
(Reims depot)   Confraternity at Saint Remy's Monastery.

Langres

BC   MSS 65-67 on confraternities are among the remains from a disastrous nineteenth-century fire.

Provins

BC   MSS 208, 221, and 258 relate to wills, confraternities, and one
     parish.

Melun

AD   H 831 is a fifteenth-century register of Saint Foy's Confrater-
     nity at Coulommiers.

Paris

BN   The Collection Dupuy, with its letters of the Pithous and
     Caracciolo, and memoirs on religious troubles in the province,
     was significant for Champagne. MS 698 is Nicolas Pithou, "His-
     toire ecclésiastique de l'église de la ville de Troyes, capitalle
     du conté et pays de Champagne, de la restauration du pur
     service de Dieu et de l'ancien ministère en la dicte église,
     contenant sa renaissance et son accroissement et les troubles,
     persécutions et autres choses remarcables advenues en la dicte
     église jusques en l'an mil cinq cent quatre-vingt et quatorze."
     The Collection de Champagne supplemented the departmen-
     tal archives on such matters as confraternities and processions.

Published Sources

Les actes de la province ecclésiastique de Reims. Ed. Thomas Gousset. 4 vols.
    Reims, 1842–1844.
The Anonimalle Chronicle, 1333 to 1381. Ed. V.H. Galbraith. Manchester, At
    the University Press, 1927.
Bailly, Balthasar. *L'importunité et malheur de noz ans.* Troyes, Claude Gar-
    nier, 1576.
Balourdet, Loys. *La guide des chemins pour le voyage de Hiérusalem et autres
    villes et lieux de la terre saincte.* Châlons, C. Guyot, 1601.
Barrillon, Jean. *Journal de Jean Barrillon, secrétaire du chancelier Duprat,
    1515–1521.* Ed. Pierre de Vaissière. 2 vols. Société de l'histoire de France.
    Paris, 1897–1899.
Barthélemy, Edouard. "Recueil des pierres tombales des églises et couvents de
    Châlons-sur-Marne." *Revue de Champagne et de Brie,* 24 (1887), 486–582;
    25 (1888), 479–563.
Batllori, M. "Un nuevo testimonio del 'Corpus de Sang.'" *Analecta sacra Tar-
    raconensia,* 22 (1949), 51–53.
Bellemère, Françoys. *Directoire de la vie humaine, contenant quatre traictez;
    le premier est du régime de la personne; le second est la forme et manière
    de soy confesser; le tiers est du remède contre scrupule de conscience; le
    quart est la forme de soy préparer à recevoir le créateur.* Troyes, Le Coq, n.d.
Benoist, René. *Traicté des processions des chrestiens auquel il est discouru
    pourquoy la croix y est elsvée et portée.* Paris, Michel de Roigny, 1572.
[Bèze, Théodore de]. *Correspondance de Théodore de Bèze.* Ed. Hippolyte
    Aubert et al. Geneva, E. Droz, 1960–.
Blaiseau, Christofle. *Coppie du sermon prononcé en l'église cathédrale de
    Troyes, au retour de la procession générale, le dimanche trentiesme iour
    d'aoust, mil cinq cens quatre vingts et sept.* Troyes, Denis de Villerval, n.d.

[Blauf, Julien.] *Annales d'Issoire*. Ed. J.-B. Bouillet. Clermont-Ferrand, 1848.

Buffet, François. *Chronique de Buffet, 1580–1588; la Ligue à Metz*. Ed. E. de Bouteiller. Paris, 1884.

Calvin, Jean. *Ioannis Calvini opera quae supersunt omnia*. Corpus reformatorum, vols. 29–87. Brunswick, 1863–1900. Reprint, 59 vols. in 58. New York, Johnson Reprint Corporation, 1964.

Camusat, Nicolas. *Promptuarium sacrarum antiquitatum Tricassinae dioecesis*. Troyes, Le Coq, 1610.

Caracciolo, Antoine. *Le mirouer de vraye religion*. Paris, Simon de Colines, 1544.

Carorguy, Jacques. *Mémoires de Jacques Carorguy, greffier de Bar-sur-Seine, 1582–1595*. Ed. Edmond Bruwaert. Paris, 1880.

Castelnau, Michel de. *Mémoires*. Ed. J. Le Laboureur. 3 vols. Brussels, 1731.

Chastellain, Georges. *Oeuvres*. Ed. Kervyn de Lettenhove. 8 vols. 1863–1866. Reprint. Geneva, Slatkine, 1971.

Chavannes, E. "Liste des réfugiés français à Lausanne, de juin 1547 à décembre 1574." Société de l'histoire du protestantisme français: *Bulletin*, 21 (1872), 463–474.

The Chronicle of Calais in the Reigns of Henry VII. and Henry VIII., to the Year 1540. Ed. John Gough Nichols. Camden Society, vol. 35. London, 1846.

Chronicle of the Grey Friars of London (1189–1556). In *Monumenta Franciscana*, vol. II, ed. Richard Howlett. London, 1882.

Les chroniques de la ville de Metz . . . 900–1552. Ed. J.F. Huguenin. Metz, 1838.

Collection des principaux obituaires et confraternités du diocèse de Troyes . . . Ed. Charles Lalore. Collection de documents inédits relatifs à la ville de Troyes et à la Champagne méridionale publiés par la Société académique de l'Aube, II. Troyes, 1882.

Cy commence une petite instruction et manière de vivre pour une femme séculière comme elle se doit conduire en pensées parolles et oeuvres tout au long du jour pour tous les iours de la vie pour plaire à Nostre Seigneur et amasser richesses célestes au proffit et salut de son âme. Troyes, Jean du Ruau, n.d.

Daval, Guillaume, and Daval, Jean. *Histoire de la Réformation à Dieppe*. Ed. Emile Lesens. 2 vols. Rouen, 1878–1879.

Demaison, Louis. "Documents sur les draperies de Reims au Moyen Age." *Bibliothèque de l'Ecole des chartes*, 89 (1928), 5–39.

Des Guerrois, Marie-Nicolas. *La saincteté chrestienne contenant les vie, mort et miracles de plusieurs saincts de France, et autres pays, qui ne sont dans les vies de saincts, et dont les relics sont au diocèse et ville de Troyes. . . .* Troyes, Jacquard, 1637.

Diario dell'assemblea de' vescovi à Poissy. Joseph Roserot de Melin, "Etude sur les relations du Saint-Siège et l'église de France dans la seconde moitié du XVIe siècle: I. Rome et Poissy (1560–1561)," *Ecole française de Rome, Mélanges d'archéologie et d'histoire*, 39 (1921–1922), 47–151.

Dobelmann, S. "Une livre de raison champenois." *Bibliothèque d'humanisme et renaissance; travaux et documents*, 5 (1944), 394–404.

Documents inédits tirés des archives de Troyes et relatifs aux Etats-généraux. Ed. T. Boutiot. Collection de documents inédits relatifs à la ville de Troyes et à la Champagne méridionale publiés par la Société académique de l'Aube, I, 1-218. Troyes, 1878.

Durand, Yves. *Cahiers de doléances du bailliage de Troyes pour les Etats Généraux de 1614.* Paris, Presses universitaires, 1966.

Erasmus, Desiderius. *Opus epistolarum Des. Erasmi Roterodami.* Ed. P.S. Allen. Vol. II (1514–1517). Oxford, At the Clarendon Press, 1910.

Estienne, Charles. *La guide des chemins de France.* Ed. Jean Bonnerot. 2 vols. Paris, H. Champion, 1935–1936.

Flamang, Guillaume. *La vie et passion de sainct Didier martir et évesque de Lengres.* Paris, 1855.

Froissart, Jean. *Chroniques de J. Froissart,* vol. X (1380–1382). Ed. Gaston Raynaud. Société de l'histoire de France. Paris, 1897.

Gower, John. *The Complete Works of John Gower.* Ed. G. C. Macaulay. 4 vols. Oxford, At the Clarendon Press, 1899–1902.

Le grand calendrier et compost des bergers avec leur astrologie et plusieurs aultres sciences salutaires tant pour les âmes que pour la santé des corps. Troyes, Jean Le Coq, 1541.

Les grandes chroniques de France; chronique des règnes de Jean II et de Charles V. Ed. Roland Delachenal. 4 vols. Société de l'histoire de France. Paris, Renouard, H. Laurens, succ., 1910–1920.

Le grant calendrier et compost des bergiers avecq leur astrologie et plusieurs autres choses. Troyes, Nicolas Le Rouge, 1529.

Guise, François de Lorraine. *Mémoires de François de Lorraine, duc d'Aumale et de Guise.* Nouvelle collection des mémoires pour servir à l'histoire de France, ed. J.F. Michaud, vol. VI. Paris, 1839.

Haag, Eugène. "Fragment de statistique officielle des églises réformées de France, trois ans avant la Révocation." Société de l'histoire du protestantisme français: *Bulletin,* 7 (1858), 22–26.

Hall, Edward. *The Union of the Two Noble and Illustre Famelies of Lancastre & Yorke.* . . . 1809. Reprint. New York, AMS Press, 1965.

Haton, Claude. *Mémoires.* Ed. F. Bourquelot, 2 vols. Paris, 1857.

Hérelle, Georges. *Documents inédits sur le Protestantisme à Vitry-le-François, Epense, Heiltz-le-Maurupt, Nettancourt et Vassy, depuis la fin des guerres de religion jusqu'à la Révolution française.* 3 vols. Paris, Picard, 1903–1908.

──────. *La Réforme et la Ligue en Champagne; documents.* . . . 2 vols. Paris, 1887–1892.

Hervet, Gentien. *Catéchisme et ample instruction de tout ce qui appartient au devoir d'un chrestien, principalement des curéz et vicaires, et tous ceux qui ont charge des églises parrochiales, en ce qui est requis au principal devoir de leurs charges.* . . . Paris, Nicolas Chesneau, 1568.

──────. *Discours sur ce que les pilleurs, voleurs et bruslers d'églises disent qu'ils n'en veulent qu'aux prestres, au peuple de Rheims et des environs.* Reims, Foigny, 1562.

──────, trans. *Le sainct, sacré, universel et général Concile de Trente.* . . . Paris, N. Chesneau, 1564.

Heures à l'usage de Sens, au long, sans rien requerir. Troyes, Jean du Ruau, [ca. 1581].

Heures à l'usaige de Troyes, au long, sans rien requerir. Troyes, Le Coq, [ca. 1514].

Histoire ecclésiastique des églises reformées au royaume de France. Ed. G. Baum and E. Cunitz. 3 vols. Paris, 1883–1889.

Inventaire des principales églises de Troyes. Ed. Charles Lalore. Collection de

documents inédits relatifs à la ville de Troyes et à la Champagne méridionale publiés par la Société académique de l'Aube, 2 vols. Troyes, 1893.

Isambert, François-A. *Recueil général des anciennes lois françaises depuis l'an
420 jusqu'à la révolution de 1789.* 29 vols. Paris, 1821–1833.

Jadart, Henri, ed. "Un troisième livret de famille rémois de 1567 à 1753."
Travaux de l'Académie nationale de Reims, 121 (1906–1907), vol. I, 259–291.

Journal d'un bourgeois de Paris sous le règne de François Premier. Ed. V.-L.
Bourrilly, Paris. A. Picard, 1910.

Lafosse, Jean de. *Journal d'un curé ligueur de Paris sous les trois derniers
Valois, suivi du Journal du secrétaire de Philippe de Bec, archevêque de
Reims de 1588 à 1605.* Ed. E. de Barthélemy. Paris [1866].

La Marck, Robert de. *Mémoires du maréchal de Florange, dit le Jeune Adventureux.* Ed. Robert Goubaix and P.-A. Lemoisne. Société de l'histoire de
France. Vol. I. Paris, Renouard, 1912. Vol. II. Paris, E. Champion, 1924.

La Place, Pierre de. *Commentaires de l'estat de la religion et république soubs
les rois Henry et François seconds et Charles neufiesme.* Ed. J.A.C. Buchon.
Panthéon littéraire, vol. XXII. Paris, 1836.

L'Estoile, Pierre. *Mémoires-journaux.* Ed. G. Brunet et al. 12 vols. Paris, 1875–
1896.

Le livre des habitants de Genève. Ed. Paul-F. Geisendorf. 2 vols. Geneva, E.
Droz, 1957 and 1963.

Louvret, Jean. "Journal, ou récit véritable de tout ce qui est advenu digne de
mémoire tant en la ville d'Angers, pays d'Anjou et autres lieux, depuis l'an
1560 jusqu'à l'an 1634." *Revue de l'Anjou et de Maine et Loire,* 3–5 (1854–
1856).

Mansi, Joannes. "Concilium Senonese." In *Sacrarum conciliorum nova et amplissima collectio,* vol. 32, cols. 1149–1202. Paris, H. Welter, 1902.

Marguerite de Navarre. *Nouvelles.* Ed. Yves Le Hir. Paris, Presses universitaires,
1967.

Matthey, Léon. "Ecoliers français inscrits à l'Académie de Genève." *Biblio-
graphie d'humanisme et renaissance; travaux et documents,* 11 (1949), 86–98,
224–241.

Mémoires et livre de famille de Nicolas Dare. Collection de documents inédits
relatifs à la ville de Troyes et à la Champagne méridionale publiés par la
Société académique de l'Aube, III, 7-164. Troyes, 1886.

Mergey, Jean de. *Mémoires du sieur Jean de Mergey, gentilhomme champenois.*
In M. Petitot, *Collection complète des mémoires relatifs à l'histoire de France,*
ser. 1, vol. 34, pp. 3–81. Paris, 1823.

Meurier, Hubert. *Le premier concile provincial tenu à Rheims, l'an 1583.* Reims,
Foigny, 1586.

————. *Traicté de l'institution et vray usage des processions tant ordinaires,
qu'extraordinaires, qui se font en l'église catholique, contenant un ample
discours de ce qui s'est passé pour ce regard en la province de Champaigne
depuis le 22 de juillet jusques au 25 d'octobre 1583. Divisé en trois sermons,
faits en la grande église de Rheims.* Reims, Jean de Foigny, 1584.

Millard, A., ed. "Le cahier des voeux du bailliage de Chaumont-en-Bassigny
pour les Etats Généraux en 1576." *Revue de Champagne et de Brie,* 5 (1878),
362–370.

More, Thomas. *Utopia.* Ed. Edward Surtz, S.J., and J.H. Hexter. *The Complete
Works of St. Thomas More,* vol. IV. New Haven, Yale University Press, 1965.

L'ordre de l'entrevue et visitation des rois de France et d'Angleterre. In Bernard de Montfaucon, *Les monumens de la monarchie françoise,* IV, 164–181. 5 vols. Paris, 1729–1733.

Palissy, Bernard. *Les oeuvres de Bernard Palissy.* Ed. Anatole France. Paris, 1880.

Parets, Miguel. *De los muchos sucesos dignos de memoria que han ocurrido en Barcelona y otros lugares de Cataluña.* Ed. Celestino Pujol y Campos. Memorial histórico español, vols. XX-XXV. Madrid, 1888–1893.

Péricaud, Antoine. *Notes et documents pour servir à l'histoire de Lyon, sous le règne de Charles IX, 1560–1574.* Lyons, 1842.

Petit, Guillaume. *Le viat de salut nécessaire et utile à tous chrestiens pour parvenir à la gloyre éternelle. . . . Composé par révérend père en dieu Monseigneur évesque de Troyes. . . .* Lyons, A. Blanchard, [1527?].

Piémond, Eustache. *Mémoires de Eustache Piémond, notaire royal-delphinal en la ville de St.-Antoine en Dauphiné (1572–1608).* Ed. J. Brun-Durand. Valence, 1885.

Pietresson de Saint-Aubin, P. *La Passion de Notre-Seigneur Jésus-Christ. Bibliothèque de l'Ecole des chartes, 85 (1924),* 310–322.

Possot, Denis. *Trèsample et abondante description du voyiage en la terre saincte dernièrement commencé lan de grace mil cinq cens trente deux depuis la ville de Nogeant sur Sene jusques à la sainct cité de Hiérusalem.* Paris, R. Chaudière, 1536.

Ces présentes heures, à l'usage de Châlons, toutes au long, sans rien requerir. . . . Paris, Symon Vostre, [ca. 1512].

Propositions, dicts et sentences contenant les graces, fruicts, prouffits, utilités et louanges du trèssacre et digne sacrement de lautel pour ceux qui le recouvrent en estat de grace: extraicts de plusieurs saincts docteurs. Troyes, Jean du Ruau, n.d.

Pussot, Jean. "Journalier ou mémoires." *Travaux de l'Académie nationale de Reims,* 23 (1855–1856), 106–179; 25 (1856–1857), 1–276.

Quicherat, J. "Lettres de rémission et de main-levée en faveur des enfants mineurs de Robert Estienne." *Bibliothèque de l'Ecole des chartes,* 1 (1839–1840), 565–573.

Les quinze effusions du sang de nostre seigneur Jésus Christ. Troyes, Jean du Ruau, n.d.

Rabelais, François. *Oeuvres complètes.* Ed. Jacques Boulenger and Lucien Scheler. Paris, Gallimard, 1955.

Regnier de La Planche, Louis. *Histoire de l'estat de France, tant de la république que de la religion, sous le règne de François II.* Ed. E. Mennechet. Paris, 1836.

Rogier, Jean. *Mémoires de Jean Rogier, prévôt de l'échevinage de Reims.* Ed. E. de Barthélemy. 2 vols. Reims, 1875.

[Sala, Gaspar]. *Proclamación católica a la magestad piadosa de Felipe el Grande. . . .* Barcelona, 1641.

Santa Cruz, Alonso de. *Crónica del emperador Carlos V,* vol. I. Madrid, Imp. del Patronato de huérfanos de intendencia é intervención militares, 1920.

Savaron, Jean. *Traitté des confrairies.* Paris, 1604.

Shaw, John. "The Life of Master John Shaw." *Yorkshire Diaries and Autobiographies in the Seventeenth and Eighteenth Centuries.* Surtees Society, vol. 65, pp. 121–162. London, 1875.

Société de l'histoire du protestantisme français. *Bulletin:*
  "Testament de Nicolas Pithou." Ed. E. Berthe. Vol. 15 (1866), pp. 108–110.
  "Liste des églises et des pasteurs réformées de France en 1660." Ed. Th. Claparède. Vol. 15 (1866), pp. 511–526, 577–582.
  "Eglises réformées de la Champagne avec leurs pasteurs et anciens, en 1571." Ed. N[athaniel] W[eiss]. Vol. 39 (1890), pp. 128–134.
  "Notes et pièces inédites sur les églises de la Champagne, Phalsbourg et Mannheim, et le collège de Sedan de 1572 à 1591." Ed. N. Weiss. Vol. 39 (1890), pp. 303–318.

Statuta synodalia, a reverendo in Christo patre ac domino Hieronymo Burgensi, episcopo comite Cathalaunensi, Franciae q̄ pari edita & promulgata, anno Domini 1557. Reims, N. Bacquenois, 1557.

Statuta synodalia civitatis & diocesis Treceñ noviter impressa ex ordinatione reverendi in Christo patris & dñi domini Odardi Hennequin Trecensis episcopi. Troyes, Le Coq, n.d.

Statuta synodi, diocesis Trecensis anno Domini 1584. Troyes, Trumeau, n.d.

Troubles Connected with the Prayer Book of 1549. Ed. Nicholas Pocock. Camden Society, n.s., vol. 37. London, 1884.

Vallet de Viriville, A. "Notice d'un mystère par personnages représenté à Troyes vers la fin du XVe siècle." *Bibliothèque de l'Ecole des chartes,* 3 (1841–1842), 448–474.

Varin, Pierre. *Archives administratives de la ville de Reims.* 3 vols. in 4. Paris, 1839–1848.

——. *Archives législatives de la ville de Reims.* 4 vols. in 2 parts. Paris, 1840–1852.

La vie et passion de Madame Saincte Marguerite vierge et martyr. Troyes, Jean du Ruau, n.d.

Vowell, John [John Hooker]. *The Description of the Citie of Excester.* 3 parts. Devon and Cornwall Record Society, 1919–1944.

La vraye confrérie selon la parole de Dieu & des saincts pères. N. pl., 1594.

Walsingham, Thomas. *Historia Anglicana.* Ed. H.T. Riley. Rolls Series. 2 vols. London, 1863–1864.

Weiss, Nathaniel, ed. *La chambre ardente.* Paris, 1889.

Wotton, Henry. *The Life and Letters of Sir Henry Wotton.* Ed. L.P. Smith. 2 vols. Oxford, At the Clarendon Press, 1907.

Selected Secondary Works

Adam, Paul. *La vie paroissiale en France au XIVe siècle.* Paris, Sirey, 1964.

Agulhon, Maurice. *La sociabilité méridionale (Confréries et associations dans la vie collective en Provence orientale à la fin du 18ème siècle).* 2 vols. Aix-en-Provence, La pensée universitaire, 1966.

Arbois de Jubainville, Henry d'. *Voyage paléographique dans le département de l'Aube.* Troyes, 1855.

Ariès, Philippe. "Contribution à l'étude du culte des morts à l'époque contemporaine." Académie des sciences morales et politiques: *Revue des travaux,* 119 (1966), 25–40.

Armstrong, Elizabeth. *Robert Estienne, Royal Printer.* Cambridge, At the University Press, 1954.

Arnaud, A.-F. *Voyage archéologique et pittoresque dans le département de l'Aube et dans l'ancienne diocèse de Troyes.* 2 vols. Troyes, 1837.

Aspects de la propagande religieuse. Etudes publiées par Gabrielle Berthaud et al. Geneva, E. Droz, 1957.

Assier, Alexandre. *Comptes de la fabrique de l'église Saint-Jean de Troyes.* . . . Troyes, 1855.

————. *Comptes de la fabrique de l'église Sainte-Madeleine de Troyes.* . . . Troyes, 1855.

Aubert, Marcel. *Le vitrail en France.* Paris, Larousse, 1946.

————, et al. *Le vitrail français.* Paris, Editions des deux mondes, 1958.

Avout, Jacques d'. *31 juillet 1358, le meurtre d'Etienne Marcel.* Paris, Gallimard, 1960.

Babeau, Albert. "Du Buisson-Aubenay, voyage d'un archéologue dans le sudouest de la Champagne en 1646." *Annuaire de l'Aube,* 60 (1886), 3–49.

————. "Un marchand de province sous Henri IV." *La réforme sociale,* 5 (1883), 324–336.

[Babel, Antony]. *Mélanges d'histoire économique et sociale en hommage au professeur Antony Babel.* 2 vols. Geneva, Impr. de la *Tribune de Genève,* 1963.

Barthélemy, Edouard de. *Diocèse ancien de Châlons-sur-Marne, histoire et monuments.* . . . 2 vols. Paris, 1861.

Baulant, Micheline, and Meuvret, Jean. *Prix des céréales extraits de la mercuriale de Paris (1520–1698).* 2 vols. Paris, S.E.V.P.E.N., 1960–1962.

Bautier, Robert-Henri. "Les foires de Champagne, recherches sur une évolution historique." In *La foire.* Recueils de la Société Jean Bodin, V, 97–148. Brussels, Editions de la librairie encyclopédique, 1953.

————. "Recherches sur les routes de l'Europe médiévale. 1. De Paris et des foires de Champagne à la Méditerranée par le Massif Central." Comité des travaux historiques et scientifiques: *Bulletin philologique et historique,* 1960, vol. I, pp. 99–143.

Bergier, Jean-François. *Genève et l'économie européenne de la Renaissance.* Paris, S.E.V.P.E.N., 1963.

Bernard, Gildas. "L'église de Villemaur." Société académique de l'Aube: *Mémoires,* 105 (1971), 1–48.

Beuve, Octave. *Le théâtre à Troyes aux quinzième et seizième siècles.* Paris, Plon-Nourrit, 1913.

Bezard, Yvonne. *La vie rurale dans le sud de la région parisienne de 1450 à 1560.* Paris, Firmin-Didot, 1929.

Bibolet, Françoise. *Les vitraux de Saint-Martin-ès-Vignes, Troyes.* Troyes, La Renaissance, 1959.

Bindoff, S.T. *Ket's Rebellion, 1549.* London, The Historical Association, 1949.

Binet, François. "Etudes sur quelques familles de la bourgeoisie troyenne au XVIe siècle." Ecole des chartes: *Positions des thèses,* 1945, pp. 51–58. Nogent-le-Rotrou, Daupeley-Gouverneau, n.d.

Biver, Paul. *L'école troyenne de peinture sur verre.* Paris, Gabriel Enault, 1935.

Bloch, Marc. "L'Ile-de-France." *Mélanges historiques,* II, 692–787. 2 vols. Paris, S.E.V.P.E.N., 1963.

Blunt, Anthony. *Art and Architecture in France, 1500–1700.* London, Penguin, 1953.

Bordier, Henri. "La confrérie des pèlerins de Saint-Jacques et ses archives." Société de l'histoire de Paris et de l'Ile-de-France: *Mémoires,* 1 (1875), 186–228, 2 (1876), 330–397.

Bossy, John. "The Counter-Reformation and the People of Catholic Europe." *Past and Present*, no. 47 (1970), 51–70.

Bourquelot, Félix. *Histoire de Provins*. 2 vols. Provins, 1839–1840.

Boussinesq, Georges, and Laurent, Gustave. *Histoire de Reims depuis les origines jusqu'à nos jours*, vol. I. Reims, Matôt-Braine, 1933.

Boutiot, Théophile. *Histoire de l'instruction publique et populaire à Troyes pendant les quatre derniers siècles*. Troyes, 1865.

———. *Histoire de la ville de Troyes et de la Champagne méridionale*. 5 vols. Paris, 1870–1880.

———. *Recherches sur le théâtre à Troyes au XVe siècle*. Troyes, 1854.

Boutruche, Robert. *La crise d'une société; seigneurs et paysans du Bordelais pendant la Guerre de Cent Ans*. Paris, Les belles lettres, 1947.

Bouwsma, William. *Venice and the Defense of Republican Liberty*. Berkeley and Los Angeles, University of California Press, 1968.

Boyer, Marjorie N. "A Day's Journey in Medieval France." *Speculum*, 26 (1951), 597–608.

Braudel, Fernand. *La Méditerranée et le monde méditerranéen à l'époque de Philippe II*. Paris, A. Colin, 1949. [Now available in an English translation by Siân Reynolds. 2 vols. London, Collins, and New York, Harper & Row, 1972–1974.]

Cameron, Richard. "The Charges of Lutheranism Brought against Jacques Lefèvre d'Etaples (1520–1529)." *Harvard Theological Review*, 63 (1970), 119–147.

Carrière, Victor, ed. *Introduction aux études d'histoire ecclésiastique locale*. 3 vols. Paris, Letouzey et Ané, 1934–1940.

Cerf, Albert. "Notice sur la relique de saint laict conservée autrefois dans la cathédrale de Reims." *Bulletin monumental*, 5th ser., 6 (1878), 5–23.

Chaix, Paul. *Recherches sur l'imprimerie à Genève de 1550 à 1564*. Geneva, E. Droz, 1954.

Champion, Pierre. "La légende des mignons." *Humanisme et Renaissance*, 6 (1939), 494–528.

Chapin, Elizabeth. *Les villes de foires de Champagne dès origines au début du XIVe siècle*. Paris, H. Champion, 1927.

Chaponnière, J.-J., and Sordet, L. "Des hôpitaux de Genève avant la Réformation." *Mémoires et documents publiées par la Société d'histoire et d'archéologie de Genève*, 3 (1844), 165–471.

Chastel, André. "L'art et le sentiment de la mort au XVIIe siècle." *Dix-septième Siècle*, nos. 36–37 (1957), 287–293.

Chaunu, Pierre. *La civilisation de l'Europe classique*. Paris, Arthaud, 1970.

Chill, Emmanuel. "Religion and Mendicity in 17th-Century France." *International Review of Social History*, 7 (1962), 400–425.

Constable, Giles. "Troyes, Constantinople, and the Relics of St Helen in the Thirteenth Century." *Mélanges offerts à René Crozet*, II, 1035–1042. Poitiers, Société d'études médiévales, 1966.

Coornaert, Emile. *Les Français et le commerce international à Anvers, fin du XVe-XVIe siècle*. 2 vols. Paris, Marcel Rivière, 1961.

Courtalon-Delaistre, Jean-Charles. *Topographie historique de la ville et diocèse de Troyes*. 3 vols. Paris and Troyes, 1783–1784.

Courtenay, William. "Token Coinage and the Administration of Poor Relief during the Late Middle Ages." *Journal of Interdisciplinary History*, 3 (1972–1973), 275–295.

Couturier, Marcel. *Recherches sur les structures sociales de Châteaudun, 1525–1789.* Paris, S.E.V.P.E.N., 1969.

Couvret, Anne-Marie. "Les Châlonnais du XVIe siècle, propriétaires ruraux." Société d'agriculture . . . de la Marne: *Mémoires,* 78 (1963), 61–81.

Crozet, René. "Les églises rurales de la Champagne orientale et méridionale du XIIIe au XVIe siècle. *Bulletin monumental,* 89 (1930), 355–397.

———. "Le Protestantisme et la Ligue à Vitry-le-François et en Perthois." *Revue historique,* 156 (1927), 1–40.

———. "Une ville neuve du XVIe siècle: Vitry-le-François." *La vie urbaine,* 5 (1923), 291–309.

Dainville, François de. "Effectifs des collèges et scolarité aux XVIIe et XVIIIe siècles dans le Nord-Est de la France." *Population,* 10 (1955), 455–488.

Dannreuther, Henri. "L'église de Vitry-le-François en août 1561, et les de Vassan." Société de l'histoire du protestantisme français: *Bulletin,* 40 (1891), 474–478.

Davis, Natalie. "Missed Connections: *Religion and Regime.*" *Journal of Interdisciplinary History,* 1 (1971), 381–394.

———. *Society and Culture in Early Modern France.* Stanford, Stanford University Press, 1975.

Delaborde, Jules. *Eléonore de Roye, princesse de Condé (1535–1564).* Paris, 1876.

Delaruelle, Etienne; Labande, E.-R.; and Ourliac, Paul. *L'église au temps du grand schisme et de la crise conciliare (1378-1449).* Histoire de l'église depuis les origines jusqu'à nos jours, XIV. 2 vols. Paris, Bloud et Gay, 1964.

———. "La spiritualité de Jeanne d'Arc." *Bulletin de littérature ecclésiastique,* 1964, pp. 17–33.

Delcambre, Etienne. *Le concept de la sorcellerie dans le duché de Lorraine au XVIe et au XVIIe siècles.* 3 vols. Nancy, Société d'archéologie lorraine, 1948–1951.

Delumeau, Jean. *Le Catholicisme entre Luther et Voltaire.* Paris, Presses universitaires, 1971.

———. *Naissance et affirmation de la Réforme.* Paris, Presses universitaires, 1965.

Demaison, Louis. *Les églises de Châlons-sur-Marne.* Caen, Delesques, 1913.

Deschamps, Jeanne. *Les confréries au Moyen Age.* Bordeaux, Bière, 1958.

Desportes, P. "La population de Reims au XVe siècle. . . ." *Moyen Age,* 72 (1966), 463–508.

Det, A.-S. "La Belle-Croix de Troyes." *Annuaire administratif . . . du département de l'Aube,* 58 (1884), 81-134.

Devèze, Michel. *La vie de la forêt française au XVIe siècle.* Paris, S.E.V.P.E.N., 1961.

Deyon, Pierre. *Amiens, capitale provinciale; étude sur la société urbaine au 17e siècle.* Paris, Mouton, 1967.

Dickens, A.G. *The Counter Reformation.* New York, Harcourt, Brace & World, 1969.

Dimier, Louis. *French Painting in the Sixteenth Century.* London, Duckworth, 1904.

Dion, Roger. "Le 'bon' et 'beau' pays nommé Champagne pouilleuse." *L'information géographique,* 25 (1961), 209–214.

———. *Histoire de la vigne et du vin en France dès origines au XIXe siècle.* Paris, Doullens, Sevin et Cie, 1959.

————. "La part de la géographie et celle de l'histoire dans l'explication de l'habitat rural du Bassin Parisien." *Publications de la Société de géographie de Lille*, 1946, pp. 6-80.

Dobson, R.B., comp. *The Peasants' Revolt of 1381*. London, Macmillan, 1970.

Doucet, Roger. *Les institutions de la France au XVIe siècle*. 2 vols. Paris, A. et J. Picard, 1948.

Drouot, Henri. *Mayenne et la Bourgogne; étude sur la Ligue (1587–1596)*. 2 vols. Paris, A. Picard, 1937.

Duby, Georges. "Les sociétés médiévales: une approche d'ensemble." *Annales: économies, sociétés, civilisations*, 26 (1971), 1–13.

Duhr, J. "La confrérie dans la vie de l'église." *Revue d'histoire ecclésiastique*, 35 (1939), 437–478.

Duparc, Pierre. "Confréries du Saint-Esprit et communautés d'habitants au Moyen Age." *Revue historique du droit français et étranger*, 4th ser., 36 (1958), 349–367, 555–585.

Du Plessis, Toussaint. *Histoire de l'église de Meaux*. 2 vols. Paris, 1731.

Elliott, J.H. *The Revolt of the Catalans*. Cambridge, At the University Press, 1963.

Emery, Richard. *The Friars in Medieval France: A Catalogue of French Mendicant Convents, 1200–1500*. New York, Columbia University Press, 1962.

Erlanger, Philippe. *Le massacre de la Saint-Barthélemy, 24 août 1572*. Paris, Gallimard, 1960.

Espinas, Georges. *Les origines du droit d'association dans les villes de l'Artois et de la Flandre française jusqu'au début du XVIe siècle*. 2 vols. Lille, E. Raoust, 1941–1942.

Evennett, H.O. *The Spirit of the Counter-Reformation*. Cambridge, At the University Press, 1968.

Fawtier, Robert. *Les Capétiens et la France*. Paris, Presses universitaires, 1942.

Febvre, Lucien. "Aspects méconnus d'un renouveau religieux en France entre 1590 et 1620." *Annales: économies, sociétés, civilisations*, 13 (1958), 639–650."

————. *Au coeur religieux du XVIe siècle*. Paris, S.E.V.P.E.N., 1957.

————. *Combats pour l'histoire*. Paris, A. Colin, 1953.

————. *Philippe II et la Franche-Comté*. Paris, H. Champion, 1911.

————. *Le problème de l'incroyance au XVIe siècle; la religion de Rabelais*. Paris, A. Michel, 1942.

————, and Martin, Henri-Jean, *L'apparition du livre*. Paris, A. Michel, 1958.

Ferté, Jeanne. *La vie religieuse dans les campagnes parisiennes, 1622–1695*. Paris, J. Vrin, 1962.

Fichot, Charles. *Statistique monumentale du département de l'Aube*. 5 vols. Troyes, 1884–1900.

Flammeront, J. "La Jacquerie en Beauvaisis." *Revue historique*, 4 (1879), 123–143.

Folz, R. "L'esprit religieux du testament bourguignon au Moyen Age." Société pour l'histoire du droit et des institutions des anciens pays bourguignons, comtois et romands: *Mémoires*, 1955, pp. 7–28.

Forsyth, William. *The Entombment of Christ: French Sculptures of the Fifteenth and Sixteenth Centuries*. Cambridge, Mass., Harvard University Press, 1970.

Fortes, Meyer. "Some Reflections on Ancestor Worship in Africa." In Third

International African Seminar, Salisbury, Southern Rhodesia, 1960. *African Systems of Thought,* pp. 122–144. London, Oxford University Press, 1965.

Fosseyeux, Marcel. "Les premiers budgets municipaux d'assistance: la taxe des pauvres au XVIe siècle." *Revue d'histoire de l'église de France,* 20 (1934), 407–432.

Fossier, R. "Rémarques sur les mouvements de population en Champagne méridionale au XVe siècle." *Bibliothèque de l'Ecole des chartes,* 122 (1964), 177–215.

Foucault, Michel. *Folie et deraison; histoire de la folie à l'âge classique.* Paris, Plon, 1961.

Fourquin, Guy. *Les campagnes de la région parisienne à la fin du Moyen Age.* Paris, Presses universitaires, 1964.

Fremy, Edouard. *Henri III pénitent.* Paris, 1885.

Friedmann, Adrien. *Paris, ses rues, ses paroisses, du Moyen Age à la Révolution.* Paris, Plon, 1959.

Gailly de Taurines, Charles. "Une représentation du Mystère de la Passion à Mézières, en 1531." *Revue historique ardennaise,* 10 (1903), 65–77.

Gavelle, E. "Les influences de l'art allemand sur l'art champenois au XVIe siècle." *Revue germanique,* 15 (1924), 265–279.

———. "Nicolas Haslins dit le flamand, tailleur d'images (vers 1471–après 1541)." *Revue du Nord,* 10 (1924), 89–116.

Geisendorf, Paul-F. *Théodore de Bèze.* Geneva, Labor & Fides, 1949.

Gennep, Arnold van. "Les funérailles." In *Manuel de folklore français contemporain,* II, pt. 2, pp. 629–824. Paris, A. Picard, 1946.

Giesey, Ralph. *The Royal Funeral Ceremony in Renaissance France.* Geneva, E. Droz, 1960.

Gilier, G. "Jametz (heures et malheurs d'une petite ville protestante au XVIe siècle)." *Société de l'histoire du protestantisme français: Bulletin,* 101 (1955), 26–32.

Gillet, Louis. *Histoire artistique des ordres mendicants; l'art religieux du XIIIe au XVIIe siècle.* 1912. Reprint. Paris, Flammarion, 1939.

Givelet, Charles; Jadart, Henri; and Demaison, Louis. *Département de la Marne. Répertoire archéologique de l'arrondissement de Reims.* 4 vols. Reims, 1885–1900.

Gluckman, Max, ed. *Essays on the Ritual of Social Relations.* Manchester, Manchester University Press, 1962.

Goody, Jack. *Death, Property and the Ancestors.* Stanford, Stanford University Press, 1962.

Gougaud, L. "Le culte de saint Fiacre, ermite." *Revue Mabillon,* 26 (1936), 197–201.

Grignon, Louis. *Description et historique de l'église Notre-Dame en Vaux de Châlons.* Châlons, 1885.

———. *Historique et description de l'église et paroisse de Saint-Alpin de Châlons.* Châlons, 1878.

———. *Statuts et historique de l'ancienne corporation des tonneliers de Châlons-en-Champagne.* Châlons, 1882.

———. *Topographie historique de la ville de Châlons-sur-Marne.* Châlons, 1889.

Groethuysen, Bernhard. *Origines de l'esprit bourgeois en France.* 1927. Reprint. Paris, Gallimard, 1956.

Guenée, Bernard. "Espace et état dans la France du bas Moyen Age." *Annales: économies, sociétés, civilisations,* 23 (1968), 744–758.

————. *L'Occident aux XIVe et XVe siècles; les états.* Paris, Presses universitaires, 1971.

————. *Tribunaux et gens de justice dans le bailliage de Senlis à la fin du Moyen Age (vers 1380–vers 1550).* Paris, Les belles lettres, 1963.

Haag, Eugène, and Haag, Emile. *La France protestante,* 10 vols. 1846–1859. Reprint. Geneva, Slatkine, 1966.

Halkin, Léon-E. *La Réforme en Belgique sous Charles-Quint.* Brussels, La renaissance du livre, 1957.

Handbuch der Geschichte der böhmischen Länder. Ed. Karl Bosl. Stuttgart, A. Hiersemann, 1967–

Hardison, O.B. *Christian Rite and Christian Drama in the Middle Ages.* Baltimore, Johns Hopkins Press, 1965.

Hauser, Henri. *La naissance du protestantisme.* 1940. Reprint. Paris, Presses universitaires, 1962.

————. *Ouvriers du temps passé (XVe-XVIe siècles).* 5th ed. Paris, F. Alcan, 1927.

Heers, Jacques. *L'Occident aux XIVe et XVe siècles; aspects économiques et sociaux.* Paris, Presses universitaires, 1966.

Henry, M.F. *La Réforme et la Ligue en Champagne et à Reims.* Saint Nicolas (Meurthe), 1867.

Hérésies et sociétés dans l'Europe pré-industrielle, 11e-18e siècles. Ed. Jacques Le Goff. Paris, Mouton, 1968.

Heymann, Frederick. *John Žizka and the Hussite Revolution.* Princeton, Princeton University Press, 1955.

————. "The Role of the Towns in the Bohemia of the Later Middle Ages." *Cahiers d'histoire mondiale,* 2 (1954), 326–341.

Hill, Christopher. *Society and Puritanism in Pre-Revolutionary England.* New York, Schocken, 1964.

Horton, Robin. "A Definition of Religion, and Its Uses." *Journal of the Royal Anthropological Institute,* 90 (1960), 201–226.

————. "Ritual Man in Africa." *Africa,* 34 (1964), 85–104.

Howe, Ellie. "The Le Be Family." *Signature,* 8 (1938), 1–27.

Hubert, L. *Notre-Dame en Vaux de Châlons-sur-Marne.* Paris, Editions du dauphin, 1953.

Huizinga, Johan. *The Waning of the Middle Ages,* trans. F. Hopman. London, E. Arnold, 1924.

Hurault, Etienne. *Les vitraux anciens de l'église Saint-Alpin à Châlons-sur-Marne.* Paris, Editions de la revue *L'art sacré,* n.d.

Imbart de la Tour, Pierre. *Les origines de la Réforme.* 4 vols. 1905–1935. Reprint. Melun, Librairie d'Argences, 1948.

International Eucharistic Congress, 9th (1894). *Congrès eucharistique de Reims.* Reims, 1895.

Jadart, Henri. *Les débuts de l'imprimerie à Reims et les marques des premiers imprimeurs, 1550–1650.* Reims, 1893.

————. *Saint-Lié, Villedommange et Jouy.* Reims, 1881.

Jolibois, Emile. *Histoire de la ville de Chaumont.* Paris, 1856.

Jones, Leonard. *Simon Goulart, 1543–1624; étude biographique et bibliographique.* Geneva, Georg & Co., 1917.

Kelley, Donald. *Foundations of Modern Historical Scholarship: Language, Law, and History in the French Renaissance.* New York, Columbia University Press, 1970.

————. "Martyrs, Myths, and the Massacre: The Background of St. Bartholomew." *American Historical Review,* 77 (1972), 1323–1342.

Kingdon, Robert. *Geneva and the Coming of the Wars of Religion in France, 1555–1563.* Geneva, E. Droz, 1956.

————. *Geneva and the Consolidation of the French Protestant Movement, 1564–1572.* Geneva, E. Droz, 1967.

————. "The Political Resistance of the Calvinists in France and the Low Countries." *Church History,* 27 (1958), 220–234.

————. "Social Welfare in Calvin's Geneva." *American Historical Review,* 76 (1971), 50–69.

Knecht, R.J. "The Concordat of 1516: A Reassessment." *University of Birmingham Historical Journal,* 9 (1963), 16–32.

Koechlin, Raymond, and Marquet de Vasselot, Jean-J. *La sculpture à Troyes et dans la Champagne méridionale au seizième siècle.* Paris, A. Colin, 1900.

Koenigsberger, H.G. "The Organization of Revolutionary Parties in France and the Netherlands during the Sixteenth Century." *Journal of Modern History,* 27 (1955), 335–351.

————. "The Unity of the Church and the Reformation." *Journal of Interdisciplinary History,* 1 (1971), 407–417.

Kolve, V.A. *The Play Called Corpus Christi.* Stanford, Stanford University Press, 1966.

Konigson, Elie. *La représentation d'un mystère de la Passion à Valenciennes en 1547.* Paris, Centre national de la recherche scientifique, 1969.

Lagarde, Georges de. *La naissance de l'esprit laique au déclin du Moyen Age,* vol. I: *Bilan du XIIIème siécle.* 3rd ed. Louvain. E. Nauwelaerts, 1956.

————. "La structure politique et sociale de l'Europe au XIVe siècle." *L'organisation corporative du Moyen Age à la fin de l'Ancien Régime,* pp. 91–118. Etudes présentés à la Commission internationale pour l'histoire des assemblées d'états. Louvain, Bibliothèque de l'université, III (1939).

Lalore, Charles. *Etat de la paroisse de Chaource avant la Révolution.* Arcis-sur-Aube, 1884.

Lebègue, Raymond. "Persistance, altération, disparition des traditions dramatico-religieuses en France." *Dramaturgie et société,* I, 247–252. Paris, Centre national de la recherche scientifique, 1968.

————. *La tragédie religieuse en France; les débuts (1514–1573).* Paris, H. Champion, 1929.

Lebrun, François. *Les hommes et la mort en Anjou aux 17e et 18e siècles.* Paris, Mouton, 1971.

Le Clert, Louis. *Le papier, recherches et notes pour servir à l'histoire du papier, principalement à Troyes et aux environs depuis le quatorzième siècle.* 2 vols. Paris, Pégase, 1926.

Ledit, Charles J. *Les hautes verrières de la cathédrale de Troyes.* Troyes, Impr. de la renaissance, 1948.

Leff, Gordon. "The Fourteenth Century and the Decline of Scholasticism." *Past and Present,* no. 9 (1956), 30–41.

————. "Heresy and the Decline of the Medieval Church." *Past and Present,* no. 20 (1961), 36–51.

————. *Heresy in the Later Middle Ages: The Relation of Heterodoxy to Dissent c.1250-c.1450.* Manchester, Manchester University Press, 1967.

Leger, François. *La fin de la Ligue (1580–1593).* Bound with Ariès, Philippe;

Chastel, André; and Charmet, Raymond. *Trois études sur le seizième siècle.* Paris, Editions de la nouvelle France, 1944.

Léonard, Emile. *Histoire générale du protestantisme.* 3 vols. Paris, Presses universitaires, 1961–1964.

Le Roy Ladurie, Emmanuel. *Les paysans de Languedoc.* 2 vols. Paris, S.E.V.P.E.N., 1966.

Lewis, Peter. *Later Medieval France: The Polity.* London, Macmillan, 1968.

Lhôte, Amédée. *Histoire de l'imprimerie à Châlons-sur-Marne, 1488–1894.* Châlons, 1894.

Loriquet, Charles. *Tapisseries de la cathédrale de Reims. Histoire du roy Clovis (XVe siècle). Histoire de la vierge (XVIe siècle).* Paris, 1882.

———. *Les tapisseries de Notre-Dame de Reims . . .* Reims, 1876.

Lot, Ferdinand, and Fawtier, Robert. *Histoire des institutions françaises au Moyen Age.* Paris, Presses universitaires, 1957-

Lovy, René-Jacques. *Les origines de la Réforme française: Meaux, 1518–1546.* Paris, Librairie protestante, 1959.

Luce, Siméon. *Histoire de la Jacquerie.* 2nd rev. ed. Paris, 1894.

———. *Histoire du Bertrand du Guesclin et de son époque.* Paris, 1876.

Lucot, Paul. *Les vitraux de l'église Saint-Etienne (église cathédrale) . . .* Châlons, 1887.

Macek, Josef. "Jean Hus et son époque." *Historica,* 13 (1966), 51–80.

Macfarlane, Alan. *Witchcraft in Tudor and Stuart England.* New York, Harper and Row, 1970.

McFarlane, K.B. "Bastard Feudalism." *Bulletin of the Institute of Historical Research,* 20 (1945), 161–180.

Maillet, Germaine. *Les vitraux de Châlons.* Châlons, Impr. du *Journal de la Marne,* 1925.

Major, James Russell. *The Estates General of 1560.* Princeton, Princeton University Press, 1951.

———. *Representative Institutions in Renaissance France, 1421–1559.* Madison, University of Wisconsin Press, 1960.

Mâle, Emile. *L'art religieux après le Concile de Trent; étude sur l'iconographie de la fin du XVIe, du XVIIe, et du XVIIIe siècles. Italie-France-Espagne-Flandres.* 2nd rev. ed. Paris, A. Colin, 1951.

———. *L'art religieux de la fin du Moyen Age en France.* 5th rev. ed. Paris, A. Colin, 1949.

Mandrou, Robert. *De la culture populaire aux XVIIe et XVIIIe siècles. La bibliothèque bleue de Troyes.* Paris, Stock, 1964.

———. "Les Français hors de France aux XVIe et XVIIe siècles." *Annales: économies, sociétés, civilisations,* 14 (1959), 662–675.

———. *Introduction à la France moderne (1500–1640).* Paris, A. Michel, 1961.

———. *Magistrats et sorciers en France au XVIIe siècle.* Paris, Plon, 1968.

Marcel, Louis. *Le cardinal de Givry, évêque de Langres (1529–1561).* 2 vols. Dijon, N. Darantière, 1926.

Marlot, Guillaume. *Histoire de la ville, cité et université de Reims.* 4 vols. Reims, 1843.

Matern, Gerhard. *Zur Vorgeschichte und Geschichte der Fronleichnamsfeier besonders in Spanien.* Münster, Aschendorff, 1962.

Mazauric, R. "La Réforme au pays messin." *Société de l'histoire du protestantisme français: Bulletin,* 95 (1948), 157–183.

Meersseman, G. "Etudes sur les anciennes confréries dominicaines." *Archivum Fratrum Praedicatorum*, 20 (1950), 5–113; 21 (1951), 51–196; 22 (1952), 5–176; 23 (1953), 275–308.

Meiss, Millard. *Painting in Florence and Siena after the Black Death.* Princeton, Princeton University Press, 1951.

Meyer, P. "Les trois Maries, mystère liturgique de Reims." *Romania*, 33 (1904), 239–245.

Mezník, Jaroslav. "Der ökonomische Charakter Prags im 14. Jahrhundert." *Historica*, 17 (1969), 43–91.

Moeller, Bernd. "Frömmigkeit in Deutschland um 1500." *Archiv für Reformationsgeschichte*, 56 (1965), 5–30.

————. *Reichsstadt und Reformation.* Gütersloh, G. Mohn, 1962.

Mollat, Guillaume. *Les papes d'Avignon (1305–1378).* 9th rev. ed. Paris, Letouzey et Ané, 1950.

Mollat, Michel. *Le commerce de la Haute Normandie au XVe siècle et au début du XVIe.* Paris. Plon, 1952. Published also as *Le commerce maritime normand à la fin du Moyen Age.* Paris, [Plon], 1952.

————. *La vie et la pratique religieuses au XIVe siècle et dans la première partie du XVe, principalement en France.* 2 parts. Les cours de Sorbonne. Paris, Centre de documentation universitaire, 1966.

————. *La vie religieuse aux XIVe et XVe siècles (jusqu'en 1449).* 2 parts. Les cours de Sorbonne. Paris, Centre de documentation universitaire, 1964.

————, and Wolff, Philippe. *Ongles bleus, Jacques et Ciompi: les révolutions populaires en Europe aux XIVe et XVe siècles.* Paris, Calmann-Lévy, 1971.

Moore, W.G. *La Réforme allemande et la littérature française; recherches sur la notoriété de Luther en France.* Strasbourg, Publications de la Faculté des lettres de l'université, 1930.

Morin, Louis. "Les calendriers des illettrés, II: L'almanach des bergers." *Revue des traditions populaires*, 5 (1890), 145–149.

————. *Histoire corporative des artisans du livre à Troyes.* Troyes, P. Noel, 1900.

Mours, Samuel. "Liste des églises réformées, avec date de leur fondation." *Société de l'histoire du protestantisme français: Bulletin*, 103 (1957), 37–59, 113–130, 200–216.

————. *Le Protestantisme en France au seizième siècle.* Paris, Librairie protestante, 1959.

Mousnier, Roland. *La venalité des offices sous Henri IV et Louis XIII.* Rouen, Editions Maugard, 1945.

Naef, Henri. *Les origines de la Réforme à Genève.* 2 vols. Geneva, E. Droz, 1968.

Neill, Stephen, and Weber, Hans–Ruedi, eds. *The Layman in Christian History.* Philadelphia, Westminster Press, 1963.

Nuce de Lamothe, M.-S. de. "Piété et charité publique à Toulouse de la fin du XIIIe au milieu du XVe siècle, d'après les testaments." *Annales du Midi*, 76 (1964), 5–39.

Nugent, Donald. *Ecumenism in the Age of Reformation: The Colloquy of Poissy.* Cambridge, Mass., Harvard University Press, 1974.

Orcibal, Jean. *Jean Duvergier de Hauranne, abbé de Saint-Cyran, et son temps (1581–1638).* Paris, J. Vrin, 1948.

Ozment, Steven. *The Reformation in the Cities* (New Haven, Yale University Press, 1975). (Appeared while my book was in production.)

Paris, Louis. *Remensiana.* Reims, 1845.

——. *Toiles peintes et tapisseries de Reims.* 2 vols. Paris, 1843.

Paris. Mobilier national. *Le XVIe siècle européen; tapisseries* (exhibition catalogue). 1965.

Paris. Petit Palais. *Le XVIe siècle européen; peintures et dessins dans les collections publiques françaises* (exhibition catalogue). 1965.

Pedrizet, Paul. *Le calendrier parisien à la fin du Moyen Age.* Paris, Les belles lettres, 1933.

Pellot, Paul. *Etude sur le testament dans l'ancienne coutume de Reims.* Paris, Rousseau, 1916.

Perroy, Edouard. *La Guerre de Cent Ans.* Paris, Gallimard, 1945.

——. *La vie religieuse au XIIIe siècle.* 4 parts. Les cours de Sorbonne. Paris, Centre de documentation universitaire, 1966.

Petit de Julleville, Louis. *Les mystères.* 2 vols. Paris, 1880.

Pigeotte, Léon. *Etude sur les travaux d'achèvement de la cathédrale de Troyes de 1450 à 1630.* Paris, 1870.

Pitz, Ernst. "Die Wirtschaftskrise des Spätmittelalters." *Vierteljahrschrift für Sozial– und Wirtschaftsgeschichte,* 52 (1965), 347–367.

Poinsignon, Maurice. *Histoire générale de la Champagne et de la Brie.* 2nd ed. 3 vols. Châlons, 1896–1898.

Poulin, A. *Les pèlerinages du diocèse de Reims.* Charleville, P. Anciaux, 1927.

——. "Les pèlerinages du diocèse de Reims à la fin de l'Ancien Régime." *Nouvelle revue de Champagne et de Brie,* 10 (1932), 152–185.

Pressouyre, L. "Sculptures funéraires du XVIe siècle à Châlons-sur-Marne." *Gazette des beaux-arts,* 6th ser., 59 (1962), 143–152.

Pullan, Brian. *Rich and Poor in Renaissance Venice.* Cambridge, Mass., Harvard University Press, 1971.

The Pursuit of Holiness in Late Medieval and Renaissance Religion. Papers from the University of Michigan Conference. Edited by Charles Trinkaus with Heiko A. Oberman. Leiden, E.J. Brill, 1974.

Rapine, Charles. *Annales ecclésiastiques du diocèse de Châlons en Champagne . . . .* Paris, C. Sonnius, 1636.

Rapp, Francis. *L'église et la vie religieuse en Occident à la fin du Moyen Age.* Paris, Presses universitaires, 1971.

Réau, Louis. *Iconographie de l'art chrétien.* 3 vols. in 6. Paris, Presses universitaires, 1955–1959.

Reichel-Dolmatoff, Gerardo, and Reichel-Dolmatoff, Alicia. *The People of Aritama: The Cultural Personality of a Colombian Mestizo Village.* Chicago, University of Chicago Press, 1961.

Rémond, André. "Quelques aspects de la vie sociale dans le théâtre, à Langres, vers la fin du Moyen Age." *Revue d'histoire économique et sociale,* 33 (1955), 19–76.

Renaudet, Augustin. *Préréforme et humanisme à Paris pendant les premières guerres d'Italie (1494–1517).* Paris, E. Champion, 1916.

Renouvier, Jules. *Des gravures sur bois dans les livres de Simon Vostre, libraire d'heures.* Paris, 1862.

Réville, André. *Le soulèvement des travailleurs d'Angleterre en 1381.* Paris, 1898.

Robert, Gaston. "Les charteries paroissiales et l'assistance publique à Reims jusqu'à 1633." *Travaux de l'Académie nationale de Reims,* 141 (1926–1927), 127–142.

Romier, Lucien. *Catholiques et huguenots à la cour de Charles IX . . . (1560–62)*. Paris, Perrin, 1924.

——. *Le royaume de Catherine de Medicis; la France à la veille des guerres de religion*. 2 vols. Paris, Perrin, 1922.

Rondot, Natalis. "Les peintres de Troyes dans la première moitié du XVIe siècle." *Revue de l'art français ancien et moderne*, 4 (1887), 147–170.

——. "Les orfèvres de Troyes du XIIe au XVIIIe siècle." *Revue de l'art français ancien et moderne*, 8 (1891), 279–393.

Roserot, Alphonse. *Dictionnaire historique de la Champagne méridionale (Aube) dès origines à 1790*. 3 vols. Angers, Editions de l'ouest, 1948.

Roserot de Melin, Joseph. *Antonio Caracciolo, évêque de Troyes. 1515?–1570*. Paris, Letouzey et Ané, 1923.

——. *Le diocèse de Troyes des origines à nos jours (IIIe s.–1955)*. Troyes, Impr. de la renaissance, 1957.

Les routes de France depuis les origines jusqu'à nos jours. Cahiers des civilisations; colloques. Paris, Hachette, 1959.

Rovira i Virgili, A. *El Corpus de sang*. Barcelona, Barcino, 1932.

Rowse, A.L. *Tudor Cornwall*. 2nd rev. ed. New York, Scribner, 1969.

Russell, Joycelyne. *The Field of the Cloth of Gold*. London, Routledge and Kegan Paul, 1969.

Salvini, Joseph. *Le diocèse de Poitiers à la fin du Moyen Age, 1346–1560*. Fontenay-le-Comte, Lussaud, 1946.

Scarisbrick, J.J. *Henry VIII*. Berkeley and Los Angeles, University of California Press, 1968.

Schickler, Frédéric. "Géographie de la France protestante." *Encyclopédie des sciences religieuses*, ed. F. Lichtenberger, V, 54–109. Paris, 1877–1882.

Shearman, John. *Mannerism*. Harmondsworth and Baltimore, Penguin, 1967.

Shimizu, J. *Conflict of Loyalties: Politics and Religion in the Career of Gaspard de Coligny, Admiral of France, 1519–1572*. Geneva, E. Droz, 1970.

Socard, Alexis, and Assier, Alexandre. *Livres liturgiques du diocèse de Troyes imprimés au XVe et au XVIe siècle*. Paris, 1863.

Socard, Emile. *Etude sur les almanachs et les calendriers de Troyes (1479–1881)*. Troyes, 1882.

——. "Rôle du ban et arrière-ban du bailliage de Troyes en 1558." *Société académique . . . du département de l'Aube: Mémoires*, 54 (1890), 233–286.

Société française d'archéologie, 113e session, Troyes, 1955. *Congrès archéologique de France*. Orléans, M. Pillaut, 1957.

Sprandel, Rolf. *Das Eisengewerbe im Mittelalter*. Stuttgart, A. Hiersemann, 1968.

Stone, Lawrence. "The English Revolution." In *Preconditions of Revolution in Early Modern Europe*, ed. Robert Forster and Jack Greene. Baltimore, Johns Hopkins Press, 1970.

Strohl, Henri. *La pensée de la Réforme*. Neuchâtel, Delachaux, 1951.

Swanson, Guy. *The Birth of the Gods*. Ann Arbor, University of Michigan Press, 1960.

——. *Religion and Regime: A Sociological Account of the Reformation*. Ann Arbor, University of Michigan Press, 1967.

Tenenti, Alberto. *La vie et la mort à travers l'art du XVe siècle*. Paris, A. Colin, 1952.

Thomas, Keith. *Religion and the Decline of Magic*. New York, Scribner, 1971.

Thomson, J.A.F. "Piety and Charity in Late Medieval London." *Journal of Ecclesiastical History*, 16 (1965), 178–195.

Tierney, Brian. *Medieval Poor Law: A Sketch of Canonical Theory and Its Application in England.* Berkeley and Los Angeles, University of California Press, 1959.

Toussaert, Jacques. *Le sentiment religieux en Flandre à la fin du Moyen Age.* Paris, Plon, 1963.

Trevor-Roper, H.R. *Religion, the Reformation and Social Change, and Other Essays.* London, Macmillan, 1967.

Trocmé, Etienne. "Une révolution mal conduite." *Revue d'histoire et de philosophie religieuses,* 39 (1959), 160–168.

Valois, Noel. "Les essais de conciliation religieuse au début du règne de Charles IX." *Revue d'histoire de l'église de France,* 31 (1945), 237–276.

———. "Vassy." Société de l'histoire de France: *Annuaire-Bulletin,* 50 (1913), 188–235.

Vaultier, Roger. *Le folklore pendant la guerre de Cent Ans d'après les lettres de rémission du Trésor des Chartes.* Paris, Guénégaud, 1965.

Vendel, Henri. *Le beau passé de Châlons, artistes châlonnais de jadis et de naguère.* Châlons, Impr. de *L'Union républicaine,* 1928.

Vernon, A. "Les comptes de la Confrérie de Sainte–Foi de Coulommiers au XVe siècle." *Bulletin de la Conférence d'histoire et d'archéologie du diocèse de Meaux,* 1 (1894–1899), 210–232.

Villages désertés et histoire économique XIe-XVIIIe siècle. Paris, S.E.V.P.E.N., 1965.

Villette, P. "La sorcellerie dans le Nord de la France du milieu du XVe à la fin du XVIIe siècle." Lille, Facultés catholiques: *Mélanges de science religieuse,* 13 (1956), 39–62, 129–156.

Viollet-le–Duc, Emmanuel. *Dictionnaire raisonné de l'architecture française du XIe au XVIe siècle.* 10 vols. Paris, 1861–1868.

Vovelle, Gaby, and Vovelle, Michel. *Vision de la mort et de l'au-delà en Provence d'après les autels des âmes du purgatoire, XVe–XXe siècles.* Paris, A. Colin, 1970.

Vovelle, Michel. *Piété baroque et déchristianisation en Provence au XVIIIe siècle.* Paris, Plon, 1973.

Wagley, Charles. *Amazon Town.* New York, Macmillan, 1953.

Walzer, Michael. *The Revolution of the Saints.* Cambridge, Mass., Harvard University Press, 1965.

Waquet, Henri. *Le bailliage de Vermandois aux XIIIe et XIVe siècles: étude d'histoire administrative.* Paris, E. Champion, 1919.

Williams, George H. *The Radical Reformation.* Philadelphia, Westminster Press, 1962.

Wilson, Monica. *Religion and the Transformation of Society: A Study of Social Change in Africa.* Cambridge, At the University Press, 1971.

Wolff, Philippe. *Histoire de Toulouse.* 2nd rev. ed. Toulouse, Privat, 1961.

Wood-Legh, K. L. *Perpetual Chantries in Britain.* Cambridge, At the University Press, 1965.

Zanettacci, Henri. *Les ateliers picards de sculptures à la fin du Moyen Age.* Paris, Compagnie française des arts graphiques, 1954.

Index

Harvard Historical Studies

85. *Patrice L. R. Higonnet.* Pont-de-Montvert: Social Structure and Politics in a French Village, 1700–1914. 1971.
86. *Paul G. Halpern.* The Mediterranean Naval Situation, 1908–1914. 1971.
87. *Robert E. Ruigh.* The Parliament of 1624: Politics and Foreign Policy. 1971.
88. *Angeliki E. Laiou.* Constantinople and the Latins: The Foreign Policy of Andronicus, 1282–1328. 1972.
89. *Donald Nugent.* Ecumenism in the Age of the Reformation: The Colloquy of Poissy. 1974.
90. *Robert A. McCaughey.* Josiah Quincy, 1772–1864: The Last Federalist. 1974.
91. *Sherman Kent.* The Election of 1827 in France. 1975.
92. *A. N. Galpern.* The Religions of the People in Sixteenth-Century Champagne. 1976.